Linsey & Mark plus Er in waiting

COOK WITH CONFIDENCE!
– affordable, appetising food for the family

Beryl Tate
"The Kitchen Doctor"

Thanks for all your encouragement - happy cooking

Beryl

SIGMA
Leisure

Published by Sigma Leisure – an imprint of
Sigma Press, 1 South Oak Lane, Wilmslow, Cheshire SK9 6AR, England.

British Library Cataloguing in Publication Data
A CIP record for this book is available from the British Library.

ISBN: 1-85058-795-7

Typesetting and Design by: Sigma Press, Wilmslow, Cheshire.

Cover Design: Sigma Press

Cover photographs: Harewood kitchen from the Schreiber range at MFI. Photograph reproduced by permission from MFI.

Printed by: MFP Design & Print

Foreword

Any chef who combines chocolate and pasta with enormous enthusiasm was bound to attract my attention. Beryl's use of her imagination in the kitchen soon guaranteed her a regular slot on my afternoon programme on BBC Essex. I remember her first visit to the studios in 1995 – wide grin, chef's whites, chequered trousers, and an enormous chocolate cake that was sure to win me over!

Her culinary skills are matched by her ability to communicate, and have made her a firm favourite with BBC Essex listeners, who love the fun she injects into the kitchen. As a fully trained and qualified chef, and former Home Economics lecturer, Beryl has a wealth of amusing anecdotes that compliment her vast professional experience.

One such 'on-air' memorable moment came as Beryl attempted to explain the correct way to stuff a Christmas turkey, noting the difference between the vent and neck end of the bird. The thick thighs also came into the conversation, and the broadcast almost turned into a scene from a pantomime, thigh slaps and all!

A summer programme saw Beryl continuing to make home-made ice cream live 'on-air' and in front of an audience, while a force ten gale, mixed with driving rain and hail, gradually tore apart our outside broadcast tent!

Finally, the sight of Beryl in a smoke-filled car, racing to the studios for a barbecue special, having previously lit the disposable barbie that was in the boot, turned many heads! Her 'whites' were slightly discoloured that day, unlike her bright red cheeks!

Steve Scruton, BBC Essex Presenter.

Acknowledgements and Dedication

Grateful thanks are due to my husband Mike in his patient endeavours while producing this book, and to all those people who have helped with their contributions, wise advice, and editorial comments. There are too many to mention by name, but they know who they are. Thank you all.

Acknowledgements are due to the organisations listed alphabetically below:

- BBC Essex Radio, Chelmsford CM2 9XB.
- BBC One, Look East Television, Norwich NR1 3ND.
- BBC Radio 2, Jimmy Young Programme, London W1A 4WW.
- East Anglian Daily Times, Ipswich IP4 1AN.
- York Festival of Food and Drink, York YO1 6WR.7

This book is dedicated to my parents, Edith and Fred.

Contents

The Kitchen Doctor
– at your service!

May I introduce myself? My name is Beryl Tate and I have over thirty years of both theoretical and practical catering experience, which I apply to my regular national and local radio appearances.

The Yorkshire Lass Who Cooks

My first memory of cooking was eagerly sitting in the hearth of my parents' Sheffield home, keenly watching the bread rise in a pancheon, which is a wide necked, narrow based earthenware bread prover. Our family did not have a conventional cooker, with an oven, four hobs, and a grill, but a double oven heated by the living room fire. This fire also heated all the hot water in a back boiler, so it was very important that the fire didn't go out. In the summer months this could be irksome, but the rest of the year it was pure joy. Apart from two gas jet burners in the kitchen, the entire household's cooking for seven people was carried out in the living room.

Once the bread dough was ready, it was carried back into the kitchen to be pummelled and shaped, before being allowed to prove again next to the fire. These are memorable nuggets of my childhood. Being the eldest daughter of five children, I was expected to take up cookery responsibilities in the kitchen, which I did, and helping to make the bread was one of them.

After a false start of wanting to be a farmer, which for a city girl was different, I settled on catering for a career. I attended the local college in Sheffield, obtained my qualifications, and I was ready to conquer anything. School meals catering was my choice, and I relished being a peripatetic cook. This involved standing in for absent cooks, and was a baptism by fire, given that I used public transport to travel the length and breadth of the West Riding of Yorkshire.

I soon married, moved south to Essex, and did many stints in any catering establishment that would have me. Eventually, I went back to college in London and obtained a degree in education, in order to teach both large-scale catering and home economics. After graduation, I lectured at the local Chelmsford polytechnic for eight years, and often taught the same courses that originally got me started in catering.

During the vacations in London, I had a taste of running my own business, which offered cookery demonstrations and outside catering. As I approached the age at which life begins, and with the full support of my husband Mike, I felt confident enough to run a restaurant. So I gave up lecturing and opened Scott's, the restaurant for non-smokers. This was extremely successful for more than a decade, and extended my skills enormously. The restaurant is now closed, so I can devote more time to the new challenge of pursuing my media activities.

What You See is What You Get

It was whilst running the restaurant that I got my first lucky break into the media. I had given a demonstration of pasta making to the village Women's Institute. The local BBC Essex radio station had heard about it and wanted to interview me. Just before we went live on air from the restaurant, the interviewer mentioned that the presenter, back in the studio, had made a derogatory remark about the chocolate pasta that I had produced. My reply was that I would have to put him right, because I thought he had broadcast his remark on air.

Anyway, the interview started, and I waxed enthusiastically about my three different flavoured soups in one bowl, my shallow fried gypsy toast, and my chocolate pasta. Eventually, I did put the presenter in his place by asking if he was wearing blinkers when he looked at food. In fact, I talked so much that the programme nearly overran and delayed the news. The outcome was that they invited me to answer live phone-in food questions, on the premise that anyone with that much rabbit deserved to be put in their place. Nevertheless, I must have got something right, because they kept on asking me back each month for many years.

It was then that I got my second lucky break. A producer from local radio moved to national Radio 2. He invited me onto the Jimmy Young Programme, initially for one hour, to replace the regular food contributor who was on holiday. Again the broadcast went well, and I was contracted to come back regularly once a month to answer food and cookery questions sent in by the listeners. Remembering that Radio 2 attracts six million daily listeners, and is the most popular radio station in Great Britain, this proposition was most exhilarating. I won warm praise from Sir Jimmy Young though, who said "Beryl's knowledge and easily digested answers to cooking problems, served up with her wonderful sense of humour, slip down a treat with my listeners." The producer claimed I'd made a big impact on the show's audience, and commented "Beryl's a real character, and completely natural. What you see is what you get. Our audience can spot a phoney a mile off, and they like the fact that not only is she funny, but she really knows her stuff. She's quite a star!" I found this all so stimulating that the seeds of this cookery book began to germinate.

The following pages capture the essence of the food I like to prepare, serve, and eat. It is simple honest food with no pretensions. The flavour and quality of the ingredients speak for themselves. Some recipes have evolved over a period of time. When cooking for the restaurant, I would consistently try to fine-tune a dish, in order to capture the taste in my imagination. Other dishes I find instinctively just work straightaway; a marriage made in heaven so to speak.

First Aid for Those Inevitable Mistakes

What makes this recipe book different from the rest? I believe that I have incorporated a great deal of my experience into this volume. I provide many tips on the equipment that you need in your kitchen, and how to choose the best ingredients for your recipes. The cookery crafts section focuses on the basic techniques that are common to a whole range of recipes. In addition, I have paid attention to any critical aspects of each recipe, such as particular ingredients, vital measurements, or crucial steps in the method.

Most importantly, I have introduced novel first aid supplements, wherever they are applicable, to help you with those inevitable mistakes that arise in the kitchen. Each supplement identifies symptoms and cures, to get you out of sticky problems such as burnt utensils or spoilt recipes, many of which are rarely found published in any cookery books.

Therefore, under '**First Aid**' headings throughout this book you will find '*Symptom:*' descriptions, each with a '*Diagnosis:*' giving the probable cause, followed by advice on corrective measures. Those headed '*Antidote:*' suggest how to rectify the problem there and then, whereas those headed '*Remedy:*' explain how to prevent the problem the next time around.

If, despite these tips you still run into trouble, I am prepared to solve your problem by E-mail or Fax. Simply describe the symptoms and send them to me either using the E-mail address **beryl@tatewise.co.uk** or the UK fax number **08701 307817** not forgetting your reply contact details. You can also visit my web site at **www.tatewise.co.uk** where you will find answers to the most frequently asked questions, corrections to any errata discovered in the book, and details of my forthcoming media appearances.

What? No Illustrations?

You may have noticed that there are no colour illustrations of my recipes. This is a quite deliberate decision. Firstly, pictures consume precious pages that I would far rather devote to extra recipes and advice. Secondly, they often depict a photographically aesthetic, but impossibly perfect result; whatever 'perfect' is! If you attempt my recipes, and for you they look right and taste right, they are right. Forget the pictures. Stamp your style on your cooking.

Abbreviations and Symbols

cm	centimetre
fl oz	fluid ounce
ft	foot
g	gram
kg	kilogram
lb	pound
ml	millilitre
mm	millimetre
oz	ounce
pt	pint
"	inch
°C	degrees Centigrade
°F	degrees Fahrenheit
*	store cupboard recipe
£	budget conscious recipe
~	approximate measurement
§	more details elsewhere – see index

Conversion Tables

These conversion tables give good working approximations.

Weights and Measures

Spoon measurements are usually rounded unless specified as level or heaped; spoon measurements of liquids are, of course, always level.

1 Dessertspoon = 2 Teaspoons   1 Tablespoon = 3 Teaspoons = 1 fl oz

Weight				Volume		
g	**oz**	**lb**		**ml**	**fl oz**	**pt**
10	½			10	½	
25	1			25	1	
50	2			50	2	
75	3			75	3	
110	4	¼		110	4	
150	5			150	5	¼
175	6			175	6	
200	7			200	7	
225	8	½		225	8	
275	10			275	10	½
350	12			350	12	
450	16	1		425	15	¾
570	20	1¼		570	20	1
700	24	1½		700	24	
900	32	2		900	32	
1,000	35			1,000	35	1¾
1,350	48	3				

Lengths and temperatures

Length				Temperature			
cm	**inch**	**ft**		**Gas Mark**	**°F**	**°C**	**°C (fan oven)**
0.5	¼			½	175	80	60
1	½			1	275	140	120
2	¾			2	300	150	130
2.5	1			3	325	170	150
5	2			4	350	180	160
10	4			5	375	190	170
15	6	½		6	400	200	180
20	8			7	425	220	200
25	10			8	450	230	210
30	12	1		9	475	240	220

What Kitchen Equipment do you Need?

They say, "A bad workman blames his tools", and even a good cook cannot achieve the best results with inferior appliances and utensils. This chapter offers my suggestions of what to look for in kitchen equipment, how to choose it, how to use it, and '**First Aid**' tips for cleaning and maintaining your equipment.

I assume everyone has certain basic kitchen facilities. At least one sink with hot and cold running water is essential, but two sinks are better, with one dedicated to food preparation, and the other to cleaning. Suitable storage cupboards are useful, although a walk-in larder, if you have one, is the best.

Appropriate Appliances of Science

Although relatively expensive, many of your kitchen appliances are essential, even if you don't do much basic cookery, and only plan to use convenience foods. The appliances considered below are presented roughly in their order of importance. I do not expect you to re-equip your kitchen, but when you have to replace an appliance, my guidelines may be useful.

The tips given here should help you to choose suitable equipment and avoid expensive mistakes. I do not recommend particular manufacturers or models because they change so quickly. Nor do I offer advice on ecological issues such as which energy source creates least pollution. Rather, I identify cookery attributes and features that you should look for in each type of appliance, and give suggestions on how to keep them in good condition.

One general tip is to try using an appliance before parting with your cash. Either borrow it, or use someone else's, to see if you like it. Consult consumer advice magazines that regularly test domestic appliances and follow their recommendations. You do not even have to buy these publications, because they are usually available at your local library. Once you do decide to buy, ensure you tell the shop if you want the appliance for something particular. Then, if it is unsuitable you can take it back. For example, you may want a bread maker machine that is particularly good at baking wholemeal bread.

Home on the Range

One of the most important appliances in your kitchen will be your cooker. They come in many shapes, sizes, materials, and colours. They offer a wide range of features, from the simplest automatic timer or stay-clean liners, to most sophisticated gadgets such as integral griddle, wok burner, rotisserie, or steaming facility. What you should ask yourself is "Am I going to use them?". The most useful gadget is a minute timer, but this could easily be bought separately. It goes without saying, that the more features, the higher the price, and the greater likelihood that things will go wrong.

Having decided on your budget, the next factor is what fuel to use. The choice is electricity, natural gas, liquid gas, and oil. Electricity is the cleanest fuel, but may take slightly longer to produce heat than gas, and may be prone to those unexpected power cuts. Gas cookers offer instant heat, but also produce much more condensation than electric cookers. Always try to have some windows open when undertaking a lot of cooking, especially in cold weather. Dual fuel cookers offer the versatility of both electricity and gas, combined in one piece of equipment. Also, I must not forget the traditional cast-iron stoves, which can use any of the fuels, may double as the central heating system, and are commonplace in farmhouse kitchens.

There are three different elements to a cooker. They are the grill, the hob, and the oven. These may be combined into one unit, or obtained and fitted separately. The advice I give below applies equally whichever alternative you choose.

Grill

The grill should be eye level, so you can see and smell what is happening; as opposed to waist height, which involves bending, and is awkward to see if the food is burning as it grills, especially if inside the oven. On the other hand, you must beware of leaning over a hot hob in order to use an eye level grill, especially if its controls are sited on the grill rather than the main hob control panel.

The grill should have two runner positions, so that your deep dishes can be accommodated, as well as shallow items such as toast.

If possible, the grill pan should have two evenly spaced handles, rather than one central handle. This ensures the weight is more evenly distributed through two hands, instead of just one.

Hob or Stove

The rings should be of a variety of sizes, so small pans as well as larger pans can be accommodated.

Ease of cleaning should be an overriding factor governing choice. Electric halogen or induction hobs are the easiest to clean. Other hobs, that involve removing pan supports in order to clean, need to be easy to disassemble and reassemble.

The control panel should feel comfortable to handle, be intuitive to operate, and be easy to clean.

Oven

Convection or zoned ovens provide different heat zones within the oven despite the thermostat. The advantage being that you can cook a variety of dishes that require different temperatures at the same time. For example, Gas Mark 6 / 200°C on the middle shelf gives a slightly higher temperature on the top shelf, and a lower one on the bottom shelf. Do not place food on the base plate of the oven, because it may burn easily.

Fan assisted ovens are the same temperature throughout the oven. This is ideal if you like to cook batches of one item such as biscuits, or pies. Fan assisted ovens are more efficient than convection or zoned ovens. Therefore, if you want to use recipes not intended for fan ovens, reduce the temperature by 20°C in order to obtain satisfactory results.

Catalytic liners or hydro-clean and pyrolytic ovens all involve self-cleaning of the inside of the oven one way or another. Well worth considering.

Look for the largest capacity of oven in relation to the overall size of the cooker, because those few centimetres or inches can make all the difference when you're trying to fit in that large turkey at Christmas.

Ovens with three shelves offer more flexibility than those with two , as they tend to have more shelf positions, as well as more available cooking space.

Try to avoid main ovens that are sited low down near the floor, as this is very inconvenient and could lead to back problems later. Built in ovens at waist height are the best for ease of access.

Modern ovens do not need a warming up period before using. They are more efficient and can be used from cold.

Keep Cool with a Refrigerator

Whether you are cooking in a bed-sit, or entertaining in a farmhouse kitchen, a refrigerator is an essential appliance. Its function is to keep food hygienically safe before consumption, but when considering what to buy, many factors such as dimensions, capacity, noise, features, style, finish, cleaning, and cost all play a part.

A fridge is essentially an insulated box with a thermostatically controlled electric pump that circulates liquid coolant around some pipe-work. Therefore, very little can go wrong with this simple mechanism.

Manufacturers have made some improvements in energy efficiency, which is measured using a letter scale. Letter 'A' rating is the most efficient, and 'G' rating is the least efficient, but since September 2001 no fridge should have been produced with a rating lower than 'C'.

There are two broad types of fridge. One has an icebox, and the other, without an icebox, is known as a larder fridge. Both have their advantages.

Ice box Fridge

This type of fridge can provide ice cubes and store small amounts of pre-frozen food. The length of storage depends on a star rating as shown in the table below.

Star Rating	Temperature	Storage Time
2 star * *	-12°C	1 month
3 star * * *	-18°C	3 months
4 star * * * *	-18°C	3 months

A 4-star version is also able to freeze small amounts of fresh food. The icebox helps to maintain an even temperature throughout the fridge.

The drawback to this type of fridge is that it needs to be defrosted manually on a regular basis.

Larder Fridge

A larder fridge does not hold frozen food because it only functions between 0°C and 5°C; but may provide a chiller compartment, which is kept cooler than the main body of the fridge, and is ideal for chilled meats or meals.

Another innovation is a cellar compartment operating at a temperature of 10°C and especially designed for the storage of wines and fruit.

A larder fridge tends to have a greater variation of temperature throughout the cabinet than an icebox fridge, and is usually cooler at the bottom. However, most models of larder fridge have an automatic defrost mechanism.

Fridge Features

Other features that should be considered when you purchase a fridge include the following.

- ◆ Castors or rollers to allow access for cleaning behind the fridge.
- ◆ Adjustable feet to make it easier to level the fridge.
- ◆ Thermometer visible from the outside, registering the inside temperature.
- ◆ Reasonable number of adjustable shelves offering flexible storage.
- ◆ Adjustable door racks offering flexible storage.
- ◆ Upright bottle store with bottle grips or rack dividers to make bottles more secure.

If your fridge is not fitted with a thermometer, I would recommend buying a separate fridge thermometer, to check that the appliance is operating between 0°C and 5°C, otherwise food is liable to deteriorate quicker than it should. You need to adjust the temperature setting of the fridge from time to time, to take account of the ambient room temperature.

Preserve Ice Cold in the Freezer

Bulk shopping and batch cooking for future consumption or simply convenience are some of the reasons why people purchase a freezer. Whether living alone or managing a large family, there is a freezer to suit your requirements; ranging from the worktop height or full height upright models to the traditional chest style.

Just like refrigerators, freezers have been given an energy rating. Letter 'A' rating is the most efficient, through to 'C', the least efficient. This is in line with the European Union commitment to be more environmentally friendly by reducing carbon dioxide emissions.

Chest Freezer

Available space is one factor governing your choice. Chest freezers take up more floor space, and are often more conveniently situated in the utility room or garage. However, some manufacturers do not recommend the latter, due to the need for a minimum ambient temperature of 10°C for freezers to work efficiently. So, unheated rooms such as garages, which can often fall below 0°C, may not be suitable.

Upright Freezer

Upright freezers are more likely to be kept in the kitchen, but siting your appliance in the wrong place will cost you more to run. Do not place it in direct sunlight, or next to a cooker or central heating boiler, as the freezer will have to use more energy maintaining the temperature at minus 18°C, necessary to keep the food inside frozen.

Freezer Features

The features that you should consider when purchasing a freezer include the following.

◆ External thermometer display to monitor the temperature of -18°C inside. If your freezer does not have this facility, I recommend that you buy an internal thermometer, to check the appliance is maintaining the temperature.

◆ Automatic defrost mechanism to eliminate tedious manual defrosting.

◆ Fast-freeze facility to allow you to freeze fresh food quickly.

◆ Warning light in case the internal temperature rises is a food safety feature.

◆ Memory button, to monitor the maximum internal temperature over several days, while you are away on holiday for instance. If the displayed maximum temperature is too high, the food is at risk and should be either discarded or cooked immediately.

◆ Adjustable number of compartments in upright models, with removable drawers or shelves to accommodate bulky items.

◆ Lockable door or lid is a useful security feature.

◆ Audible alarm if the door or lid is not closed properly is a food safety feature.

◆ Castors or rollers to allow access for cleaning behind the freezer.

◆ Adjustable feet to make it easier to level the freezer.

◆ Reversible door hinges and handles are a convenience.

Shopping, Freezing, and Thawing

For safety tips and advice on purchasing, freezing, storing, and thawing frozen foods see the later '**Refrigeration and Freezing**' section on page 92.

Fast Food from a Microwave Oven

When I think of a piece of equipment in the home that has significantly transformed the lives of the owners, the microwave oven is up there with the automatic washing machine, dish-washer, vacuum cleaner, television, and radio.

The microwave oven works by producing invisible electromagnetic waves, which agitate water molecules in food. Amazingly, this agitation produces enough friction to generate heat in the food. I always think this process is like rubbing your hands together. It does not matter how cold your hands are; rubbing them together always makes them warmer.

The key to successful microwave cooking is to eliminate any cold spots, so that the food is cooked uniformly. The electromagnetic waves do not radiate evenly within the oven, so most will have a turntable to rotate the food through the waves.

Basic Microwave Oven

You can purchase just a basic microwave oven, which will cook the majority of foodstuffs acceptably, and is ideal if you simply want quick results, or to reheat food prepared by another method. The biggest drawback of these basic models is that they cannot brown or crisp raw foods.

Combination Oven

If you want speedy cookery but with traditional results, a combination oven may be the solution. This is a microwave oven with the convenience of a conventional oven and grill built in. Some foods cooked in a basic microwave oven can be limp and soggy, such as jacket potatoes. With a combination oven, the food can take on a familiar cooked appearance; jacket potatoes gain a crisp skin, but retain a soft textured interior.

In theory, a combination oven could replace your main oven as the primary source of cooking. You can use the grill, conventional oven, or microwave features independently, or in any combination. However, the space inside such ovens is often relatively small.

What you need to remember is to experiment with your new oven. It is like any novel piece of equipment. You need to get to know it inside out, its limitations, and all the facilities. It is important to read the manufacturer's instruction booklet to get the best from your acquisition, then you can cook with confidence.

Whiz That Food Processor

I consider a food processor to be a necessity if you enjoy cooking, because it takes on the role of a second pair of hands in the kitchen. It will speed up mundane food preparation processes, allowing you to get on with the more enjoyable aspects of cooking.

A food processor offers a wide range of functions, from shredding, slicing, grating, chopping, chipping, and grinding to liquidising, puréeing, whisking, and kneading. The downside is that, the more functions provided, the more attachments need to be washed up and stored.

Make sure your choice of processor fits the space available on your worktop, and blends into the overall kitchen design. It is of no use hiding this valuable piece of equipment in a cupboard, because you will not use it as often as when it is at your elbow, begging to be utilised.

In order to get the most out of your machine, familiarise yourself with all the attachments, read the instructions avidly, know how to assemble and disassemble all the parts, and use it as often as possible.

Take the Plunge with a Deep Fat Fryer

Greasy, carbon black, chip pans that smoked as though they were sending signals, were the norm in the kitchen when I was younger. Now safety, sophistication, and size make the deep fat fryer dominant, consigning the traditional chip pan to the dustbin.

The deep fat fryer is easier, cleaner, safer, and less smelly to use than the time-honoured chip pan. Features to look for include the following.

- Temperature controls take the guesswork and hazard out of assessing when the oil is ready for frying. You set a dial and an indicator light tells you when the oil has reached the required temperature.
- Automatic timer will eliminate the need to keep a check on the food being fried.
- Easy to use controls let you lower the food into hot oil after you have closed the lid. This is safer for the user, as any splattering from hot oil is eliminated, and escaping steam is kept to a minimum.
- Removable filter designed to reduce the escape of frying smells.
- Frying capacity varies between models and determines how much you can fry and the amount of oil required.
- Ease of cleaning affects how easy it is to strain and drain used oil. Check that the parts are dishwasher friendly.
- A viewing window is meant to allow you to see what is happening in the oil without opening the lid, but is of limited use because of the steam produced while frying.

For safety tips and advice on '**Deep Fat Frying**' see page 86.

Bread Maker to Give Us the Dough

The waft of freshly baked bread conjures up memories of honey coloured, pleasingly risen loaves, with crisp crusts, soft textured crumb, and a superb taste.

If you don't have the time to undertake your own bread making, or indeed may not the have the skill in your hands, you can always fall back on commercially produced hand-baked bread.

Another alternative is to use an electric bread-making machine. This involves placing the ingredients into the non-stick pan supplied; then you put the pan in the machine, plug it in, switch on, and finally set the programme. At the touch of a button, you can have fresh bread within 2 – 2½ hours using an accelerated rapid programme. Otherwise, for slightly better results, just wait 3 – 4 hours for basic white bread, or 4 – 5 hours for the wholemeal bread cycle.

One of the main advantages is the certainty of knowing exactly what goes into making the loaf, because you choose the ingredients. This also means you can be creative in your selection of herbs, spices, seeds, nuts, and fruit to customise your dough.

You will need to read and follow the manufacturer's instructions to the letter, especially the order the ingredients are placed into the baking pan. Before purchase, check that the machine can make at least one basic loaf that calls for all the ingredients to go in at the beginning of the process. Otherwise, you cannot leave the machine to complete the job unattended.

If you want to use your bread maker specifically for baking a particular type of loaf, tell your retailer before purchase, because some machines are more efficient than others at producing certain varieties of bread. Most machines are good at baking white bread, but wholemeal bread and enriched doughs often produce poor results in some machines.

Remember that you must have a suitable worktop space for this additional appliance. It must be easily accessible with a handy power socket. You may also find the machine somewhat annoying, as kneading and mixing dough are not silent procedures.

Ice Cream Maker must Churn its Keep

"Stop me and buy one" was the slogan of the travelling ice cream vendor. I'm sure, if you were like me, you would take up that challenge, but these days the slogan is rarely heard. This is because ice cream, which was once considered a treat or even a luxury, has now become ubiquitous, with a myriad of flavours.

You may think that with this amount of choice, no one would want to make their own ice cream, let alone pay hard cash for a machine to do the job for them. One reason is that you know exactly what goes into making the product, by using fresh ingredients like double cream, egg yolks, and fruit. It will not contain any of the emulsifiers or flavourings that commercial products must have to give them a smooth and creamy texture. Nor will it have any synthetic preservatives or stabilisers to increase its freezer life. Therefore, home-made ice cream should be stored for no more than a week, because then it will start to lose its flavour.

Another reason for choosing to make your own ice cream is that you can customise the result, by using the fruit from your garden, or the spoils of a family foray into the countryside. There is nothing quite so comforting as knowing that, the dish you are savouring was produced exclusively by you. That is self-satisfaction with a big S.

Although home-made ice cream can taste just as good as some of the luxury shop bought creations, don't think that it will be cheaper, because it won't – especially if you have purchased an ice cream maker. You can make ice cream without a machine, but some of the recipes are time consuming, due to the process of stirring the mixture several times during freezing, to avoid the formation of ice crystals and achieve a smooth consistency. There are recipes that do not require this tedious procedure, and I have included some of these later in the book.

Ice cream makers work by gradually freezing the raw ingredients whilst constantly moving or churning the mixture. This produces a smooth texture and eliminates large ice crystals that cause graininess.

The choice of machine will be governed by cost. The more expensive models have their own freezer unit and can be operational within five minutes of switch on. They comprise a ½ litre (1 pint) bowl that will freeze and churn your ice cream with motorised paddles and be ready within half an hour. Such models are ideal for the impulsive cook. However, this is a bulky piece of equipment that does not like being moved around due to the refrigerant. Therefore, you need to allocate precious space on your worktop for it.

The cheaper models have a detachable churning bowl with coolant sealed inside its double skin. This needs to be pre-frozen in your freezer for up to 18 hours before use. Ideally, you should keep the bowl in the freezer permanently until needed, if you can spare the space. Most of these models have either a motorised bowl or motorised paddles to churn the ice cream once the machine has been assembled. It will take approximately 15 – 30 minutes to churn ½ litre (1 pint) of ice cream. If you want a variety of flavours, you may have to re-freeze the coolant in the bowl between each flavour.

One final piece of advice is to find a friend or neighbour who has an ice cream maker, and ask to try it out before putting your hand in your pocket. This may avoid an expensive mistake, and will give you the opportunity to see whether it is worth investing in another precious gadget.

Useful Utensils or Gimmicky Gadgets?

Although utensils are usually less expensive than appliances, they can soon make a sizeable hole in your pocket. The greater the variety of cooking that you plan to undertake, the more utensils you will probably need. Although good kitchen equipment can be expensive, most items will last a lifetime. It is pointless to spend a fortune on matching kitchen fixtures, and stint on the tools you need to do the job. However, beware of the plethora of gadgets that clutter up cook shops. Many are more expensive than the basic tool, but are often less efficient and more difficult to clean.

Rattle Those Pots and Pans

First I will focus on all those pots and pans that are the starting point for many recipes, and try to remove some of the mystique from the abundance of choice you are bombarded with in cookery shops.

Heat Conductivity

Cooking pots and pans need to equalise the heat across their surfaces, without hot spots, and so transfer the heat evenly to the food inside. Each material has a heat conductivity coefficient that governs the speed at which the heat is spread.

Material	Heat Conductivity (Calories per cm per sec per °C)
Copper	0.94
Pure aluminium	0.53
Cast aluminium	0.33
Steel	0.16
Cast-iron	0.12
Stainless steel	0.05

To avoid hot spots, low conductivity material such as cast-iron must be thicker than high conductivity material such as copper. However, other factors also govern your choice of cookware as outlined below.

Saucepans

You need a range of saucepans, plus lids, if you are into any style of cooking. However, although a matching set of saucepans may be aesthetically pleasing, ideally you should choose a variety of sizes and types in order to get the best performance from each one.

Before you even introduce food to a brand spanking new saucepan, you need to follow the manufacturer's instructions on how to season that new pan. Otherwise, you will be in for a sticky time. Believe me, it is worth the time and effort to follow those instructions, if you want to achieve problem-free cooking. Another tip, for the best cooking results, is to use your pans on a low to medium heat. This will also preserve the life of the saucepan.

Copper Saucepans

Copper pans are lovely to look at, are expensive to buy, and are high on maintenance (both keeping clean and re-lining the tin). However, they are excellent conductors of heat, and therefore give good results with food, but watch out for those hot handles.

Non-stick Saucepans

Non-stick surfaces are offered on a variety of products; some endorsed by celebrity chefs, which is always a good sign, because they have their reputation to think of. Choice is governed by what you intend to use the pan for. If just boiling milk, the cheapest will do, but sauce making, porridge, and scrambled egg need quality pans. Non-stick pans are most useful for foods that are notoriously sticky such as all egg-based dishes, milk dishes, porridge, and sauces.

Look out for a pouring lip, for ease of pouring, and handles that are angled away from the heat source, to protect your hands. Rounded base pans are best as this makes stirring around the bottom easier. Check the non-stick coating is guaranteed for life. Ensure the lid is tight fitting but has a steam outlet.

Stainless Steel Saucepans

Stainless steel makes me think of bright and shiny, easy to clean, and light to handle saucepans. They are ideal for certain methods of cooking such as boiling vegetables and pasta, but not for sauce making or stewing as the sauce tends to burn onto the thin walls of the pan.

Enamelled Cast-Ironware

Enamelled cast-iron visually has a rustic charm about it, with its chunky design, choice of strong colours, and heavyweight feel. They are extremely efficient at spreading and retaining the heat, allowing you to cook at a lower setting, but they do take longer to heat up initially.

The heaviness can be a disadvantage, because when full of hot food, you are certainly made aware of how weighty they can be. The enamel rim can become chipped; exposing the cast-iron beneath, which in turn can rust. Prolonged use will eventually wear away the enamel coating. I have worn out one set of these saucepans. Wooden handles, if fitted, are easy to char by mistake, if the heat source is too fierce.

Cast-Aluminium Saucepans

Cast-aluminium saucepans are good all-round performers, very hard wearing, and easy to clean. Their thick base conducts the heat evenly, with no hot spots. They are the workhorses of saucepans. Anodised aluminium gives a non-stick finished, and is often known as hard anodised cookware.

First Aid

There are two points to watch out for when using aluminium saucepans.

Symptom: *Aluminium pans are stained.*
Diagnosis: *These pans are prone to staining with certain foods.*
Antidote: *Boil up water in the pan with either lemon juice or vinegar. Use 1 litre (2 pints) of water to two tablespoons of acid.*

Symptom: *Foods take on a metallic taste or an unusual colour.*
Diagnosis: *Food has been allowed to steep or stand for some time.*
Remedy: *Do not store food in aluminium pans for a long time.*

Frying Pans

Non-stick Frying Pans

A variety of non-stick coated frying pans are available. You should choose those endorsed by celebrity chefs, as they will only put their name to products that are tried, tested, and approved. Look out for non-stick pans that can cope with metal implements being used on them.

Cast-iron Frying Pans

Cast-iron frying pans are, and always will be, the best choice for frying. Once properly seasoned, so that they become non-stick, they will last a lifetime.

Seasoning and Care

Seasoning is essential when you first purchase a cast-iron frying pan. This is done by burning thin layers of oil onto the surface of the pan. The pan must be heated to a high temperature and a coating of oil swilled around the surface. This process should be repeated several times to build up a non-stick layer.

Each time you use the pan, heat it to a high temperature, before adding a little oil to cover the whole surface. Use a piece of kitchen paper or a pastry brush to distribute the oil evenly. Use the pan exclusively for frying food with oil or fat.

To clean the pan, never use a metal scourer, or you will undo all your hard work in achieving a non-stick coat. Also, never leave the pan to soak in water, as it may go rusty. Preferably, you should simply wipe out the pan with kitchen paper. Alternatively, add a teaspoon of salt to the dry hot pan, and use kitchen paper screwed into a ball to rub the salt around the pan until the salt turns grey. Discard the salt, and wipe out with a clean piece of kitchen paper.

Wok

'The blacker the wok, the better the cook' highlights the versatility of this piece of equipment. You can steam, braise, boil, stir fry, shallow fry, and deep fry in this large semicircular pan.

Woks are usually made from mild steel or anodised aluminium. If it is mild steel, follow the instructions for seasoning and care of a cast-iron frying pan given above. The non-stick anodised aluminium variety does not require seasoning. They can be purchased with one long handle or two shorter ones. Choose whichever feels most comfortable for you.

Omelette Pan

An omelette pan is a small frying pan with rounded sides. It should be kept solely for making omelettes, or in an emergency, for frying eggs. A 15 cm (6") diameter pan will hold a two-egg omelette mix, whereas an 18 cm (7") pan will take a three egg mixture.

Whether you prefer copper, cast-iron, enamelled cast-iron, aluminium, or anodised aluminium, the base of the pan should be thick, so that it will retain the heat, and cook the eggs quickly.

Anodised aluminium, or non-stick, omelette pans do **not** require seasoning. However, all the other types do, and to obtain the best results when using your pan, follow the instructions for seasoning and cleaning frying pans given above.

Pancake or Crêpe Pan

This little frying pan with shallow sides shouts, "I'm a pancake pan and want to remain exclusive!" and that is how you should treat this special piece of equipment.

It can be made from copper, cast-iron, or anodised non-stick aluminium. If you buy the copper or cast-iron variety, you will need to follow the seasoning and cleaning instructions given above for frying pans.

Because this pan is a miniature frying pan, it usually has a short stubby handle. This can get very hot, especially if made of metal, so be aware and take care not to burn yourself.

Griddle Pan

This pan is very fashionable in giving food that black striped effect that says; "I've been griddled". The griddle is used exactly like a frying pan, but it has raised ribbed ridges. These keep the food above any excess oil or fat, which is a healthier method of cooking.

Griddles are made of cast-iron, and should be heated before being used; otherwise, the food may stick. If possible, oil the food to be griddled rather than the griddle itself. This will reduce the amount of oil splattering and smokiness from surplus cooking oil.

Roasting Tins, Trivets, and Bags

You need roasting tins made of solid, heavy-gauge metal, to avoid them buckling at high temperatures. You should obtain at least two sizes of tin. Choose roasting tins that incorporate handles, as these give something to grip when the tins are in action.

A trivet is a metal grid that sits snugly inside the roasting tin. It is a useful addition when roasting poultry, game, or meat, because it allows the food to sit above the fat. Therefore, the food is not shallow frying, but truly roasting.

Roasting bags can be purchased at large supermarkets. You can also use microwave bags as an alternative to roasting bags. Their purpose is to roast food without it drying out, and reduce splattering, which saves soiling of the oven. The idea is that you place the food to be roasted in the bag, allowing sufficient air space around the food, and then place the bag in a deep roasting tin. Tie the bag loosely to allow steam to escape, or partially slit the top of the bag with scissors. After cooking, completely slit the top of the roasting bag, and remove the food carefully. Any residue juices can be used for the sauce.

Casserole Dishes

You could braise or casserole food in an old tin can with aluminium foil acting as a lid, but the most effective and efficient casserole dishes conduct heat well and distribute it evenly to the food. A tight fitting lid is essential, so that moisture and flavour are retained, and the food has less chance of drying out.

A variety of materials is used, including Pyrex® (which is toughened glass), white porcelain, glazed earthenware, stainless steel, enamelled cast-iron, and enamelled mild-steel.

Ideally, the food should first be sealed or browned in the casserole dish you intend to use. This ensures that all the residue and sediment acquired during the sealing process is utilised during braising, and no flavour is lost.

Quality stainless steel, and enamelled cast-iron or mild-steel casseroles are ideal because they can initially be used on the hob for sealing, as well as in the oven for braising. They are durable, hard wearing, and can look attractive when used as oven-to-table-ware.

Whereas, Pyrex®, white porcelain, and glazed earthenware cannot be used directly on a heat source. Therefore, the initial sealing of food must be done else-where and transferred to the casserole dish.

Baking Utensils – Shake, Rattle and Roll

Whether you are a novice or a master baker, you will certainly need a nucleus of baking equipment, which should include the following items.

Pastry Blender

This is a hand held gadget, made of stainless steel, with five or six thin, semicir-cular wires attached to its handle. It is used when making pastry, to mix the fat into the flour, whilst aerating the mixture. It is particularly useful if you have hot hands, to avoid touching the pastry mix.

Rolling Pin

Rolling pins can be made from wood, polyethylene, stainless steel, or marble. Some can be filled with water to prevent the pastry sticking. They should all be smooth, long, straight, and feel comfortable to handle.

Flour Dredger

Dredgers can be fine- or coarse-holed depending on the desired coverage of the contents. Usually they are used for flour, cocoa powder, and castor or icing sugar.

Pastry Brush

Brushes must be soft bristled, so as not to damage the product. They are very versatile and used for many tasks, from spreading oil on baking tins, to egg washing bread rolls. However, watch out for loose bristles when the brush is used.

Pastry Cutters

These are sold in sets of seven and made of plastic, stainless steel, tinned steel, or aluminium. Plain cutters are for savoury items, and fluted cutters for sweet items. Therefore, it is easy to identify whether the product is sweet or savoury.

Baking Trays and Mats

Baking trays can be made from carbon steel, aluminium, or non-stick materials, but must be heavy in relation to their size, so that they do not buckle under the heat.

Baking mats or baking parchments are reusable non-stick baking sheets that save cleaning and prevent damage to delicate patisserie products. They are easy to use, and easy to clean, simply by wiping with a damp cloth after use.

Baking Tins

Patty and Quiche Tins

There is a variety of sizes, shapes, and materials , depending on the ultimate use. Look for the tins with loose bases, as these are more practical for service. This is because the base can be used as a substitute plate after the flan or quiche has been baked. All baking tins should be stored in dry conditions, and in an orderly manner, to avoid damage.

Individual Basins

These individual basins come in a variety of shapes and sizes, but the most popular are dariole moulds and ramekin dishes.

Dariole moulds look like pudding basins that have shrunk in the wash. They are individual containers for sweet and savoury puddings, mousses, jellies, and sponges. They can be made from aluminium or boilable plastic, and hold approximately 150 ml (5 fl oz) of liquid. The plastic variety usually also come with a lid.

Ramekin dishes are made in porcelain or glassware in a range of sizes. They are straight sided similar to miniature soufflé dishes. They can be used for the same sort of dishes as dariole moulds, but can go directly from the oven to the table.

Sandwich Tins

These sponge cake tins are usually purchased in pairs, in either 15 cm (6") or 18 cm (7") or 20 cm (8") diameter versions. Buy tins with loose bases, to make it easier to remove the sponges from the tins, and made from brushed aluminium or anodised aluminium. The tins can also be used for baking bread, flans, Chelsea buns, and shortbread. After use you should wash and dry them thoroughly, and store in dry conditions.

Bread Tins

I've used a variety of containers to bake bread, including terracotta flower pots, non-stick sandwich tins, and cast-iron rectangular terrines, as well as the more traditional ½ kg (1 lb) and 1 kg (2 lb) loaf tins.

First Aid

Symptom: *Bread tends to stick in the baking tin.*

Diagnosis: *Not greased sufficiently.*

Remedy: *Lightly coat the inside of the container with vegetable oil and line the base with non-stick greaseproof or parchment paper.*

Skewers

From the humble rosemary twig through to the exotic handcrafted gold tipped variety, skewers are ideal for holding food in place whilst cooking.

Wooden skewers should always be soaked in water for at least half an hour before threading with food, to prevent the wood catching fire while cooking.

The cheap metal variety is good for testing if food is cooked. When testing poultry, insert the skewer into the thickest part of the thigh, and the juices should run clear. To test if cakes are baked, insert the skewer, and it should come out clean. Another use for skewers is to heat them over the hob, sprinkle icing sugar over cakes or biscuits, and scorch the sugar to give a decorative caramelised pattern.

Whisks and Mixers Beat off Opposition

If you are into making sauces or baking cakes these versatile utensils will help you effortlessly blend your ingredients together.

Hand Whisks

Whisks can be made from stainless steel, polyethylene, wood, or tinned steel. I have three whisks each of different size and construction. I use a large stainless steel whisk for aerating eggs, a medium polyethylene whisk to remove lumps from sauces, and a small wooden whisk for mixing small amounts of liquid.

First Aid

Symptom: *Non-stick pans have become scratched and contents are sticking.*

Diagnosis: *Probably you have used metal utensils in the pans.*

Remedy: *Only use plastic or wooden utensils in non-stick pans.*

Electric Whisk

Being easy to use and clean, makes this one of the 'must have' gadgets in the kitchen. Before buying, try to handle several models to see which is the most comfortable to use and hold.

Electric Blender

This is another kitchen tool that is invaluable in sticky situations. For example, it is great at smoothing lumpy sauces, puréeing soups, blending egg based mixtures, frothing sauces, and even chopping small amounts of herbs, vegetables, or fruit. Whether you only undertake these tasks occasionally, or you cook incessantly, a hand-held blender is a useful piece of equipment. It can replace or enhance the functions of the bulkier and more expensive food processor. Especially since the hand blender is compact enough to be used in situ, right inside the cooking saucepan, as long as it is away from direct heat. If space is at a premium, this nifty gadget is a must.

When buying this handy implement, you should look for the following features. It should be easy to operate and clean, and feel comfortable to handle, with sturdy controls and a streamlined design. Ideally, it should be able to stand unaided when not in use. Some models provide a range of operating speeds, a whisk attachment in addition to the standard blender, an enclosed chopping bowl, or a liquidising beaker. If there were enough features, you may even decide not to invest in a food processor.

The one golden rule, when using this time saving gadget, is not to remove the blending foot from the mixture, until the power has been switched off, and the motor has stopped. Otherwise, everyone and everything gets to taste the mixture, and the time you thought you'd saved has been lost in cleaning up!

Electric Liquidiser

This is a covered goblet with a small set of motorised blades in the bottom, which is used to liquidise soups and sauces, or blend liquids. A liquidiser is limited in the tasks it can undertake, and you would be better with a hand-held electric blender, which is more versatile, more compact, and easier to wash-up.

Kitchen Forks and Spoons

You need a large fork for jobs such as beating eggs, making pastry, fluffing cooked rice, tossing salads, testing pasta and vegetables to see if they are cooked, and of course steadying hot roast meat for carving.

Large kitchen spoons are ideal for basting meat, poultry, and vegetables. They are also used for portioning cooked dishes, and stirring mixtures without fear of burning your fingers.

Both utensils can be made from wood, plastic, or metal. Try not to use metal utensils with non-stick pans to avoid scratching the surface.

Slices and Spatulas Lift and Separate

Lifting and separating, just like the bra advert, is how I view slices and spatulas.

Fish and Cake Slices

Slices can lift items like poached fish, shallow fried eggs, or baked pizza, and separate pieces of cake, fruit pie, or meringues. This shows the versatility of this small piece of equipment, where two or three different sized slices, perhaps of varying shapes, are useful tools to have in the kitchen. They come in a variety of materials, for instance honed hardwood, plastic, stainless steel, aluminium, and silver.

Spatulas

Spatulas are made of plastic or rubber, so that they can reach into every corner or crevice, removing every last drop of mixture from any container. They are also useful for spreading and lightly combining mixtures.

Kitchen Tongs

These are used instead of your fingers for turning and holding hot foods such as fish, steaks, sausages, meat balls, and vegetables, where you may not want to pierce the food. They can be made from stainless steel, chrome, plastic, and hardwood.

Knives and Graters in at the Sharp End

"I see you've been in the knife box again", is a northern saying that means you are as sharp as the contents. Let's hope so!

Kitchen Knives

If you care about quality in the kitchen, you have got to be sharp, and stay sharp when cooking. The same applies to knives. My earliest recollection of knives at home, was hearing my dad sharpening a yellow bone-handled, stiletto shaped, knife on the back door step.

Very sharp knives show that the person using them means business. Serious cooks, having purchased a sharp, well balanced, comfortable, kitchen knife, will continually use the butcher's steel or knife sharpener to maintain that razor sharp edge. It is easier to cut yourself with a blunt knife, as more pressure is required to do the job, causing the knife to slip.

One of the main factors in choosing a knife is that it should feel right in your hand, almost like a glove. Does it feel comfortable, well balanced, with a good grip? Handle several different makes of knife. Feel the weight. Weightier knives do not necessarily mean better. The trend today is towards lighter weight, forged from stainless steel or even ceramic, but what you must identify is the means of keeping that edge on the blade. Do you need a special steel or sharpening equipment, or will a standard 25 – 30 cm (10 – 12 inch) long butcher's steel be sufficient?

As well as feeling balanced in your hand, a good knife should have the tang (the extension of the blade) running through the entire handle to give rigidity. The handle itself should be non-slip, or made from non-slip material, to avoid accidents when your hands become wet or greasy. If you use a dishwasher, check that your knives are dishwasher safe.

Cook's Knife

Choose a cook's knife with a blade that is not too long, otherwise you will have difficulty in maintaining good control. It is better to start with an 18 – 23 cm (7 – 9 inch) blade to master basic skills, and move on to a larger knife if you feel the need arises.

Vegetable Knife

A smaller version of a cook's knife, with similar attributes except for a shorter 8 cm (3") blade, is known as a vegetable knife. It is easier to handle and control when undertaking more precise work. Along with its big brother, it is invaluable in the kitchen.

Serrated Knife

A serrated knife is ideal for slicing acid loving foods such as tomatoes and citrus fruit. The acid affects the performance of straight edged knives, whereas serrated edged knives are unaffected. They vary in size, but one similar in length to a vegetable knife will do nicely.

Knife Block

After use, store all sharp knives in a knife block or rack to avoid damage to the knives and to yourself.

Sharpeners

You can judge a cook by the knives they use. I do not mean just the quality though. Quality can be bought, but you can't buy permanent sharpness. The difference between a committed cook and an indifferent one is the edge on their knives.

Blunt knives can tear, crush, rip, or simply not cut food cleanly, so the product suffers. The person using a blunt knife can also suffer, as they are more prone to accidents, due to the extra amount of pressure required in using a dull knife.

All knives, even the most expensive, need sharpening at some time. Choosing a sharpener, that is compatible with you, will depend on the amount of time and effort you are willing to spend honing the dulled edge; for like any skill there is a knack to master.

Knife Sharpener

The easiest to use is an electric or a manual knife sharpener, where drawing the blade between rotating grinding wheels sharpens the knife. The electric version can cope with all sizes of knife, but the smaller manual variety is most effective on small knives. With just a few strokes, the edge on the knife should be soon restored.

Sharpening Steel

If you fancy looking like a professional, a butcher's or sharpening steel is a must. This resembles a shrunken version of a sword, where the blade is cylindrical similar to a poker, but engraved with a hatched sharpening pattern. The handle should feel comfortable to use, be non-slip with a good grip, and have a generous hand guard. Steels vary in length from 18 cm (7") up to 30 cm (12"). Choose one that does not feel too cumbersome.

There is a technique in using a sharpening steel. Hold the knife in one hand and the steel in the other hand, with the knife-edge resting on the steel at a slight angle. Run the knife towards you along the steel, whilst stroking the steel the entire length of the knife blade, but without damaging the knife-edge. Repeat this action on both sides of the blade. The angle of sharpening can vary between 10 and 25 degrees depending on the knife maker's instructions. You will know whether you are using the right angle by looking at the knife blade. Scratch marks indicate the angle is not correct; whereas a smooth clean blade shows promise. The best test is to carefully feel across (not along) the knife-edge with your finger, or simply try using the knife. Once you've mastered the technique, three or four quick flicks should be sufficient to sharpen your knife.

Whetstone

A whetstone is used for sharpening all edged implements, such as knives and scissors. It is usually made from silicon carbide, and needs to be wetted with oil or water before use. The whetstone is the most difficult sharpener to use, and requires the most skill. Eventually, the surface wears down to a concave shape, and will need to be levelled off to remain serviceable.

Chopping Boards

These items are a must in the kitchen, from both hygiene and safety points of view. They will save your work surfaces from damage and costly replacement.

People ask me how many boards do they need in their kitchen. The answer is a minimum of two, so you have one for raw foods and one for cooked foods, thus avoiding cross-contamination. Ideally, you should have easily distinguishable boards, either colour coded, or made of different materials, so there is no mistake in usage.

Boards are easily discoloured through constant use, and are prone to odour taints. This can quickly be rectified by wiping the board with neat bleach or baby sterilising fluid, leaving for 10 – 15 minutes, before rinsing thoroughly with clear water. Allow to air dry, before placing in a rack or hanging up. Try not to stack boards on top of each other, because they will be prone to mould growth, due to a lack of circulating air.

You can purchase boards made from a variety of hardwoods, plastic, glass, melamine, and rubber.

First Aid

Symptom: *Chopping board wobbles or slides when in use.*

Diagnosis: *Board or work surface is uneven.*

Antidote: *Place a damp, clean, tea towel underneath the board to hold it firm.*

Kitchen Scissors

Every kitchen needs scissors, whether you are snipping cooked bacon, removing fish fins, or trimming greaseproof paper to line cake tins. You can buy specialist poultry shears, which look like scissors with attitude, but for general-purpose needs, a sturdy, non-slip, comfortable pair is all you will require. Hang them in a convenient place, and be methodical, always return them to their home, so you can find them next time and save frustration on your part.

Graters

The purpose of this equipment is to shred food with varying degrees of coarseness. They can take the form of specialist graters used exclusively for individual food items such as nutmeg, ginger, chocolate, and even garlic, although this is usually more pressed than grated. The other end of the scale is the general, all-round, box grater, with a different coarseness on each side. There are also micro-graters available in two grades, one fine and one coarse, which are at the cutting edge of technology and work very effectively.

Cleaning and drying a grater can be difficult, but I use an old toothbrush for cleaning into every nook and cranny, followed by careful wiping with a dry tea towel, and leaving somewhere warm to dry completely.

Channelling Knife

This little tool is used for removing a continuous strip of peel from citrus fruit or cucumber. It can give the fruit or vegetable an attractive pattern, as well as supplying laces to tie certain foods together, such as pancakes or bunches of fresh beans. The knife looks like a small bottle opener, but with a sharpened kink on an inside edge for removing a strip of peel.

Mincers and Grinders Extract Flavours

The instructions with this group of utensils are for bumping and grinding, or squeezing and squashing.

Citrus Zester

The zester is a gadget for removing the flavoursome rind from citrus fruits, without the bitter pith. An alternative is to grate the fruit on a fine mesh grater.

Citrus Squeezer

Having removed the zest, cut the fruit in half widthways, and extract the fruit juice by twisting the fruit halves on a citrus squeezer. Another way of obtaining the fruit juice is to stab the cut fruit with the prongs of a fork, and twist to remove the juice.

Pestle and Mortar

This consists of a pear-shaped crusher, known as the pestle, and a bowl, which is the mortar. When used in unison they crush herbs, spices, nuts, and ice, along with blending liquid mixtures. Both the pestle and mortar should be made in the same material, which can be either glass, wood, cast-iron, marble, or stone.

Pepper Mill

A pepper mill reduces whole peppercorns to a fine or coarse powder. Look for a mill that is easy to use, easy to refill, as well as easy on the eye.

Garlic Press

If you love washing-up, a garlic press may be a good choice. Otherwise, it is better to crush garlic using the flat of a knife blade, or a smooth heavy object. Add a pinch of salt to help break down the garlic cells, and work the squashed garlic into a paste with the flat tip of the knife.

Sieves and Strainers Sort Out the Best

Whether making food lighter by introducing air, or removing surplus liquids, sieves and strainers are gadgets that enlighten or refine precious foodstuffs.

Sieves

I use different sieves for various procedures. Sieving flour requires a fine plastic mesh. Straining any food needs a stainless steel mesh. Puréeing sauces and soups also needs a stainless steel mesh. Ideally, they should all be dishwasher proof.

Colander

A colander is mainly used for washing delicate raw foods, and draining away liquids, but may also be improvised as a steamer over a saucepan of boiling water. They can be made from stainless steel or plastic. Look for a colander with one long handle, or two diametrically opposed handles, for ease of handling and lifting.

Salad Basket

A salad basket is a collapsible mesh basket used for washing and draining salad leaves and some vegetables. However, you could manage with just a colander and a clean tea towel or kitchen paper to dry off the contents.

Measures Keep Things in Proportion

Measuring devices such as scales, jugs, timers, and thermometers are all needed to take the guesswork out of cooking.

Weigh Scales

There is such a choice here.

At one end of the spectrum are the traditional and accurate balance scales. With these, the food is placed in the scale pan opposite the required balance weights, until equality is achieved.

At the other end of the spectrum are the digital, quick response scales, where the readout is instantaneous. Ensure you position these scales where you can easily read the digital display.

I think your overall kitchen design and personal preferences have an influence on your final choice of scales.

Measuring Jugs

If you are going to attempt almost any sort of cookery, you need at least one measuring jug, for calculating the capacity of liquids. Some jugs also identify the weight of sugar and flour, so you might be able to manage without weigh scales.

You can purchase glass, plastic, or stainless steel jugs, but make sure that the scale is clearly marked and easy to read. Always stand the jug on a horizontal surface when measuring liquids, so that the surface of the liquid is level.

The best jugs should also have a comfortable handle, an easy to pour spout, and be well balanced.

Kitchen Timer

A timer is a valuable piece of gadgetry to avoid burnt biscuits, cremated cakes, and sunken soufflés. If you haven't a timer built into the cooker, I recommend you buy one. It will save you time and heartache, if you remember to use it regularly.

Thermometers

These are specialist pieces of equipment for registering temperature. This could be to check that your freezer is at -18°C, the fridge is between 0°C and 5°C, the oven thermostat is working, the Sunday roast is cooked through, or some melted sugar has achieved the correct stickiness.

Apart from the thermometers incorporated into their appliances, most cooks will not use any other type of thermometer, unless cooking roast dinners, or making preserves and boiled sweets. In which case, a special meat thermometer probe, or sugar thermometer will be invaluable.

However, to reduce the risk of food poisoning, if your freezer or fridge does not have a built-in thermometer, you will need to buy one to monitor their operating temperature. These can be purchased from supermarkets, cook-shops, and hardware stores.

Are You Picking the Best Ingredients?

The saying goes, "You can't make a silk purse out of a sow's ear", and similarly a cook needs the best ingredients to obtain creditable results. This chapter contains my best tips on buying all your food items, ranging from groceries, through fruit and vegetables, to fresh fish and meat. Of course, if you grow your own produce, it will probably be better than whatever you could buy in the shops.

When buying anything, you should use all your five senses to help you make the best selection, and avoid expensive mistakes.

Sight: Let your eyes do the walking and scrutinise the product. Check the colour, and overall appearance, while looking out for signs of damage or bruising. Read the label and note the use-by or best-before date.

Touch: You need to handle fresh goods, as juicier produce weighs more than the same size drier or stale ones. All perishable goods will change in texture over time. They may be firm when fresh, but softer, flabbier, and not so heavy when stale.

Smell: Many fresh foods will change in smell or aroma as they ripen, the classic example being fruit. Those that smell the most are usually the ripest. On the other hand, fresh fish or meat has little smell, but develops a powerful aroma as it ages. If fish smells of ammonia, it is stale and should not be used. Meat tends to smell sweet, as it becomes stale.

Hearing: "As fresh as when the pod went pop" is a slogan that sells frozen peas. Popping pea pods, snapping French beans, and squeaking greens are some of the sounds that tell you that the food is at its peak of perfection. As it ages, so it loses its turgidity and ability to make a sound.

Taste: The most enjoyable of the five senses is the sensation of taste. Your taste buds will enjoy food that is at the peak of freshness, but any food that borders on staleness is munched with indifference.

Use all of your senses every time you shop, and eventually you will improve and get satisfaction from selecting the best ingredients.

At the start of this chapter I focus on store cupboard groceries; the sort of things that everyone has in their larder, and which form the basis of a selection of quick and easy recipes given later in the book.

Packets, Jars, and Tins

Food packaging has come a long way since 1810, when metal cans were made to meet the needs of Napoleon's troops. Now it's the ring pull can, with best-before date, ingredients list, cooking instructions, nutritional values, storage information, actual and drained weight, plus a complaints procedure should you not be entirely satisfied with the contents.

The same rules apply to packets and jars. Therefore, the consumer is able to make an informed choice when comparing one product with another. That is the theory anyway, but in reality other factors such as branding, personal taste, snob value, and perceived value for money, all figure largely when choosing between two or more similar products.

When buying any groceries, always check the use-by date or best-before date, and look for a long lead-time if you are not going to use the product straight away. This is because once that commodity gets into your store cupboard, it seems to migrate to the back of the shelf, never to appear until its time limit has just expired. The difference between the use-by and best-before date marks is an important one when handling, cooking, and consuming food. Food safety is at the heart of use-by dates, as they are found on highly perishable foods that are likely to be a source of food poisoning. Do not consume such foods that have passed their use-by date, unless they have been kept suitably frozen since soon after purchase. Conversely, the best-before date mark is found on non-perishable foods, which can safely be kept beyond their date stamp, although the texture and quality of the food may slowly deteriorate. However, both types of date mark assume that you follow the supplier's storage instructions.

Packets of foodstuffs need to be checked, before purchase, to make sure that no visible damage has occurred, before you put your hand in your pocket and part with your money. Any cartons or tins that appear rounded at the end where you would open them, so that they don't sit level on the shelf, may be 'blown'. This occurs when harmful bacteria have multiplied in the product creating internal pressure. Such cartons or tins should be discarded. Do not purchase dented tins, for this very reason, because there is more likelihood of air getting into the product and contaminating the contents.

I have had first-hand experience with a blown Tetra-Pak® fruit juice carton, which was within its use-by date, but completely over pressurised. Any food product you are not happy with, you should take back to the store and get your money back, which is what I did with the tetra-pack. In recent years, customer service in all food outlets has improved beyond recognition. I remember, as a young girl, taking back a shopping bag half full of potatoes, which I had purchased just an hour before, with a message from my mum, that the potatoes were all rotten inside, and she wanted her money back. The shopkeeper said that he would not give any money back because he could not see inside the potatoes when he bought them. Happy shopping days!

Store Cupboard Hide and Seek Items

When cookery programmes refer to store cupboard items, what groceries do they expect to be in the larder? Well, they say beauty is in the eye of the beholder, and the same goes for store cupboard essentials. If your diet consists only of breakfast cereals, boxes of the same are ambrosial, and you want nothing else. Whereas, if you want to eat well and varied, storing the essentials that enable you to do so, plus those little nuggets that make or break a dish are invaluable. So, what items you keep in your larder is always down to personal taste, how much money you are prepared to invest, and the amount of storage space you have available.

However, here is a list of what I would consider store cupboard essentials that I will be using in the later recipe section on '**Dishes from Store Cupboard Items**'. The dishes chosen are quick and easy to prepare, and tasty to eat. The list is: flour, bread, eggs, cheese, milk, butter or margarine, cooking oil, salt, pepper, sugar, and jam or marmalade. These are the very basic ingredients that I expect every person will have in their larder.

Flour is a Staple of Life

Flour is one of the staples of life and the most versatile of foods. With flour, you can make a wide variety of breads, pastries, cakes, biscuits, batters, pastas, and noodles. It is also used as a thickener for liquids, and as a seal to lock in flavour and moisture.

There is a vast choice of types and brands of flour available, but the underlying consideration is what you want to make with it. The various cereals such as wheat, rice, maize, soya, barley, rye, buckwheat, chickpea, sorghum, and oats govern the types of flour. Each of these cereals is associated with certain regions of the world and the local cuisine. Chickpea or gram flour is used for flat breads in Middle Eastern and Indian cookery. Rye flour used in Northern Europe and Scandinavia produces close textured dark bread. The grey, blackish buckwheat flour, which is not strictly a cereal, but a fruit of the dock plant family, is popular in Japan, America, Northern Europe, and Russia. Cornmeal or maize flour is used a great deal in America for baking needs, as well as in Italy for polenta. It is in Africa that the grain sorghum is used in making flat breads. In Britain, wheat flour is the cereal most commonly used for cooking. What you really need to consider is the type of flour for your chosen dish.

White Flour

This contains approximately 75 per cent of the wheat grain. The manufacturer has removed the bran and wheat germ to be used in other products.

Plain Flour

Plain flour is low in a protein called gluten, which makes it ideal for pastries, biscuits, and sauces.

Sauce Flour

Sauce flour is ideal for people wanting to reduce their fat intake, as you can thicken a sauce without the use of fat. The flour readily disperses into any liquid, giving a smooth sauce with very little effort.

Self-raising Flour

Self-raising flour has added raising agents (calcium phosphate and sodium hydrogen carbonate). It is ideal for items that need an airier result such as cakes, puddings, and scones.

Strong Bread Flour

Strong flour or bread flour is the flour to use for making bread and all yeast-based products, puff pastry, choux pastry, and strudel pastry. This is because the flour has an abundance of gluten, which gives elasticity to the mixed paste or dough, and acts like scaffolding holding up a structure. It is more expensive than other flour because the gluten rich grain has to be imported from Canada.

Brown Flour

This contains approximately 85 per cent of the whole grain; having only some of the bran and wheat germ removed. It is usually only available as **strong bread flour** and gives bread a lighter texture than wholemeal flour.

Wholemeal Flour

This flour contains the whole of the wheat grain and is often known as 100 per cent extraction flour. Nutritionists recommend using this flour in baking because it increases your fibre intake. It is available as **self-raising flour** or **strong bread flour** with similar uses as described above.

Additives

In Britain, flour producers are required by law to fortify **white flour** and **brown flour** with calcium, iron, and B vitamins (niacin and thiamine). However, **wholemeal flour** already contains these nutrients, as well as being a good source of fibre.

Storage of Flour

Keep flour in a cool airy cupboard. **White flour** will keep up to 9 months, whereas **brown flour** and **wholemeal flour** will keep for just 3 months.

Do not mix old and new flour because the quality diminishes over time. Try to maintain efficient stock rotation.

Loaves of Bread

Bread can be purchased in a vast array of shapes, sizes, and textures. This ranges from the mass produced, white sliced, sandwich shaped, cotton-wool confection, to the hand made, specialist flour, wood baked, unique tasting, dough ball. There is a kind of bread for every taste.

When buying and storing fresh bread the following guidelines. Check that the packaging is intact. The best-before date should have some longevity, in order to enjoy the product at its best. The back label should contain a list of ingredients, nutritional information, freezer notes, and a customer care-line.

Bread can be frozen for a maximum of one month, before deterioration through dryness sets in. Once thawed, use the bread within 24 hours to avoid loss of quality, and do not refreeze. Store fresh or defrosted bread in a cool dry place.

Do not eat mouldy bread. If in doubt, throw it out.

Eggs is Eggs

Eggs can be cooked in a variety of ways, including shallow fried, scrambled, baked, poached, or made into an omelette. I consider these last two techniques the most culinary challenging. Therefore, in the later recipe section, I have given you some tips on how to get satisfying results with poached eggs and omelettes.

Hen eggs are the eggs most commonly used in cookery. They can be purchased in a variety of forms.

Dried Egg

Dried egg is pasteurised and guaranteed salmonella free. It is available as whole egg or just egg white. Once reconstituted, by following the manufacturer's instructions, it can be used instead of fresh eggs in any dish requiring beaten egg.

Chilled Eggs

Chilled hen eggs are pasteurised and guaranteed salmonella free. They are sold in six-packs of whole egg, egg white, or egg yolk. Use as for fresh eggs.

Fresh Eggs

Whole, fresh, hen eggs are by far the most popular form, and are graded by size as small, medium, large, and extra large. Double-yolked eggs are identified and sold separately.

Look for the Lion Brand on eggs, denoted by a little lion stamped on the shell. This guarantees that the eggs have been produced to a higher code of practice than required by European Union regulations, with better standards of hygiene and animal welfare. The hens have all been vaccinated against salmonella. All eggs with the Lion Brand logo are British.

Eggs are sold in boxes of six, and apart from battery hens, the farming method is specified on the box.

Battery

This farming method will not be identified on the box, but accounts for the majority of the UK egg market. The hens are kept in cages in a completely artificial indoor environment.

Barn or Perchery

The hens have perches and feeders at different levels, and the hen-house floor is covered in deep straw or wood shavings. The hens are held in an indoor environment.

Free Range

Here the hens have continuous daytime access to open air runs, with a maximum stocking density, and which contain vegetation.

Columbus

This is similar to free range, but produces healthier eggs, because the hens are fed omega-3 fatty acids in their diet. Omega-3 fats help maintain a healthy heart.

Organic

This is also similar to free range, where the runs are organic pastures, and at least 70 per cent of the feed must be from an organic source. There is less likelihood of organic eggs containing pesticides and antibiotic residues.

Duck Eggs

Duck eggs are 50 per cent larger than the average hen egg.

Quail Eggs

Quail eggs are miniature eggs, used mainly for garnishing and impact. You would need five of these tiny eggs to match the size of a medium hen egg. They can be used as for hen eggs and have a similar flavour.

Egg Storage

Eggs should be refrigerated immediately after purchase. Eggshells are porous, and in theory absorb strong smells, so do not store eggs near pungent aromatic food. The eggs should be kept in their boxes, with their pointed ends downwards, and used in rotation in date stamp order.

When ready to use, remove the eggs from the fridge 30 minutes before you need them, to allow them to return to room temperature and perform efficiently.

You should always wash your hands before and after handling eggshells.

Dirty or cracked eggs should not be used, due to the risk of contamination.

See **'Get Cracking on Eggs'** later in this book, for more tips on using eggs.

Hard and Soft Cheese

You are spoilt for choice when it comes to cheese. You can select from the old established classics through to many new varieties, as well as all the vegetarian alternatives.

Cheese is made by the coagulation of milk, or milk products, obtained mainly from cows, sheep, goats, and water buffalo. It can be classified in a variety of ways, but one of the most common is by the country or region of origin. You need to be sure of your geography and cheese history, to avoid being duped, and sold a cheese without any provenance. How the cheese is manufactured also plays a significant part in its classification, whether it is hard, semi-hard, blue-veined, soft, cream, or processed.

From a novice's viewpoint, the easiest and most effective way of categorising cheese is by sinking your teeth into a tasty morsel. Use your senses to study its appearance, aroma, taste, and texture. This can be undertaken at any delicatessen, specialist cheese shop, or supermarket, where tantalising titbits are displayed in the hope of luring you to buy.

From a cook's perspective, when buying cheese, you consider how you are planning to use it in the meal. Whether it's going to take centre stage or play a supporting role. You also want to know how well it performs once heated or cooked. Does it melt readily, as required for Welsh rarebit, or does it hold its shape well, as in grilled goat's cheese? As a rule, look for cheeses with a high fat content, that are not too hard or dry, to give good melting results.

Choosing Cheese

Loose Cheeses

If buying loose cheese, select a freshly cut piece that looks moist. If the surface appears dry or hard, it tells you the cheese has been hanging around too long since the last portion was removed.

It is better to purchase soft cheeses, such as Brie or Camembert, which are just ripe, and allow them to ripen at home, rather than over-ripe, or runny, because their shelf life will be zero. These soft cheeses should yield slightly when pressed, as this indicates ripeness. Brie that has a chalky and under-ripe centre will never ripen satisfactorily at home, because the maker carries this out under controlled conditions. If you are unsure about the quality and taste of a cheese, ask for a sample before you buy.

Cheeses can be pasteurised or unpasteurised, and should be labelled accordingly, at the point of sale. The vulnerable, such as babies, young children, pregnant women, and the elderly should not eat unpasteurised cheese. Only buy small quantities of cheese, to enjoy at their best, and in prime condition.

If buying prepacked cheese, look for those wrapped in waxed paper, which allows the cheese to breathe, rather than plastic shrink-wrap, which seems to encourage the cheese to become sweaty and wet.

Soft Cream Cheeses

This group of cheeses is adaptable and easy to use in sweet and savoury dishes. They vary enormously in fat content, taste, and mouth feel. The range consists of high fat varieties including mascarpone and cream cheeses; lower fat alternatives such as curd, ricotta, and fromage frais; plus the dieter's friends of cottage cheese and quark.

If you have to watch your calorie intake, quark may be the answer. This is a low fat, skimmed milk, curd cheese containing only 0.2 per cent fat. It has a bland taste, making it suitable for both sweet and savoury dishes, and it can replace any other soft cream cheese. It is half the price of the alternativess.

Storing Cheese

Wrap loose cheese in cling film or waxed greaseproof paper, place in an airtight container in the fridge, away from easily tainted foods such as milk and cream. Check the use-by date, and do not exceed it.

You can cook with cheese past its best, but it will not enhance the dish. Bland, under-ripe, or poorly kept cheese will reveal itself in the finished dish. For eating, cheese is best served at room temperature, to enjoy its aroma, taste, and texture fully. Place the cheese on the service plate or board approximately one hour before consumption. Unwrap it, but cover it loosely with greaseproof paper or cling film. Do not leave cheese in shrink-wrap plastic once out of the fridge, otherwise it will sweat and become wet. Remove the shrink-wrap and lightly cover. After use, rewrap the cheese and return it to the fridge promptly.

Cheese freezes well, especially when grated, where it can be used straight from the freezer.

See the later section for tips on '**Cooking With Cheese**'.

Milk, Cream, and Yoghurt

Doorstep delivery of milk, cream, and yoghurt is fast becoming a thing of the past. Now these dairy products can be obtained in supermarkets, garage fore-courts, and a wide range of other shops. The choice on offer is immense.

Milk

There are many different types of milk. The most popular type is from cows, but there is also milk from goats and ewes, and vegetarian soya milk. Cows milk is identified by the amount of fat content. Channel Island being the highest at approximately 5 per cent, down to skimmed milk at 0.1 per cent. Homogenised milk has a fat content of about 4 per cent, but has the added bonus of being distributed throughout the liquid. This is of benefit when serving beverages, as you will not see any globules of fat floating on top of the hot drink. All milk sold by dairies and shops is now pasteurised, that is heat treated to destroy harmful micro-organisms.

Sterilised and long-life or ultra-heat-treated (UHT) milk has been processed to extend its shelf life. Milk is also sold with reduced water content, in condensed, evaporated, or dried forms, which are ideal where space and weight are at a premium. All these are useful store cupboard items.

Cream

The cream of the crop refers to the best, and that is how cream is viewed. It is the richness or fat content in cows milk, which when drawn off and left to ripen, produces a buttery flavoured cream. Today, fresh cream is not allowed to ripen and develop flavour, but is pasteurised immediately in order to kill bacteria. Cream is classified by the amount of fat it contains and this in turn governs how you use it in cooking.

Type	Legal Minimum Fat %	How to Use
Single cream	18	This can only be poured.
Soured cream	20	Similar to single cream.
Crème fraiche	30	Similar to single cream.
Whipping cream	35	This is ideal for whipping.
Double cream	48	Adds creaminess to a dish.
Clotted cream	55	This can only be spooned.

Yoghurt

Yoghurt is made from milk, to which friendly culture or bacteria are added, then left to ferment. This produces its characteristic texture and taste. While yoghurt can be made from goat, ewe, mare, water buffalo, and camel milk, the majority in this country is made using cows milk.

As with milk and cream, yoghurt is graded according to how much fat is present. The very low fat varieties are made from skimmed milk. At the other end of the scale, the creamy thick types have added cream. So, you need to read the label before buying if you are counting calories.

Yoghurt is seen as a health promoting food, as it is more digestible than milk. This is advantageous for people who suffer from lactose intolerance.

Storage

Before buying, always check and adhere to use-by dates as indicated. Refrigerate all dairy products in the container they were delivered in, and keep away from strong smelling foods. Do not add surplus old milk, cream, or yoghurt to any fresh new dairy product. It is better to keep products in their original container, and use them up quickly.

Once opened, keep well covered to protect from dust and pests. Opened long-life products should be treated as for fresh products.

See the later section for tips on '**Using Milk, Cream, and Yoghurt**' for cooking.

First Aid

Symptom: *Dairy product is showing signs of going off.*

Diagnosis: *Usually caused by poor refrigeration.*

Antidote: *Check the use-by date. Use your nose to assess for freshness. Aroma is a good indicator of what is good or not. Taste a very small amount, and if it is more acidic than when it was first used, it probably is past its best.*

Remedy: *Always have a stock of store cupboard long-life dairy products for situations like this.*

Butter, Margarine, and Fats

A simple method of differentiating fats and oils is that fats are solid at room temperature, whereas oils are liquid. While fats are frequently seen as the culprits of health problems, a life devoid of fats limits the enjoyment and pleasure that they bring to food. They make food more palatable, adding smoothness and tenderness to the product. Fats also carry flavour, contribute to the mouth feel of juiciness, as well as extending keeping qualities of food.

Butter

Butter is made by churning cream, and therefore is a dairy product. It can be purchased salted, slightly salted, or unsalted. The salted variety has a longer shelf life than unsalted, but you need to check the use-by date before purchasing.

Butter should be refrigerated and brought out to room temperature before use in cooking or spreading. As butter burns easily when used in shallow frying, always add the same amount of oil to reduce this tendency.

Margarine

Margarine may be made from pure vegetable oil, or a mixture of vegetable and animal fats. It can be purchased in a hard variety, or the softer polyunsaturated variety, as well as the health conscious low-fat spreads.

Some types of margarine have limited use in cooking, and the manufacturers' recommendations should be followed carefully. Some are not ideal for shallow frying, due to a tendency to splutter and spit. Margarine should be kept refrigerated, but some can be used straight from the fridge for cooking and spreading.

Cooking Fat

Cooking fat is also known as shortening, and originated in the USA as a lard substitute. It is used for pastry making, some cake making, and shallow frying. Always store it in the fridge.

Lard

Lard is made from pigs' fat. It is used for pastry making, some cake making, and shallow frying. Store lard in the fridge.

Suet

Suet is made from the fat surrounding lamb or ox kidney, which has been shredded and coated with flour. A vegetarian alternative is also available, which is made from hydrogenated vegetable oil coated in rice flour.

Both types of suet need to be stored in a cool dry place. Suet is used for steamed sweet and savoury puddings. The beauty of this fat is that it needs no rubbing in; it is simply stirred into the dry ingredients.

Vegetable and Nut Oils

The explosion of foreign travel, consumerism, and cookery programmes has all contributed to the widespread knowledge and use of oils in the kitchen. Whereas forty years ago, chips would be fried in beef dripping or lard, now it's groundnut or vegetable oil in the deep fat fryer.

Attitudes have changed towards the use of oil in cooking; now we have cakes and biscuits that use oil in place of fats; hot or cold dressings have replaced the heavier sauces; and oils are the choice when frying.

There are two categories of oil on offer, either unrefined or refined. The former is more expensive, having a pronounced fruity aroma, better flavour, and distinctive colour. This is because the oil is pressed naturally and left to mature, before being put on sale.

Olive Oil

Olive oil is known as the classic oil in cooking. It is identified by its country of origin, and the region where it was produced – very much like wine. There is a vast gamut of flavours, and you need to experiment to find those you like best. As a guide, olive oil from Spain, the largest producer, has a strong peppery taste, and is green to gold in colour. The nuttiest tasting is golden coloured Italian oil; whereas, Greek oil is viscous, green, and strongly flavoured. French oils are lighter coloured and fruity in style.

All olive oils are classified by how they are processed or treated. Extra virgin oil and virgin oil are the purest, being taken from the first pressing of the olives. Extra virgin oil guarantees a low acidity, with less than 1 per cent of oleic acid. Oils with 3 per cent oleic acid are classed as pure olive oil or simply olive oil.

Because extra virgin oil is the finest, with a pronounced aroma and flavour, it is the most expensive. It is ideal for salad dressings and mayonnaise, but would be wasted if used for frying, as its flavour is too strong. Also the smoke point of extra virgin is about 155°C, whereas the ideal frying temperature is 175°C. If an oil is heated to its smoke point it deteriorates or breaks down quicker; making the oil useless.

Olive oil is mainly a monounsaturated oil, and is considered beneficial in helping to reduce blood cholesterol.

Oils for Frying

The best oils for deep fat frying have a smoke point temperature that is much higher than 175°C, which is the ideal frying temperature. The packaging will usually say if an oil is suitable for frying. See 'Deep Fat Frying' on page 86.

Groundnut Oil

Groundnut oil, also known as peanut or arachide oil, has a less pronounced flavour than olive oil. It is ideal for deep fat frying or stir frying, as it has little smell, a high smoke point, and is relatively inexpensive. Strictly speaking, groundnuts are not nuts but legumes, because they grow underground. Beware of people with nut allergies.

Corn or Maize Oil

The taste of corn, or maize, oil tends towards a neutral flavour, and it can be used in all forms of cooking. Like groundnut oil, it is ideal for frying.

Blended Vegetable Oil

Oil blended from a number of sources is also known generically as vegetable oil. It is always a refined oil, and is designed for economy. It has a high smoke point, making it particularly suitable for deep fat frying. The blends most commonly include oils such as soya, cottonseed, rapeseed, palm, and coconut. Both palm and coconut oils are high in saturated fats, which is bad news for low cholesterol diets.

Oils For Flavouring

Nut and seed oils pressed for their flavour are intended for use in small quantities in dressings and marinades. They are often fairly expensive, and burn quite easily.

Sunflower, Safflower, and Rapeseed Oil

These seed oils are all low in saturated fat and therefore ideal for anyone wanting to follow a low cholesterol diet. The taste tends towards a neutral flavour, and they can be used in all forms of dressings and in baking. Sunflower oil is the cheapest, and can help to eke out the more expensive oils.

Sesame Oil

Sesame seed oil is used in Middle and Far Eastern cooking. It has a very pronounced flavour, so use it sparingly. Since it burns readily, if you want to use it for stir frying, always add it at the last minute, or mix it with another oil.

Individual Nut and Seed Oils

Individual nuts or seeds are pressed to extract oil that has a distinctive taste. Use sparingly or mix with other oils, otherwise their flavour can be overpowering. These include walnut, almond, hazelnut, pumpkinseed, mustard seed, and linseed oil. In particular, linseed or flaxseed oil is high in omega-3 fatty acids and often used as a health supplement. All these nut and seed oils burn readily.

Fat Structure

Many nut and seed oils are high in monounsaturated or polyunsaturated fats and therefore ideal for anyone wanting to follow a low cholesterol diet. However, there are some notable exceptions such as coconut and palm oils, as shown in the following table.

Percentage Fat Content

Oil Type	Saturated	Monounsaturated	Polyunsaturated
Safflower oil	9	9	82
Walnut oil	10	19	71
Sunflower oil	13	25	62
Corn oil	14	26	60
Rapeseed oil	8	62	30
Olive oil	15	82	3
Sesame oil	16	39	45
Groundnut oil	20	41	39
Chicken fat	31	48	21
Pork lard	42	47	11
Palm oil	51	38	11
Butter	66	30	4
Beef dripping	56	40	4

Storing Oils

Always store oil in a cool dark place.

Check the use-by date, and never use an oil if it has developed a rancid taste. Buy oil in small quantities, especially those for flavouring, rather than large amounts, because the oil may go stale or rancid before it can be used up. Oil with a high saturated fat content keeps the longest.

If oil is kept in a cold place, it can solidify. The oil becomes cloudy, and solid deposits form at the bottom of the bottle. This is not harmful, and it will return to its natural state as the temperature is raised.

If deep fat frying, strain the oil after each use. This will extend its life, so that it can be used 3 or 5 times more. If the oil begins to foam, bubble, or smoke unduly, it is past its best and should be changed. You will notice that its smoke point decreases with each use until it becomes unusable.

Rock Salt and Sea Salt

Sodium chloride is essential to life. It is found in comparatively small amounts in all foods that have not been processed. However, in many manufactured foods, it is used extensively. It is also used in the kitchen, where it may be added to foods during cooking, or sprinkled onto dishes just before consumption.

Rock Salt

Most salt is mined from underground dried-up lakes. It can be sold as large coarse crystals, or ground and refined into the customary table salt and cooking salt.

Sea Salt

Sea salt is obtained by the evaporation of seawater. Such salt is presented in attractive flakes or crystals, and prized by connoisseurs. The flavour of the product is more pronounced, therefore you use less to achieve the same taste. Maldon in Essex is the home of one of the best producers of sea salt.

Versatile Commodity

For the cook, salt is a versatile commodity, with a multitude of uses. It can clean and season pots and pans. If food is appropriately seasoned with salt, it will usually enhance the flavour. A tiny amount of salt can even improve the flavour of sweet puddings and cakes.

Salt can draw out moisture from raw foods, as when pickling vegetables or meats. However, this can sometimes be a disadvantage, as when baking potatoes on a bed of salt to produce a crisp outer skin, where the inside texture can be dry due to the osmosis effect.

When deciding how much salt to add to various dishes during cooking, always consider the saltiness of the ingredients, especially where anchovies, soy sauce, and olives are involved. Remember that some people are more tolerant of a salty taste than others, and you need to season to your personal taste. Generally, it is better to under season rather than over season. Salt added to a liquid that is to be reduced, will result in a concentration of saltiness. Therefore, add the salt after the reduction of the liquid.

Pungent Peppercorns

Along with salt, pepper must be the most widely used condiment, both on the table and in the kitchen. Peppercorns are the fruit of a climbing vine from Asia and the West Indies. The fruit is picked while still green, and dried either in the sun or over a fire, to produce black peppercorns. For white peppercorns, the fruit is allowed to ripen on the vine, then soaked in water to remove the outer skin. The most pungent are black peppercorns.

Peppercorns can be bought whole, cracked, coarsely ground, or finely ground. You should try to use freshly ground pepper, rather than the ready ground varieties. This is because all spices are at their most pungent and fragrant when newly ground, so you need less to obtain the same effect.

Sugar, Syrup, Treacle, and Honey

Sometimes seen as a hidden menace by the health conscious, sugar appears in many foods, both naturally and by artificial means. It is one of the most important ingredients in cooking, for apart from adding sweetness, it is a preservative in jams, jellies, chutneys, candied food, and curing.

Sugar is mostly obtained from sugar cane or sugar beet, and provides energy, but nothing else. Cane sugar can be purchased unrefined as sugar and syrup products, with a distinctive flavour and darker colour. It is also available as refined white sugar in various grades of crystal. Beet sugar can only be purchased as white refined sugar. Sugar is usually sold in 500 g, 1 kg, or 2 kg bags.

Preserving Sugar

Preserving sugar is produced in large crystals, which dissolve quickly into liquids. Pectin is added to aid the setting of jams and jellies. This is especially useful for fruits low in pectin that only give a medium set without assistance, such as plums, greengages, blackberries, and raspberries. Alternatively, you can add lemon juice, or some other fruit rich in pectin and acid, such as cooking apples, gooseberries, damsons, blackcurrants, or redcurrants.

Granulated Sugar

Granulated sugar is supplied in small crystals, and is the most widely used, general purpose, and the cheapest sugar.

Castor Sugar

This sugar is aptly named, because of its perfect fineness for use in the sugar sifter or castor. It is ideal for making sponge cakes, as it dissolves so readily.

Icing Sugar

Icing sugar is also known as confectioner's sugar, and has the finest crystals. As its name implies, it is ideal for making cake icing and other cake confectionery.

Muscovado Sugar

This is the crudest and strongest tasting of all the brown sugars, and is also the most expensive.

Soft Brown Sugar

Brown sugar can be light or dark brown in colour. It is used in cooking to give flavour and a degree of colour.

Demerara Sugar

This is a mid-brown gritty textured sugar, which only dissolves slowly. It is often used on the top of cakes, or to coat biscuits, to give a crunchy finish.

Golden Syrup

Syrup is a pale yellow, sticky, flowing liquid used in baking to give a soft texture and a very sweet taste. It can be purchased in either tins or jars.

Black Treacle

Treacle is a thick, dark, unctuous liquid. It gives a distinctive flavour and sweetness to any food. Traditionally, it is an ingredient of gingerbread and parkin. It is usually only sold in tins.

Honey

Honey ranges from the cheapest blended types to the expensive sort derived from a specific flower variety. It can be used as an alternative to sugar in cooking, or as a spread on bread. Use a cheaper blended honey in baking, because heat quickly destroys the flavour. If honey is used to replace sugar in a recipe, the food will be darker, due to the honey sugar caramelising more readily than normal sugar. It also improves the keeping qualities of the food, because honey is moisture absorbent, and keeps the product moist. Honey is usually available in 250 g or 500 g jars.

First Aid

Symptom: *Icing sugar not in the cupboard, when needed for icing a cake.*

Diagnosis: *Forgot to check that all ingredients available before starting a recipe.*

Antidote: *Put granulated or castor sugar into a food processor or liquidiser, and whiz until as fine as icing sugar. Note that home-made icing is never as white as the commercial variety.*

Symptom: *Brown sugar is hard, solid, and difficult to mix into a fruitcake.*

Diagnosis: *Sugar has dried out too much, or been on the shelf for too long.*

Antidote: *Place the sugar in a glass bowl and microwave for about 15 seconds, until it becomes soft. Alternatively, place the sugar in a glass bowl, cover with a damp cloth, and leave overnight.*

Remedy: *Keep brown sugar in an airtight container for storage.*

Symptom: *Syrup and treacle are messy to weigh out.*

Diagnosis: *Too thick to spoon easily.*

Antidote: *Put the open tin in a saucepan of hot water to make contents more fluid. Line the scale pan with cling film, spoon the syrup or treacle onto it, gather up the cling film, and squeeze out into the required mixture.*

Symptom: *Clear honey has gone cloudy in the jar.*

Diagnosis: *The honey has got cold and started to crystallise.*

Antidote: *Put the open jar in a saucepan of warm water, or put the open glass jar in the microwave oven for 20 second bursts, until the honey goes clear.*

Remedy: *Store honey at room temperature, not in the fridge.*

Jam and Marmalade Preserves

Preserves include jams, curds, jellies, and marmalades, which are simply jams based on citrus fruit. A thick doorstep of freshly baked bread smothered in jam, or some other preserve, is one of those simple pleasures in life.

When buying jam, look at the fruit content, which will be displayed on the ingredient list. A high fruit content will give you a better flavour. Compare jam varieties on price as well as fruit content.

Preserves are mixtures of fruit and sugar boiled together until a gel is formed. Traditionally jam was made with 70 – 72 per cent sugar levels, but these have been reduced to as low as 65 per cent. This is due to changes in public taste and attitudes such as healthy eating, reduced sugar intake, and a liking for less sweet jam. The lower the sugar contents, the greater the chance of spoilage and moulds. This explains why it is recommended that, once a jar of any preserve is opened, it should be stored in the fridge. Another reason is that homes are warmer nowadays, due to more efficient insulation and central heating, which creates ideal conditions for mould and yeast growth.

Choosing Chocolate

The type of chocolate you choose depends on what you are going to do with it. The four basic categories are confectionery, cooking, couverture, and white chocolate.

Confectionery Chocolate

This is what most people eat as a bar of chocolate for pleasure. It can be used in cooking to give a basic chocolate flavour, and is ideal if cooking for children, as it tends to be sweeter with less cocoa mass than the intensely bitter cooking chocolate. However, if you use confectionery chocolate for piping, coating sweets, or making chocolate moulds you will find it difficult to work with, as it remains fairly viscous.

Cooking Chocolate

You can identify cooking chocolate by its intense, pronounced taste, and the amount of cocoa solids present. Look for 50 per cent or higher for plain chocolate, or 30 per cent for milk chocolate. The price you pay will also be significantly higher. It is worth it though, because cooking chocolate will give you a superior flavour and respond well to melting, piping, and coating your products.

Do not be duped into buying chocolate-flavoured covering, which should be left on the shelf. It is low in cocoa solids, high in hydrogenated fat and stabilisers, and relatively cheap. It also has a poor flavour and poor cooking qualities.

Couverture Chocolate

This is not readily available. Its principal users are professional confectioners, who choose it for its high cocoa butter content, which makes it runnier and less viscous when melted. Luxury cooking chocolate from supermarkets is the nearest equivalent, and like couverture, is the most expensive.

White Chocolate

Although something of a novelty, this is not really chocolate at all, because it contains no cocoa solids. It is made from cocoa butter, milk solids, sugar, and flavourings. I do not recommend using white chocolate in cooking, unless you want a special effect, because it is quite difficult to work with.

Bakers' Yeast for Baking

Yeast can be purchased either fresh or dried. Dried yeast also comes in an easy blend, fast action form with added Vitamin C (ascorbic acid). Whichever yeast you use, it must be in good condition, not stale or old. If in any doubt, test it by placing a teaspoonful of the yeast into lukewarm water. It should start to activate and froth within 15 minutes in warm conditions. If it doesn't, it is probably past its best, and should be thrown away. However, beware that too much heat can kill yeast. So ensure the water is never too hot.

See the '**Bread Making**' section later in this book for details of using yeast.

Remember to use bakers' yeast for baking and brewers' yeast for brewing!

Fresh Yeast

Fresh yeast should be available at supermarkets that have an in-store bakery (ask the assistants), as well as health food shops, and traditional bakers. It has the appearance and texture of crumbly Cheshire cheese, but is light beige in colour. The smell is pleasant, sweet, and fruity.

Fresh yeast that has gone stale is dark brown in colour on any exposed edges, smells musty, does not crumble easily, and has the texture of putty.

It should be stored, wrapped in cling film, in the refrigerator, and will keep in that condition for up to two weeks. If you want to keep it for longer, it is best frozen, wrapped in kitchen foil, where it will keep for up to three months. You can use it straight from the freezer by grating it into a bowl, then adding the required liquid. The conventional way of activating fresh yeast is to place it in a small bowl and cream it with a small amount of the measured lukewarm liquid. The remaining liquid and perhaps a teaspoon of sugar are added to help it along.

Dried Yeast

Dried yeast is the dehydrated equivalent of fresh yeast and is available in most supermarkets and other food stores. Check the use-by date before purchase to ensure it is not old stock. In its original packaging, dried yeast will keep at least until its use-by date, but once the container or sachet is opened you should use it as soon as possible.

Like fresh yeast, it is blended with lukewarm water and a little sugar before it is ready for use. It is alive and ready when a frothy head appears on top of the water, similar to the froth on a head of beer. This should take about 10 to 15 minutes in warm conditions, or slightly longer if the room is cool. If no head or froth appears on the water, the yeast is inactive, and should be discarded. Start again, using new yeast. Check the temperature of the water, which should feel just the same temperature as your little finger when placed in the water.

Easy Blend or Fast Action Yeast

This is a variant of dried yeast with added Vitamin C (ascorbic acid), which speeds up the fermentation process. Its availability and storage characteristics are the same as for dried yeast.

The beauty of this yeast is that it is added directly to the dry ingredient mix, usually flour. It does not first need to be reconstituted like the other yeasts. Any other ingredients are added, such as salt, fat, and lastly the water. In this case the water needs to be slightly hotter (hand hot), because the yeast is in a mixture. The reason people choose easy blend or fast action yeast is that it allows them to cut out the activation process, as well as one of the proving processes. Therefore, it is a great time saver.

Pick of the Bunch of Fruit and Vegetables

When purchasing any short shelf life food , before you touch it, let your eyes to do the work and sell it to you. This is just as true whether the produce is a white cauliflower with its crunchy outer dark leaves, or a peach with its downy sun-kissed skin. What you are looking for is freshness, that peak of quality, and that subliminal ready-to-eat sign, which will be rewarded in pleasurable eating. All you have to do is follow some simple guidelines to buying fruits and vegetables. These suggestions apply to most of them with only one or two exceptions.

Use Your Eyes

Let your eyes seek out produce that is unblemished, bruise free, with no unsightly damage or leaching. The chosen product should be the anticipated colour. For example tomatoes should be red, not green indicating they are under-ripe.

Check the Smell

Certain fresh fruits or vegetables give off aromas when ripe and ready to eat. So pick up and smell produce such as pineapples, melons, strawberries, fresh garlic, and tomatoes, and compare with similar choices available. The ones that smell the most are usually the ripest.

Feel the Weight

Try to handle your potential purchase. Pick it up, feel its weight, and compare it against others, preferably using a weigh scale. This gives you its density or water content, which translates into juiciness. The heavier the item the more likely it is juicier than a similar lighter weight item.

Texture is Tricky

Judging texture is difficult; especially the softness of stoned fruit. It is better to buy fruit that is slightly under-ripe, and ripen it at home. The reason is that there is less chance of bruising, which can occur by poor handling, being tossed and turned like something in a tumble dryer, if left to ripen fully in the shop. When you get the fruit home, place it inside a paper bag with a banana. This works particularly well with avocado pears. Alternatively, sit the fruit on a soft cloth, such as a tea towel, without the fruit touching each other. This is especially good for nectarines, peaches, melons, and avocado pears.

However, most vegetables need to be firm in texture when purchased; especially root vegetables, courgettes, aubergines, asparagus, onions, celery, brassicas, beans, and tubers. If they are soft and bendy, they have been around for too long, and should be left where they are.

Listen As Well

While trying to make you aware that you use all your senses, especially when purchasing anything fresh with a very limited shelf life, the sense of hearing cannot apply to the majority of fruit and vegetables. There are exceptions though.

The squeak of fresh cabbage leaves as soon as you start to handle them reminds me of squeaking piglets. Older leaves offer no such delights. Coconuts, when shaken, indicate the presence of 'milk', which is in fact a watery liquid making a refreshing drink. The sound of this liquid is another indicator of freshness, because as the coconut ages, evaporation takes place, and eventually it will be devoid of all moisture.

A sound from my childhood is the rattle of pips when a Cox's apple is shaken. I looked forward to sinking my teeth into the first of the crop, but was always told to shake the Cox apple first, in order to hear the pips dancing around inside the apple waiting to be released into the outside world. I still maintain this custom.

Avoid Sogginess

Do not purchase anything that appears to be unduly wet, as this speeds up mould growth and rot.

Thin Fruit Skins

Some varieties of citrus fruit are at their juiciest when the skin is thin and smooth. Limes for example – especially if the skin changes from dark green to a lighter, almost yellowish green. Bananas also – the fruit becomes more fragrant and riper as the skin becomes thinner. Bananas easily bruise, and don't like the cold, so don't store them in the fridge, because it affects their colour and texture.

First Aid

Symptom: *Apples look fine, but on peeling, the flesh is speckled with brown spots.*

Diagnosis: *This is 'bitter pit', caused by calcium deficiency and uneven watering of the tree at crucial times.*

Antidote: *Unless badly marked, it does not usually show once peeled and cooked. It is not harmful to eat.*

Remedy: *Before you buy, look carefully at the apples for tiny sunken pits on the skin that cover the blemishes.*

Symptom: *Avocado pears or other stoned fruits are too hard and need ripening.*

Diagnosis: *The fruit is under ripe and inedible.*

Antidote: *Place the fruit in a bag with a ripe banana and leave for two or three days to ripen.*

Symptom: *Avocados, apples, bananas, potatoes, and celeriac soon discolour once cut open.*

Diagnosis: *Air discolours the flesh of many fruit and vegetables due to oxidisation.*

Antidote: *Keep any skin intact as long as possible, rub the cut flesh with lemon or lime juice, wrap in cling film, and refrigerate.*

Bunches of Grapes

When buying grapes, the quickest and easiest way to tell whether they are past their best is to pick up the bunch and give it a little shake. If grapes fall off, it indicates that the bunch is past its best. What you are looking for is intact bunches of grapes with no visible mould. Green grapes turning to greenish yellow indicate sweetness and ripeness, but the best way is to taste one or two of the grapes.

Juiciest Pineapples

On the subject of buying a ripe pineapple, most people know that to judge ripeness you should tug at one of the spiky leaves and, if it is ready for eating, the leaf will detach easily from the body of the fruit. That is only one indication though, and there are several more signs to consider before you part with your money.

Firstly, don't touch the pineapple – just look! The spiky leaves should be green, indicating freshness. Yellowish brown leaves tell you that the pineapple has been knocking about for too long. With regard to skin colour, orangey yellow is what you are looking for, with no visible brown, bruised or over-ripe patches.

Having sized up the pineapple visually, handle it. Smell it for a fruity aroma. Look at the base of the fruit, opposite to the leafy end. There is a small stem or core that runs all the way through the pineapple to the leaves. This is what attached the pineapple to the mother plant, similar to the stalk of an apple. Make sure the base of that core is not mouldy or soft in anyway, as over-ripeness in pineapples tends to occur from the middle core and work towards the outer skin. A mouldy core will accelerate that ripening.

After making these preliminary observations, and selected the best, now is the time to weigh similar sized fruits against each other. The heaviest fruit of similar size and foliage will be the juiciest.

As pineapples age, the weight reduces due to evaporation, the skin colour changes to an autumnal brown, and the leaves turn to grey. The flesh takes on the flavour of wine, and becomes stringier in texture.

Fresh pineapples should be stored in the refrigerator until required, then brought out and allowed to return to room temperature before eating, to maximise taste and texture. Do not use for mousses, jellies, or anything containing gelatine as the raw pineapple breaks down the gelatine and prevents setting.

Exceptional Passion Fruit

These are the size and shape of plums, dark purple in colour, with thick hard inedible skins. As they ripen the inedible skin becomes more wrinkled, and the more wrinkled the greater the chance of aromatic, sweet, juicy pulp inside. The pulp is laced with small black, crunchy, edible seeds. If these seeds are not to your liking, sieve them out before serving the pulp in a fruit salad or as a sauce.

Fresh Salad Leaves

Salad leaf produce is very delicate and easily crushed, so great care should be taken to ensure that the leaves are not damaged in any way. Mixed salad leaves, that are purchased already bagged, are prone to condensation spoilage causing the leaves to become slimy and limp. You need to check the use-by date carefully, especially if you are forward planning meals.

Root Vegetables

When purchasing potatoes, look out for any visible signs of greening, which indicates that they have been exposed to light. Reject these potatoes, as they can be harmful to eat, especially if you are pregnant.

Ideally, buy potatoes and other root vegetables unwashed, as the attached soil prolongs their shelf life. Excessive soil or mud should be knocked off if possible; otherwise, you are paying for something that you do not want.

Know Your Onions

The saying "know your onions" applies literally to culinary use, when choosing firm sound onions. To test one, press the opposite end to the root, which is known as the neck end. It should be solid and not at all soft, as this indicates ageing. The papery outer skin that covers the juicy layered inner skins should be tightly attached, as loose papery skins is another indicator of ageing.

Mouth-watering Mushrooms

The choice of fresh cultivated mushrooms extends beyond the common button, open, and flat types to the exotic oyster, enokitake, shiitake, wood-ear, and truffle varieties. Any mushroom purchased in a supermarket or shop should be safe to eat. However, beware of specimens picked from woods or meadows by the untrained amateur. If you go mushroom gathering, you must be experienced in identification in order to avoid serious consequences.

All fresh mushrooms should be firm to touch, dry, with no visible bruising or discoloration. They should feel heavy in relation to their size, with no holes in the stem of the mushroom. When it comes to economy and flavour, the large diameter flat mushrooms have the edge over the others.

Dried mushrooms are a store cupboard delight for a canny cook. Just a small handful of these dried, wizened, bark-like morsels can transform the ordinary mushroom dish into a taste sensation. The flavour and colour are released once hot water is poured onto the mushrooms, and their texture is reconstituted. Make use of the water, wherever possible, as it shouts flavour and colour.

Find the Freshest Fruits of the Sea

"You shall have a fishy, on a little dishy, when the boat comes in." When buying fish have this song in your head, and you will not go far wrong. Have an open mind, because the fish available will depend upon what could be caught. You are looking for the freshest, finest quality, and best value to give you that taste of the river or sea.

Fish can be categorised in several ways.

◆ Where it lives: sea, lake, or river.

◆ By its shape: round, flat, or shellfish.

◆ Where the oil is found: with white fish oil is only found in the liver, whereas oily fish has it distributed throughout its darker flesh.

When it comes to purchasing fish, if the exact fish suggested in the recipe is not available, try to select another from the same group, so the flavour and texture will be similar.

White Fish

White fish can be round or flat, and form the largest choice, ranging from the humble whiting, through everyday haddock or plaice, to the luxurious halibut. All white fish are low in fat and easier to digest than oily fish.

Oily Fish

Oily fish are identified by always being round in shape, and the flesh is dark in colour, never white. They range from tiny whole whitebait, through shiny silvery herring, to majestic wild salmon. Scientific studies have shown that people who regularly eat oily fish containing omega-3, are significantly less likely to suffer from heart disease. It is recommended that you should include oily fish in your diet two or three times a week. Tinned oily fish includes tuna, sardines, mackerel, salmon, and pilchards.

Buying Fresh Fish

When choosing fresh fish make sure the flesh is firm and stiff, with shiny smooth skin. Avoid any fish that has a flabby limp body, with dry dull skin that dents when you touch it. Ensure the eyes are prominent and bright, not dull and sunken, as this indicates old stock. The gills should be bright red, not pale. Any natural skin markings should be distinct, not faded; for example, plaice markings should be orange not dull brown. There should be no pronounced smell, as a fishy smell indicates decay. On scaly fish, look for an abundance of scales, because these fall off as the fish starts to decay.

When buying fresh river fish or oily sea fish, make sure they are as fresh as possible, as they tend to decay quicker than other types. Whitebait in particular must be absolutely fresh, because it is not gutted before cooking.

All fresh fish, including shellfish, should be consumed on the day of purchase. Keep it loosely wrapped in the fridge until you are ready to cook it.

Buying Shellfish

Shellfish may be sold either fresh or cooked. Live shellfish should be undamaged and lively, reacting quickly when touched. If cooked, try to handle them before buying, if possible, to assess their weight in relation to size. If they have been poorly cooked, and are full of water instead of flesh, they are poor value for money.

Buying Smoked Fish

Smoked fish can go mouldy, so examine it carefully. The skin must be glossy, the flesh firm, and there should be no unpleasant smell. When buying smoked fish, select the paler naturally smoked products, rather than the vivid yellow or orange dyed varieties, with the dreaded 'E' numbers, which leech the colour into the cooking liquid along with some of the flavour. If you are thinking of buying smoked salmon, for optimum flavour choose Atlantic or Scottish varieties, rather than the Pacific variety, because they are usually better quality.

Buying Frozen Fish

At one time, frozen fish was considered as second rate, but improvements in technology and handling have put good quality frozen fish on a par with fresh fish. When buying, look for thick, well sealed, undamaged packaging. Avoid any fish that shows signs of freezer burn, which appears as slightly discoloured and dry looking patches, especially around the edges or on the thin ends of fillets.

Storage of Fish

Do not exceed the use-by date.

Live shellfish such as lobsters, crabs, scallops, oysters, clams, and mussels should be wrapped in a damp cloth in the fridge, and used on the day of purchase.

All fresh fish and shellfish should be kept in the fridge, loosely wrapped, until ready to cook. If you detect a smell of ammonia, this means the fish is stale.

Frozen fish should be stored in the freezer, until you are ready to use it. Follow the manufacturer's instructions on how to defrost and cook. As a guide, fresh white fish and smoked fish can be frozen in your freezer and kept for up to 3 months. Fresh oily fish and shellfish can be similarly frozen, but only kept for up to 2 months.

Thaw frozen fish in a covered container overnight in the fridge. Do not refreeze raw fish after thawing. However, you can cook it, and it can be refrozen, as long as you cool it down to room temperature and into the freezer within 1½ hours.

Tinned fish, once opened, or frozen fish that has been defrosted, becomes as perishable as when it was fresh, and needs to be consumed quickly.

Meat Your Match and Play the Game

It was not very long ago that the choice of meat available was limited to what the local butcher could lay his hands on. Whether this was new season lamb in May, hare from October through to February, or turkey in November and December. These were real family treats, special occasions that you looked forward to with anticipation and excitement.

The meteoric rise in supermarkets, and the diversity of their food range, has led to a lack of the seasons' treats, and smothered one's yearning for seasonal foods. The supermarkets can supply a wide choice and variety of all categories of food, with meats no exception. As well as the standard fare that you would find in independent butchers, supermarkets may also stock what I call 'zoo food' or exotic meats such as alligator, ostrich, and kangaroo, which cater for the more eclectic taste.

Whether you purchase meat from an independent retailer or a large multi-national, what you want to know is – How is it going to perform on the taste and texture fronts? What methods of cooking will best suit your chosen cut of meat? What are the storage requirements? How long will it safely keep without affecting quality? Are there any special preparation requirements?

If you support an independent retailer, your friendly, knowledgeable butcher can answer all these questions, but you need to open your mouth and ask. Such butchers are extremely accommodating in what they can supply, from rare breed meats to customised cuts prepared ready for cooking or marinated barbecue delights. The only condition is that you must give the retailer sufficient notice. Remember that he wants your custom.

Meats bought in supermarkets already have cooking, storage, and shelf life information printed on their packaging.

When buying for eating quality, look for producers that have humane animal husbandry and welfare policies. This may be in the form of outdoor reared, or organically produced, or RSPB/RSPCA endorsed products. These endorsements tell you that the animal was neither intensively farmed nor seen solely as profit, but that the animals' well-being and environment were also considered.

Stress-free animals, allowed to roam and forage for themselves, build fat as well as muscle. It is this fat or 'marbling' in the muscle or meat that gives taste and texture. Without fat, meat tends to be prone to dryness, and is easily overcooked.

Perfect Poultry

When you think of poultry, you instantly think of chicken, but don't forget guinea fowl, duck, goose, and turkey. Whilst chicken is readily available in a myriad of sizes, cuts, and breeds, for optimum taste, buy fresh organic or corn fed birds. Endlessly versatile, and quite healthy once the skin has been removed, chicken is more popular today than ever before. However, guinea fowl (known as educated chicken between you and me) or turkey, can both be substituted in chicken dishes.

When choosing fresh oven-ready chickens, look for a soft flexible breastbone, plump breast with a faint blue tinge, and no visible signs of bruising. Bruising is identified as red or brown blotches just under the skin. Although fresh chickens are superior in flavour and texture to frozen birds, these do offer a cheaper alternative. If properly thawed and cooked, frozen birds can be very good.

Remember that chicken thighs and drumsticks are the most economical cuts of a chicken to buy, because the majority of people want breast meat. So, look out for those bargains!

When purchasing frozen poultry, make sure the bag covering the bird is unbroken and there are no marks or discoloured dried up patches on the skin. This is freezer burn and will damage the flavour and texture of the meat.

It is absolutely essential that any frozen poultry is completely thawed before cooking, otherwise you run the risk of salmonella food poisoning. Remove any pre-packed giblets, and defrost the poultry overnight, either in a clean empty sink, or in a suitable container in your refrigerator or a cold room. You must make sure that the inside of the bird is thawed as well as the outside. You need to feel the flesh, which should be soft and pliable. Once thawed, store in your refrigerator until required.

After handling raw poultry, fresh or frozen, you must immediately wash your hands in hot soapy water before undertaking any other task.

Gorgeous Game

Wild animals and birds hunted and killed for their flesh are known as 'game'. Because they are wild, you do not know what they have eaten, nor their age, or pedigree; unlike farmed animals where there is now full traceability.

Frozen game is available throughout the year, but fresh game is only available in season. Out of season, the law protects game animals against hunting. When buying fresh game use a reputable licensed poulterer (game butcher), whose advice and expertise you can rely on.

Best of Bacon

When buying bacon, look for dry cured products, rather than the cheaper wet cured varieties that are more readily available.

The dry cured method uses salt and seasonings that are rubbed into the product and left to cure. The bacon shrinks slightly due to osmosis and so makes it a little more expensive. However, when you cook it, no further shrinkage takes place. What you are left with is a tastier meatier product that is easier to cook, without any residue in the pan.

Wet cured bacon is steeped in water and salt, known as brine. When you cook with this bacon, it releases the water and salt, and some of its flavour into the pan, causing a white scum. Instead of shallow frying or grilling, you are in fact boiling the bacon, which shrinks noticeably on releasing the brine.

Marvellous Red Meat

Whilst people are more health conscious, and may be reducing the amount of red meat they consume, roasting joints or steaks benefit from some 'marbling' – a light distribution of fat throughout the flesh – to aid texture and taste. On some cuts of meat, fat is artificially wrapped around it, because the animal has been bred to be lean, due to customer demand.

Alternatively, if you want a naturally low-fat red meat with bags of flavour, venison is the answer. This has very little fat distributed through the meat. Therefore, it is dense in texture and high in protein. It requires light cooking for a relatively short time because of its compact nature. Venison is usually served pink, otherwise it tends to toughen up due to its lack of fat, and what you end up with is expensive shoe leather. If you want to roast venison, this is best done in a roasting bag § to prevent it completely drying out, or it needs to be coated in streaky bacon before roasting and basted frequently.

Storage of Meat

Perishable foods, like fresh meat and poultry, have very limited storage life, unless subsequently frozen. The best place to keep fresh meat and poultry is a refrigerator, between 0°C and 5°C, to ensure that bacteria, mould, and enzyme activity is reduced, because it is these organisms that cause food to go off. If you don't have a fridge, buy any perishable foods daily, as you need them. Buy just the amount you need to avoid any surplus from sitting around too long before being eaten.

Offal and processed meat, such as mince, has an even shorter shelf life than cuts or joints of the same animal. Always use within the use-by date or, if buying unpackaged from an independent butcher, follow the guidelines below.

Once home, remove the meat from the packaging, and place in a suitable container to avoid any drips. If it is wet, wipe dry with kitchen paper. Cover lightly with the wrapping paper or foil, and place in the fridge as soon as possible. Store near the bottom of the fridge, below any cooked foods to avoid cross-contamination.

Type of Meat	Storage Time
Raw Meat and Bacon	
Bacon rashers	5 – 7 days
Fresh joints	3 – 5 days
Steaks / chops	2 – 4 days
Braising meat	2 – 4 days
Offal / mince	1 – 2 days
Cooked Meat and Bacon	
Cooked joints	3 – 5 days
Casseroles	2 – 3 days
Made-up dishes	2 – 3 days
Raw Poultry and Game	
Whole birds	2 – 3 days
Jointed birds	2 – 3 days
Cooked Poultry and Game	
Whole birds	2 – 3 days
Jointed birds	2 – 3 days
Made-up dishes	1 day

If the meat is vacuum-packed when you purchased it, follow the instructions for storage. Frozen meat and poultry should be held in its frozen state at -18°C in the freezer. Make sure that all packaging is intact to avoid freezer burn. The manufacturer will identify storage times on the packaging. Unless advised otherwise, all frozen meat and poultry should be thoroughly thawed before being cooked. Thaw it in the refrigerator, or a cool larder, on a suitable tray to catch the melting water, and empty the tray regularly. Allow at least 24 hours for the meat to defrost completely.

How do you Cook With Confidence?

An admiring fan once asked the international golfer Gary Player, how was it that when the shot really mattered, he was always lucky and the ball went home? Player replied that the more he practised, the luckier he became! The same basic rule applies to cooking. You might have an aptitude, but it is only by making mistakes and learning from them, that you improve your skill and understanding of the task. Even basic cookery techniques can quickly go awry, especially in inexperienced hands. It is very easy to cook even the simplest of dishes poorly. Experts have climbed this steep learning curve in order to improve their skills and become better cooks.

The experienced cook does not just depend on a recipe with ingredients, timings, and instructions, but also cooks with affection. When you cook anything, you rely on your five senses to tell you when that item is cooked. You may have a recipe, with a time allocation for cooking, but you have to remember that it is only a guide. What you must really bank on are your five senses.

Sight: Look at its colour before food goes into the oven. It will change colour when cooked; darker as in the case of bread, sponges, and biscuits; lighter as in the case of fish, poultry, and meat.

Touch: Texture will change from raw to cooked. So it may be soft when raw, but firm when cooked, such as bread, sponges, and milk pudding; or hard when raw, but soft when cooked, such as apple, and potato.

Smell: Food will change in smell or aroma when cooked. Raw onions have an acrid smell that makes you cry. Whereas, cooked onions have a sweet caramelised smell.

Hearing: Some foods make an audible sound when cooked. Frying pumpkin, sunflower, or mustard seeds, or spices will pop and jump. Fruit cake will sing when nearly cooked, but fall silent when completely cooked.

Taste: All food tastes different in the raw state compared with their cooked state. This is the most enjoyable of the five senses, when trying to decide if food is cooked or not.

By using all of your senses every time you cook, eventually you will improve the finished product, and get satisfaction from a job well done.

This chapter starts by focussing on a variety of basic cookery crafts, which will be needed if you intend to try the recipes given at the end of the book. It supplements these skills with trouble-shooting remedies to correct those inevitable mistakes. Later in the chapter, I have provided some tips of the trade for a range of culinary techniques. These are followed by guidelines on hygiene and safety, not only in the kitchen, but also in the garden for your al fresco barbecues.

Conquer Crucial Cookery Crafts

Some cookery techniques occur repeatedly in basic recipes. This section describes such skills as home-made bread, puréed soups, roast meats, braised casseroles, sauces, pastries, and cakes. I attempt to explain the importance of the ingredients, together with how and why the techniques work, plus professional tips that you will rarely find published in cookery books. The skills in this section are arranged in much the same order as their associated recipes that appear later in the book.

Where appropriate I have included trouble-shooting entries to explain how to correct the more common place problems that often arise. In other words, they offer first aid in the kitchen for rescuing dishes that have a problem, and suggest suitable solutions with advice on how to avoid the problem in the future.

Therefore, throughout this chapter, under the heading of '**First Aid**' you will find descriptions of a particular '*Symptom:*' and its '*Diagnosis:*', with advice on corrective measures. Those headed '*Antidote:*' suggest how to rectify the problem with the current ingredients, whereas those headed '*Remedy:*' explain how to correct the problem the next time the technique is employed.

Bread Making

I can think of nothing more hunger inducing than the yeasty smell of fresh bread baking. You have to be strong willed to resist that enticing aroma, that makes you think "Break out the butter, we are in for a treat". If you could bottle that heady smell, you could use it as a kitchen air freshener or an aid to selling your house, but you'd be denied the pleasure of getting your hands sticky pummelling dough (and I don't mean the paper variety).

Ingredients

Flour

Strong plain wheat flour, which has a high gluten content, is the substance that gives bread its volume and texture. There are many varieties of strong flour; white, wheat-meal, whole-meal, and granary. In general, brown flour used just on its own does not give such a large volume or light texture as white flour. If you like the close texture of brown whole-meal bread that is fine, but if you prefer a lighter loaf with a whole-meal flavour, replace some of the whole-meal flour with white flour. Up to half the amount of white flour will still give a good texture, colour, and taste.

Yeast

The raising agent used in bread making is yeast, which is a living organism called **saccharomyces cerevisiae**, and is only visible under a microscope. Yeasts are found growing wild everywhere; on the skins of fruit, in the air, and in the soil. Wild yeasts cause jams and fruit to ferment, producing alcohols and carbon dioxide gas. It is these properties that have been put to use in the brewing and baking industries, which have developed cultivated yeasts. All yeasts can be used for both brewing and baking, but now yeasts cultivated for brewing produce more alcohol, while those for baking produce more gas. If you should use brewers yeast in bread making it will make the bread taste bitter.

Yeast feeds on carbohydrates found in starches and sugars. When it is combined with flour and given the correct conditions of warmth, moisture, food, and time, it grows rapidly and gives off carbon dioxide, which permeates the dough making it spongy in texture. This process is called fermentation and is why the mixed dough is left to rise at least once, if not twice, before baking. It is during this phase that the alcohols and acids are produced that help develop the bread's flavour. Therefore, the longer the time and slower the fermentation, the better will be the flavour.

The amount of yeast required varies according to the type of bread being made. Enriched breads, whole-meal breads, and wheat-meal breads need more yeast than white breads.

Fresh Yeast is a putty-coloured crumbly paste, and should have no visible dark brown dry patches indicating old age. It is not so readily available. There are three ways to use it.

◆ Dissolve with the mixing liquid; either milk or water.

◆ Rub into the flour.

◆ Make into a sponge batter with all the liquid and some of the flour.

Dried Yeast is also known as **Baker's Yeast**. Do **not** buy Brewer's Yeast or Tonic Yeast, which is used only in the brewing industry. There are two ways to use **Dried Yeast**.

◆ Dissolve in sweetened warm water 104°F / 40°C until frothy, and add to the flour mix.

◆ Make into a sponge batter with all the liquid and a third of the flour. Stand in a warm place until it rises like a sponge and doubles in volume. Then add the rest of the flour and salt.

Fast Acting / Quick Action Yeast is always added dry to the flour before adding any liquid.

Quantities

The recommended ratio of yeast to flour is not constant. The proportion of yeast reduces as the quantity of flour increases, as shown in the table below.

Flour	Fresh Yeast	Dried and Fast Action Yeast
225 g (8 oz)	10 g (½ oz)	5 g (¼ oz) *or* 2 level teaspoons
450 g (1 lb)	25 g (1 oz)	10 g (½ oz) *or* 1 level tablespoon
1.5 kg (3 lb)	50 g (2 oz)	25 g (1 oz) *or* 2 level tablespoons
3 kg (6 lb)	75 g (3 oz)	40 g (1½ oz) *or* 3 level tablespoons

Salt

This brings out the flavour of the flour, strengthens its gluten, controls the rise, and makes a crisp crust. Salt should never come into direct contact with the yeast as it dehydrates its natural moisture. Too much salt can kill the yeast. Use about 1 level teaspoon per 450 g (1 lb) of flour. Enriched doughs and sweet buns do not require as much, so always follow the amounts given in the recipe.

Sugar

Sugar is food for the yeast; traditionally, a small amount was added to activate fresh yeast by creaming the two together. This has now been found to be detrimental to the yeast and the resultant dough. It gives the bread a strong yeasty taste. Therefore, unless you like that taste, do not use this method. Never exceed the amount of sugar recommended in the recipe. Use brown sugar or honey in place of white sugar, as yeast grows better with the former.

Fat

Bread can be made without the addition of fat. Whether the fat is butter, margarine, or lard, it enriches the dough, gives the bread a softer crumb, and also delays staling. As a rule, use about 25 g (1 oz) of fat per 450 g (1 lb) of flour.

Liquid

Water, milk, or a mixture of both can be used in bread making. What you must consider is the temperature of the liquid. It can be cold 50°F / 10°C which will give a cold rise that will develop flavour and texture but take longer to rise. The optimum temperature is 104°F / 40°C, so that the mixed dough will be warm enough to start the yeast fermenting immediately. This temperature can be achieved by boiling one third of the required quantity of liquid and mixing with the other two thirds of cold liquid. Do not make the liquid any hotter otherwise it will kill off the yeast cells. Use 275 ml (10 fl oz) of liquid per 450 g (1 lb) of flour.

Traditional Bread Ingredients

	450 g (1 lb)	strong white &/or brown bread flour
	1 level teaspoon	salt
	1 level teaspoon	white sugar or brown sugar or honey
	25 g (1 oz)	lard or margarine or butter or vegetable oil
	25 g (1 oz)	fresh yeast
		or
		10 g (½ oz)
		dried yeast
or	10 g (½ oz)	sachet of fast / quick action easy blend yeast
	275 ml (10 fl oz)	water &/or milk – hand hot
	1	beaten egg for glaze

Traditional Bread Method

Sieve the flour and salt into a large mixing bowl. Rub in the fat thoroughly.

Fresh Yeast Option

Add the sugar to the dry mix. Cream the fresh yeast with half the warm liquid. Add the creamed yeast to the flour mixture with the remaining warm liquid.

Dried Yeast Option

Put half the warm liquid in a jug; stir in the sugar and dried yeast, and leave to froth for 10 – 15 minutes. Add the frothy yeast to the flour mixture with the remaining warm liquid.

Fast Action Yeast Option

Add the sugar and fast action yeast to the flour mixture and stir well. Add all the hand hot liquid in one go.

Kneading

Mix together with your hands to make a soft elastic dough, ensuring all the ingredients are well combined. Turn out the dough onto a clean worktop and knead for about 10 – 12 minutes until smooth, elastic, and free from stickiness. Add a little more flour or water if necessary to achieve the desired consistency.

First Proving

If using fast action yeast you can omit this first proving completely.

Lightly oil the mixing bowl, return the dough to the bowl, and lightly oil the top of the dough. Cover the bowl with a clean damp tea towel, and leave in a warm place to rise for 1 – 1½ hours until doubled in size.

Turn out the risen dough onto a clean worktop, knock out the air bubbles, and knead for about 5 minutes until it regains its original size. This is commonly known as 'knocking back'.

Final Proving

Shape the dough and place into a greased loaf tin, or divide and shape the dough into rolls and place on a greased baking sheet. Leave in a warm place to prove for 10 – 15 minutes until increased in size by about a third.

Baking

Bake in a hot oven at Gas Mark 7 / 425°F / 220°C (200°C for fan oven) for about 35 minutes for a loaf, or 10 – 15 minutes for rolls. Place a roasting tin of water at the bottom of the oven to improve the flavour and texture of the bread. After about 5 minutes, remove the bread and glaze with the beaten egg, return it to the oven until golden brown and firm to the touch.

First Aid

Symptom: *Fast action yeast not added to flour mix before the water.*

Diagnosis: *Forgetfulness – a common problem.*

Antidote: *Do **not** sprinkle the fast action yeast on the dough, hoping it will work. It's better to add the yeast to a small amount of flour, say 100 g (4 oz), and add just enough water to make a pliable dough. Now add the yeasty dough to the yeast-less dough, and knead for 10 minutes. I know from experience that this works!*

Symptom: *Bread dough will not rise when proving.*

Diagnosis: *May have forgotten to add yeast, or yeast maybe too old, or could have killed yeast with too much heat.*

Remedy: *Check the recipe to see if you have used the stated amount of yeast. Fresh yeast should not be dark brown, but the colour of putty or a light fawn brown. Check the use-by date on dried yeast.*
When adding liquid make sure it is hand hot or about 104°F / 40°C because anything much above this temperature is likely to kill the yeast. Do not place the dough to rise in a too hot atmosphere. Too much heat kills yeast.

Symptom: *Bread is soft when first baked, but quickly becomes dry and stale.*

Diagnosis: *Not enough liquid used in the dough can make the dough too stiff. Quickly made bread, with only one rising, goes stale quicker than bread with two risings.*

Remedy: *Check the recipe carefully and use the correct liquid quantity for the amount of flour: either 275 ml (10 fl oz) liquid per 450 g (1 lb) flour or alternatively 1 cup of liquid per 3 cups of flour. The cup can be a teacup, old tin can, etc, as long as you use the same measure for both ingredients. This is a guide and depends on the flour strength and how long it has been stored.*
Allow two risings of the dough to allow alcohols produced by the yeast to develop and aid keeping qualities.

Symptom: *Bread tastes very yeasty after baking.*

Diagnosis: *Too much yeast used in relation to flour.*
The sugar was creamed directly with fresh yeast.
Warm rise doughs tend to have a yeasty flavour, especially if over-heated during rising.

Remedy: *If doubling the recipe quantities, do not double the amount of yeast, but increase by half. See the 'Quantities' given above.*
The old fashioned method of creaming the sugar with fresh yeast should not be used as this kills some of the yeast cells.
Try to prove the dough in a cold room as this adds flavour to the dough, but not a yeasty taste. The cooler rising will take longer but the taste will be better.

Symptom: *Bread seems very dense and heavy after baking.*

Diagnosis: *Too much liquid was added, making the dough too soft and sticky. Insufficient kneading of the dough.*

Remedy: *You need to check the liquid quantities in relation to the dry ingredients. As a guide, use 275 ml (10 fl oz) liquid per 450 g (1 lb) flour or 1 cup of liquid per 3 cups of flour.*
You must knead the dough consistently for 10 minutes; treating the dough firmly.

Basic Purée Soups

The value of soups lies in the fact that they act as an appetiser, by increasing the flow of saliva and gastric juices. All soups should be served at their correct temperature; either hot, or the other extreme, chilled, to enhance the flavour. Apart from bags of flavour, the correct consistency, freedom from grease, and colour all need to be considered. We have all consumed soups that may have one of the above attributes, but lack the others. I was once served spinach and nutmeg soup that was admittedly at the correct temperature, but looked like wet washing with the colour of khaki green.

Soups are classified or grouped according to their consistency or thickness. Thin or clear soups are consommé, broth, and chowder. Thickened soups are purée, cream, velouté, brown, and bisque.

Basic Purée Soup Ingredients

40 g (1½ oz)	margarine
350 g (12 oz)	your choice of vegetable as primary ingredient
110 g (4 oz)	any mixture of leek, carrot, Swede, parsnip, onion
40 g (1½ oz)	plain flour
850 ml (1½ pt)	vegetable stock
1	bouquet garni § (see page 78)
	salt and pepper to taste

Basic Purée Soup Method

Melt the margarine in a large saucepan. Roughly chop your primary choice of vegetable and the mixture of vegetables, and add them to the saucepan. Cook until soft but without colouring (called 'sweating').

Stir in the flour off the heat until thoroughly combined. Place the saucepan back on the heat and add the preheated vegetable stock, stirring all the time until the stock is used up.

Add the bouquet garni, cover the pan with a lid to prevent excess evaporation, and simmer the soup for about half an hour, until all the vegetables are soft and cooked. When the vegetables are cooked, remove the bouquet garni.

If you want a smooth consistency, liquidise the soup with a blender or in a food processor; otherwise, for a coarser soup, leave the vegetables as cooked.

Adjust the seasoning and consistency as necessary. This quantity of soup will serve about 3 or 4 people.

First Aid

Symptom: *Soup is too greasy.*

Diagnosis: *Imbalance of ingredients. Not enough flour to fat or too fatty meat used.*

Antidote: *If only a small amount of fat: Allow the soup to cool, add ice cubes, and when the fat solidifies on the ice cubes, remove them with the fat. Alternatively, lay kitchen paper over the surface of the soup to mop up globules of fat.*
If larger amounts of fat: Leave the soup to cool completely, to allow the fat to solidify, and scoop off the excess fat.

Remedy: *Check ingredients for any visible lumps of fat and discard.*

Symptom: *Soup is over-seasoned.*

Diagnosis: *Being over zealous with the salt and pepper.*

Antidote: *If too peppery, add yoghurt or cream to counteract the peppery taste. If that does not work and it is chunky vegetable soup, strain off the vegetable chunks and rinse well, discard some of the soup and replace with fresh water or stock, and finally return the chunks to the soup.*

If too salty, add a peeled potato cut into large pieces to absorb the excess salt. Remember to remove the potato pieces before serving.

Symptom: *Soup has little or no flavour.*

Diagnosis: *No seasoning added, or insufficient ingredients for amount of liquid.*

Antidote: *Add one of the following: chopped herbs, Marmite®, Tabasco® sauce, Worcestershire sauce, mustard, or tomato purée. Alternatively, finely chop some more of the main ingredients, add them to the soup, and simmer until just soft.*

Boiled Chicken

Chicken forms the basis of so many succulent dishes that, with just one boiled chicken, you can be extremely crafty, and see how far it can stretch.

Ingredients
~1.25 kg (~2¾ lb)   fresh *or* frozen chicken (thoroughly defrosted)

Method

Remove the chicken from its wrapping, remove and discard the innards.

Place the chicken in a saucepan and just cover it with cold water. Cover with a lid and boil for one hour, until the chicken is just tender.

Carefully remove the chicken from the liquid, and allow the chicken to cool slightly before removing the skin, bones, and any gristle. Remember to keep the liquid chicken stock.

Chop the chicken meat fairly finely, divide into even sized portions, about 100 g (4 oz) each, and freeze or refrigerate until required.

Succulent Roast Meat

There is nothing more traditional than sitting down to a full roast dinner, with all the vegetables; whether it be roast beef and Yorkshire pudding, golden chicken with parsley and lemon stuffing, or glistening loin of pork with crispy crackling. With all meats and poultry, it is all about timing and personal preferences such as how you like your meat cooked.

When buying meat to roast, allow 100 – 175 g (4 – 6 oz) per person for a boneless joint, or allow 200 – 350 g (8 – 12 oz) per person if the meat is still on the bone.

Method

Below is a guide to the appropriate temperatures and timings to roast meat. The **Cooking Times** show the roasting duration in minutes per pound plus an extra number of minutes. So a 4 lb chicken will need 20 min x 4 + 20 min = 100 minutes. Remember to convert the metric weight of a joint to pounds by dividing by 450 grams. You can also use a meat thermometer, which takes some of the guesswork out of deciding if the meat is cooked to your liking. The probe sticks into the cooked meat and registers the result on a visible scale, and is a worthwhile investment if you love roasts. The **Meat Probe Scale** indicates the readings for two types of meat probe thermometer; one uses words such as 'Beef Rare' or 'Lamb Well-done' and the other uses core temperatures.

Meat	Temperature	Meat Probe Scale		Cooking Times
	Mark / °F / °C (fan oven)	*Words*	*°F / °C*	*min per lb + min*
Chicken	Gas 5 / 375 / 190 (170)	Medium	170 / 76	20 + 20
Beef	Gas 4 / 350 / 180 (160)	Rare	140 / 60	15 + 20
		Medium	160 / 71	25 + 25
		Well-done	170 / 76	30 + 30
Lamb, Veal	Gas 4 / 350 / 180 (160)	Medium	180 / 82	25 + 25
		Well-done	190 / 87	30 + 30
Pork	Gas 4 / 350 / 180 (160)	Medium	190 / 87	30 + 30
		Well-done	200 / 94	35 + 35

If you roast a joint weighing less than 1.25 kg (2½ lb), you need to add an extra 5 minutes per 0.5 kg (1 lb) to the overall roasting time. However, this is just a guide. It depends on your oven and how you like your roast meat done.

All meats and poultry benefit from a resting time of 10 – 15 minutes once the joint is cooked to your liking. The joint should be lightly covered with foil to keep warm and let the juices be absorbed into the meat before carving.

First Aid

Symptom: *Roast meat is dry or tough.*

Diagnosis: *Insufficient fat in the meat, or intensively reared meat that lacks any natural fat.*
Possibly over-cooking.
Not allowing the meat to rest before carving.

Antidote: *Add a dash of wine or stock to the roasting pan if the meat looks dry before it is ready. Cover with foil, lower the temperature slightly, and allow its full cooking time.*

Remedy: *Look for traditionally reared meat that has natural fat marbling throughout the joint. Add additional fat to joints by larding. This is threading strips of pork fat into lean meat to imitate natural marbling. Ask your butcher to do this.*
Check the weight of the joint, the cooking times, and the roasting temperatures. Purchase a meat thermometer.
Carving immediately the joint comes out of the oven results in the meat losing all its natural juices as they are still bubbling and rising to the surface of the meat. Some meats can start to curl or roll up as you carve, so it is good practice to let the meat relax; just like you!

Symptom: *Roast joint looks cooked but is pink inside.*

Diagnosis: *Only beef or venison are ever served rare. All other meats are served just cooked or well done. The joint has not been cooked long enough, or the oven was too hot and only roasted the outside.*

Antidote: *Return the joint to the oven and continue to roast to your liking.*

Remedy: *Either purchase a meat thermometer (and use it), or use a skewer to stick into the thickest part of the joint to see if the juices run clear. Check your cooking time and temperature.*

Braised Casseroles

These are slowly stewed dishes where meat, game, poultry, or fish are cooked in a tightly closed container with liquid, which can be stock, water, wine, or milk.

Ingredients

450 g (1 lb)	chosen meat *or* game *or* poultry *or* fish
25 g (1 oz)	lard
110 g (4 oz)	chosen vegetables – sliced *or* chopped – such as carrot, celery, leek, parsnip, Swede, *&/or* peas. § (see page 79)
110 g (4 oz)	onion – sliced *or* chopped §
2 cloves	garlic – crushed (optional)
25 g (1 oz)	flour
570 ml (1 pt)	stock *or* water *or* wine
1	bouquet garni § (see page 78)

Method

To prepare meat, trim to remove excess fat and cut into either thin slices, or even-sized cubes or portions. Melt the lard in a shallow pan and quickly fry the meat until it is sealed and lightly brown. Place the sealed meat in the casserole dish.

To prepare fish, cut it into either thin slices, or even-sized cubes or portions.

To prepare the vegetables, wash, peel, and slice or chop into even-sized pieces. Fry the vegetables and onions (plus crushed garlic if desired) in the lard until lightly brown. Sprinkle the flour into the vegetables and stir until all the lard is absorbed. Add hot stock, water, or wine to the vegetable mixture and stir thoroughly until the flour absorbs all the liquid.

Pour the thickened vegetable mixture into the casserole dish, either to cover the meat, or to place the prepared fish on. Add the bouquet garni §.

Cover the dish with a tightly fitting lid and place on the middle shelf of the oven at Gas Mark 4 / 350°F / 180°C (160°C for fan oven) for about 1½ – 2½ hours depending on the type of meat, or for about 1 hour for fish.

Test to see if the meat or fish is tender by tasting a piece, and season to taste before serving.

First Aid

Symptom: *Casserole sauce is too thin and runny.*

Diagnosis: *Too much liquid or uneven recipe balance. Ideally, a casserole recipe should contain the correct amount of liquid to allow it to thicken through natural evaporation, without drying out any of the contents. However, if the consistency is not satisfactory I have a number of tips to help you thicken a casserole.*

Antidote: *Remove the solid ingredients of meat or fish, and vegetables, and boil the liquid to reduce and thicken it slightly.*

> *You can add kneaded butter or beurre manié § (see page 77) towards the end of cooking until the required consistency is achieved.*
> *Another tip is to blend cornflour and cold water into a smooth paste, and stir into the casserole about 10 minutes before the end of cooking. But beware – it could become gloopy, thick, and cloudy.*

Remedy: *One trick I used in the restaurant was to place one whole peeled potato into the casserole with the other ingredients and allow it to slow cook in the oven. At the end of cooking, I'd fish out the cooked potato and liquidise it with some of the liquid and use this to get the required consistency of sauce. You can similarly liquidise any of the vegetables in a casserole, especially if you want a smooth sauce.*
If using meat in your casserole, you can dust it with seasoned flour before sealing in hot fat. This will aid the thickening of the sauce.

Symptom: *Casserole sauce lacks flavour.*
Diagnosis: *Insufficient seasoning.*
Antidote: *Add salt and pepper and retaste. Other improvements to the flavour may be obtained by adding one of the following: Worcestershire sauce, Tabasco® sauce, mint sauce, horseradish sauce, or mustard.*

Symptom: *Casserole sauce is greasy.*
Diagnosis: *Too much fat on the braised meat, especially with lamb or mutton dishes where the fat produced 'sleeps' on the top of the liquid.*
Antidote: *If only a small amount of fat, allow the dish to cool and add ice cubes. The fat solidifies on the ice cubes, which can be removed with the fat. Alternatively, lay kitchen paper over the surface of the sauce to mop up globules of fat.*
If larger amounts of fat, leave the casserole to cool completely, to allow the fat to solidify, and scoop off the excess fat.
Remedy: *Need to remove some of the visible fat before braising; but beware that meats without any fat are prone to becoming dry or tough when cooked.*

Symptom: *Casserole meat is under-cooked and chewy.*
Diagnosis: *Cooking time too short or temperature too low.*
Antidote: *Need to continue to cook &/or raise temperature slightly.*

Symptom: *Casserole meat is dry or tough.*
Diagnosis: *Over-cooking at too high a temperature, or wrong cut of meat, or poor quality meat, or lack of fat in the meat.*
Remedy: *Check temperature is Gas Mark 4 / 350°F / 180°C (160°C for fan oven) for braising, and obtain a reliable meat source.*

Perfect Béchamel White Sauce *

Sauce making is a most important part of cooking, because a good sauce enhances the food it accompanies.

◆ It brings out the flavour of the food e.g. parsley sauce and steamed fish.

◆ It adds extra flavour and goodness e.g. cheese sauce and macaroni.

◆ It provides a pleasant contrast to the texture of more solid food e.g. mint sauce and roast lamb.

Sauces can be thickened in a variety of ways, but one of the foundation or mother sauces is a white sauce; also known by its French name of béchamel.

Here I explain how to achieve that perfect smooth roux-based sauce. This is a sauce whose thickening agent is flour which, when combined with fat, produces the roux. It is this roux, when heated with hot liquid, that gives body to the liquid by changing its consistency. This is because the starch in the flour has swelled, burst, and thickened the liquid.

The ingredients of a white béchamel sauce are whole milk, fat, and flour. The ratio of milk to fat and flour governs the consistency of the sauce. The thinnest is a pouring sauce; next is a coating sauce; and the thickest is a binding or panada sauce.

You will need a wooden or plastic balloon whisk, a wooden spoon, and either two saucepans for the traditional method, or one saucepan for the all-in-one method.

Ingredients for 1 pint of sauce

570 ml (1 pt)	whole milk (not skimmed)
1 small peeled	whole onion (for traditional method)
	salt and pepper to taste

Pouring Sauce

40 g (1½ oz)	butter *or* margarine
40 g (1½ oz)	plain white flour

Coating Sauce

50 g (2 oz)	butter *or* margarine
50 g (2 oz)	plain white flour

Binding or Panada Sauce

110 g (4 oz)	butter *or* margarine
110 g (4 oz)	plain white flour

Traditional Method

Place the milk and a small peeled whole onion in a saucepan. Bring to the boil, leave to infuse for 15 minutes.

Gently melt the butter or margarine in a separate saucepan, but do not allow it to colour. Add an equal quantity of the flour and, on a low heat, stir together until the flour has absorbed all the fat, and the roux moves round the saucepan like wet sand.

Remove the onion from the warm milk. Gradually add tablespoons of the warm milk to the roux, on a medium heat, beating until a smooth consistency is achieved, before adding more milk.

Bring the sauce to the boil, and leave to simmer for approximately 5 minutes. Add seasonings and check the taste.

All-in-one Method

Place all the ingredients, cold milk, fat, and flour, in a saucepan. On a medium heat, whisk the sauce until it starts to thicken and bubble. With the spoon, stir the sauce right into the corners to eliminate lumps of flour. Whisk the sauce again until smooth and thick, with no taste of uncooked flour. Add seasonings and check the taste.

First Aid

Symptom: *White sauce is too lumpy.*

Diagnosis: *Adding cold milk to the hot roux (flour and fat mixture) too quickly, or insufficient mixing of the ingredients.*

Antidote: *Need to heat the liquid to the same temperature as the roux, then they will amalgamate more readily. Add hot liquid in small amounts and beat well until thoroughly smooth before any more additions. If all that fails, blend in a food processor or liquidiser, or use a sieve.*

Symptom: *White sauce is thin and dull.*

Diagnosis: *Insufficient cooking of the flour in the sauce, poor beating of the sauce, or incorrect measuring of the ingredients.*

Antidote: *Raise the temperature of the sauce whilst beating vigorously, but taking care not to burn the sauce. If that does not work, add kneaded butter or beurre manié § (see page 77), or stir in a little cornflour dissolved in milk, and cook until the desired consistency is achieved. Always check quantities accurately to achieve the right consistency of sauce.*

Symptom: *White sauce has too thick a consistency.*

Diagnosis: *Poor measuring of ingredients.*

Antidote: *Remove half the roux mixture to use at a later date, add more liquid to the remaining roux until the correct consistency is achieved.*

Symptom: *White sauce lacks flavour.*

Diagnosis: *Insufficient seasoning.*

Antidote: *Season with salt and pepper, then retaste. Other improvements to the flavour can be achieved by a number of additions:*

    – Add a small onion to simmer in the sauce, then discard the onion before serving sauce.

    – Add a small amount of mustard, or Tabasco® sauce.

> – *Add any herb such as rosemary, bay leaf, or thyme, which must be removed before serving.*
>
> – *Add just a knob of butter.*

Symptom: *White sauce contains burnt bits, appearing as brown flecks.*

Diagnosis: *Saucepan is too thin, or heat source is uneven.*

Antidote: *Remove from the heat immediately and sieve into a clean pan, with a heavier base if possible.*

Cheese Sauce *

A white sauce can be easily adapted to a cheese sauce by adding finely grated strong cheese to taste, plus a teaspoon of Dijon mustard. I use about 100 g (4 oz) of cheese to half a litre (1 pint) of sauce, but you can customise this to your own taste. I think it is better to use a cheese with some bite to its flavour, because in the long run you need less of it to feel it biting!

Ingredients for 1 pint of sauce

570 ml (1 pt)	pouring white sauce § (see above)
110 g (4 oz)	strong Cheddar cheese – grated
1 teaspoon	Dijon mustard (optional)

Method

Make up a pint of pouring white sauce. Off the heat, stir in the grated cheese and mustard. Mix until everything is combined, and use as required.

First Aid

See the '**First Aid**' section for '**Perfect Béchamel White Sauce**'.

Symptom: *Cheese sauce appears stringy and oily.*

Diagnosis: *Cheese was overheated by boiling and released its fat.*

Remedy: *Add the cheese off the heat and stir until just melted.*

Symptom: *Cheese sauce does not taste of cheese.*

Diagnosis: *Too little mild flavoured cheese used.*

Antidote: *Add sufficient cheese to achieve a savoury taste.*

Remedy: *Use strong flavoured cheese.*

Baked Egg Custard *

This light-textured, milk-based, set custard is versatile enough to be either sweet toothed or have that savoury piquant edge, depending on which recipe you follow.

The sweet variety can form the basis of egg custard tart, queen of puddings, bread and jam pudding, and burnt cream or crème brûlée.

The savoury variety can be used for any quiche filling, cheese pudding, and savoury bread and butter pudding.

Ingredients to serve 4 people

570 ml (1 pt)	milk
4 large	eggs

Sweet Flavour

1 pod	vanilla
or ½ teaspoon	vanilla extract
4 tablespoons	golden granulated sugar

Savoury Flavour

1 teaspoon	Dijon mustard
	salt and pepper
2 tablespoons	Parmesan cheese – freshly grated

Method

Place the milk in a saucepan.

Sweet Flavour

If using a vanilla pod, cut the pod lengthways with a small sharp knife and scrape out all the seeds from inside. Place all the seeds and pod into the milk. Bring the milk to the boil, remove it from the heat, and leave to infuse for 10 minutes. Remove the vanilla pod halves.

If using vanilla extract, add it straight to the boiled milk.

Break the eggs into a large bowl with the sugar, and whisk until thoroughly combined. Add the vanilla milk and mix well. Strain the mixture into a jug.

Savoury Flavour

Bring the milk to the boil. Break the eggs into a large bowl and mix with the mustard, salt and pepper. Add the hot milk and mix well. Strain the mixture into a jug. Add the freshly grated cheese and stir well.

Baking

Divide the mixture evenly between four dariole moulds § or pour it all into a pie dish. Place the moulds or dish into a roasting tin half full of hot water.

Bake at Gas Mark 3 / 325°F / 170°C (150°C for fan oven) for 35 – 45 minutes until the custard is just set. Remove from the hot water, and leave to cool before refrigerating.

If using dariole moulds, they can be turned out just before serving.

First Aid

Symptom: *Egg custard mixture not set after baking for the allotted time.*

Diagnosis: *The ratio of milk to egg in the ingredients is important.*
The material of which the baking dish is made can affect the oven temperature and especially the baking time.

Remedy: *Check the recipe to ensure the correct number and size of eggs are used for the specified quantity of liquid.*

Check the oven temperature and baking time, and adjust according to the material of the baking dish. Glass and earthenware are poor conductors, and may need longer cooking times than metal, which is a good conductor.

Symptom: *Egg custard has tiny holes throughout and oozes liquid after baking.*

Diagnosis: *The custard has been baked at too high a temperature without sufficient protection from the roasting tin water bath.*

Remedy: *Check the oven temperature, and ensure the roasting tin is at least half to three-quarters full of water.*

Sweet or Savoury Pancakes *

My top tip for pancakes is to leave the batter to rest overnight in the fridge. This allows the flour starch more time to be released into the milk and gives greater cohesion. Therefore, you can produce thinner pancakes. So, with a little forethought, you will get more pancakes from the basic batter mix. Now there's Yorkshire thrift at work!

Ingredients

Batter

110 g (4 oz)	plain flour
1 pinch	salt
2 large	eggs
150 ml (5 fl oz)	milk
150 ml (5 fl oz)	water

Pancakes

1 tablespoon	vegetable oil
	sugar and lemon juice *or* marmalade *or* jam
or	grated cheese and cheese sauce

Flavours

1 dessertspoon	spices such as ginger, cinnamon, *or* mixed spice
or 2 tablespoons	finely grated citrus zest of orange, lime, lemon, *or* grapefruit
or 1 dessertspoon	black poppy seeds *or* mustard seeds
1 dessertspoon	sun-dried tomato paste *or* curry paste
or 2 tablespoons	roughly chopped herbs such as chive, parsley, thyme, coriander, dill, basil, *or* mint

Method

Prepare Batter

Sieve the flour into a mixing bowl and add the salt. Make a depression in the centre of the flour, break in the eggs, and add the milk. Use a whisk or wooden spoon to draw in the flour whilst beating continuously.

Gradually add the water while whisking, until the mixture is a smooth thick batter, free from lumps. The batter should look like single cream.

Pour the batter into a jug and leave in the refrigerator overnight to relax.

Make Pancakes

Place a tablespoon of vegetable oil in a saucer. Use a pastry brush to coat the surface of a pancake pan §, or small frying pan, until the pan just glistens. When you tip the pan, there should be no visible sign of running oil.

Heat the pan until a faint blue haze appears just above the surface. Pour enough batter from the jug to coat the surface of the pan thinly. Allow the pancake to set around the edge, flip it over with a flick of the wrist, or use a palette knife or round-ended knife to turn the pancake over. Similarly, lightly cook the other side. Turn the pancake out onto a warm plate. Repeat with the remainder of the batter.

For sweet pancakes, dredge with sugar; then simply drench in lemon juice or spread with marmalade or jam, and finally roll them up like a cigar.

For savoury pancakes, fill with grated cheese; then roll up like a cigar, coat with cheese sauce, and brown under the grill.

Add Flavours

Why not pep up the basic pancakes by stirring flavourings into the batter just before use? If you choose the sun-dried tomato paste or curry paste, blend a little batter into the paste until evenly coloured, before stirring into the rest of the batter.

First Aid

Symptom: *Pancake batter looks lumpy with balls of dry flour floating in it.*

Diagnosis: *The flour was not sieved before use, or the liquid was added too quickly without sufficient beating.*

Antidote: *Strain the batter through a sieve to remove the excess lumps. Alternatively, use a blender, or place the batter in a food processor and whiz until smooth.*

Symptom: *Pancake batter will not hold together and the pancakes are brittle.*

Diagnosis: *Recipe imbalance with too much liquid for the flour.*
Insufficient resting of the batter before use.

Remedy: *Check your recipe against my pancake ingredients.*
Rest the batter for at least 30 minutes, but preferably overnight, before use, to allow the starch in the flour to swell into the milk and form a mesh.

Symptom: *Pancakes are thick, difficult to handle, and taste heavy, chewy, and leathery.*

Diagnosis: *Recipe imbalance with insufficient liquid for the flour.*
Pancakes cooked at too low a temperature.

Remedy: *Check your recipe against my pancake ingredients.*
Make sure the pan is hot with a blue haze before you add the batter. Try to get the batter just to coat the pan. Swirl the pan if necessary. Fry the pancake on a medium heat.

Baking Potato Pastry

If you hate making pastry because you feel it's too much fuss, or you have had unsuccessful results, potato pastry is the pastry for you! This light, soft textured pastry requires very little skill to make and handle. It never cracks when rolled, and can be used in both savoury as well as sweet dishes; so, in my eyes, it's a cook's best friend.

Ingredients

110 g (4 oz)	peeled weight of potatoes
110 g (4 oz)	melted butter *or* margarine *or* vegetable oil
225 g (8 oz)	self-raising flour

Method

Cut the peeled potatoes into even sized pieces, so they will cook evenly. Place them into a saucepan, and just cover with water. Put on the saucepan lid, and bring to the boil. Boil the potatoes until soft when tested with a sharp knife.

Drain off all the water, and return the saucepan to the heat to dry off any remaining liquid. Using a fork or potato masher, mash the potatoes until smooth and free from lumps.

Add the fat and combine well. Add the sieved flour and stir until thoroughly combined. The potato pastry should form into a ball.

Leave the pastry to cool completely before use.

At this stage the pastry can be wrapped in cling film, and refrigerated for up to 2 days until needed.

Roll out and bake as for other pastries (see below).

First Aid

Symptom: *Potatoes cause stomach-ache, nausea, or vomiting after being eaten.*

Diagnosis: *A toxic substance called solanine is sometimes found in potatoes.*

Remedy: *Avoid using green potatoes and old potatoes with eyes.*

Symptom: *Pastry is insufficient for the size of the dish.*

Diagnosis: *In recipes, pastry is quoted in terms of the weight of its flour content. It is not the weight of all the ingredients.*

Remedy: *When a recipe requires say 8 oz of potato pastry, that defines the weight of flour, to which must be added 4 oz of potato, and 4 oz of fat.*

Baking Shortcrust Pastry

"I can't make shortcrust pastry." How often has someone we know uttered these words? Usually, when you enquire further, either the recipe they are following is unbalanced, or their technique needs improving. Shortcrust pastry is probably the most used home-made pastry, because it is quite simple to make.

Ingredients

225 g (8 oz)	plain flour
1 level teaspoon	salt
50 g (2 oz)	lard
50 g (2 oz)	margarine *or* butter
8 teaspoons	cold water

The basic recipe includes:

Plain Flour

Sieve to incorporate air, the raising agent, which expands when heated.

Salt

Improves the flavour and strengthens the gluten in the flour. Use roughly 1 level teaspoon of salt per 225 g (8 oz) of flour.

Fat (Lard with Margarine or Butter)

Usually equal quantities of lard, which gives a crumbly texture, and margarine or butter, which both add flavour and a flaky, crunchy texture.

Water

Should be as cold as possible, and be just enough to bind the pastry. Use about 1 teaspoon per 25 g (1 oz) of flour.

Method

A good shortcrust pastry should crumble easily. To achieve this, keep everything cold: the ingredients, the equipment, and your hands! If you have hot hands, you have to work extra quickly and lightly. Alternatively, use a food processor, or invest in a pastry blender §. The secrets of success are:

◆ Keep everything cool.

◆ Handle ingredients as lightly as possible.

◆ Introduce as much air as possible. Sieve the flour and salt. Rub the fat into the flour using your fingertips only, and lift the mix level with the rim of the bowl. Alternatively, use a pastry blender §, or sharp bursts of a food processor. The mixture should resemble ground almonds or breadcrumbs.

◆ Add the cold water. Form the pastry into a ball by hand, or with sharp bursts of the food processor. Cover in cling film, and allow the pastry to chill for at least 30 minutes before rolling.

◆ Roll lightly with short, even, forward strokes without undue stretching.

◆ Bake at Gas Mark 6 / 400°F / 200°C (180°C for fan oven) for about 10 minutes until just firm, and then reduce to Gas Mark 5 / 375°F / 190°C (170°C for fan oven) for about 15 minutes until cooked.

First Aid

Symptom: *Pastry is blistered and hard.*

Diagnosis: *Too much handling when rolling out the pastry.*

Remedy: *Handle the pastry lightly. Do not turn the pastry over when rolling out, nor use too much flour on the work surface. Roll as evenly as possible with short sharp strokes.*

Symptom: *Pastry is hard and tough.*

Diagnosis: *Too much water added to bind the pastry and over handling.*

Remedy: *Use about 1 teaspoon of cold water per 25 g (1 oz) of flour as a guide.*

Symptom: *Pastry shrinks when baked.*

Diagnosis: *Pastry not allowed to relax before baking, or over stretched before baking.*

Remedy: *Chill the pastry for at least 30 minutes to let it relax before baking. Try not to pull the pastry to fit its dish.*

Symptom: *Pastry is insufficient for the size of the dish.*

Diagnosis: *In recipes, pastry is quoted in terms of the weight of its flour content. It is not the weight of all the ingredients.*

Remedy: *When a recipe requires say 225 g (8 oz) of pastry, that defines the weight of flour, to which must be added salt, 110 g (4 oz) fat, and water.*

Baking Sugar Pastry

Once you have mastered potato pastry and shortcrust pastry, you are ready to progress to sugar pastry.

Ingredients

225 g (8 oz)	self-raising flour
1 pinch	salt
110 g (4 oz)	butter
50 g (2 oz)	castor sugar
1 large	egg

Method

All the techniques for shortcrust pastry apply equally to sugar pastry.

Keep everything cool, and handle the pastry as lightly as possible.

Sieve the flour and salt into a mixing bowl. Cut the butter into pea sized pieces.

Rub the butter into the flour until it looks like ground almonds or breadcrumbs.

Stir in the sugar, add the egg, mix together well, and form into a ball.

Wrap in cling film, and chill for at least 30 minutes before rolling out.

Roll and bake as for shortcrust pastry above.

Baking Pastry Blind

This refers to baking an empty pastry flan base, before adding a filling for a quiche or tart.

Roll out the pastry to line a flan ring. To stop the pastry rising, place a piece of greaseproof paper over the pastry, and fill with 2 tablespoons of raw lentils or rice. Bake in a preheated oven at Gas Mark 6 / 400°F / 200°C (180°C for fan oven) for about 10 minutes until just firm. Remove the greaseproof paper and lentils or rice.

Baking Cakes and Sponges

The best way of marking an occasion is by producing a cake. You've all sunk your teeth into a piece of gooey birthday cake, or savoured a sliver of dark moist wedding cake cocooned in marzipan and icing. Then there's that favourite aunt who always offers huge wedges of deliciously decadent chocolate cake. This is by far the most memorable and nicest approach to categorising cakes, but there are more traditional ways.

Categories

The various types of cake are most commonly identified by the method or process adopted to achieve the finished product. Occasionally, more than one method can be combined in making a cake.

- **All-In-One Method**. All the ingredients are mixed together, often using a food processor. It is the easiest method, and ideal if you are new to cake baking.
- **Boiling Method**. The fat, sugar, and fruit are boiled together, then the eggs and flour are mixed in. It is usually used for fruitcakes.
- **Melting Method**. The fat and sugar, or syrup, are gently heated together until the fat has dissolved, then the other ingredients are added. It is used for gingerbread, parkin, and malt loaf.
- **Rubbing-In Method**. The fat is rubbed into the flour, before adding the other ingredients. This is used for rock cakes, raspberry buns, and large cakes.
- **Whisking Method**. The eggs and sugar are whisked vigorously until thick and creamy in texture; usually becoming lighter in colour than when first combined. This method is used for sponge sandwich, Swiss rolls, and sponge drops.
- **Creaming Method**. The fat and sugar are creamed together until soft in texture, and usually change to a lighter colour once thoroughly combined. It is used for fairy cakes, Victoria sponges, butterfly buns, and rich fruitcakes.

An alternative way of categorising cakes is by the amount of fat involved relative to the amount of flour.

- **No Fat Sponges**. These contain no fat at all. Usually the whisking method is used.
- **Plain Cakes**. The amount of fat is not more than half the amount of flour. Usually the rubbing-in method &/or melting method is used.
- **Rich Cakes**. The amount of fat is more than half the amount of flour. Usually the creaming method or all-in-one method is used.

Ingredients

Cakes are made from a mixture of flour, sugar, eggs, fat (usually), and liquid. They can vary enormously in taste and texture, depending on the proportions of the ingredients used, and the method of preparation and cooking. The aim when making a cake is to produce something that has an attractive appearance, a pleasant flavour, and is uniformly risen with an even open texture. The choice of ingredients plays a vital part in achieving this aim.

Flour

Use soft, weak, or specially manufactured sponge flour, with a high starch and low gluten content. This will help produce uniformity of texture. For rich, dark, heavily fruited celebration cakes, and often for whisked sponges, use plain flour. For most other cakes utilise self-raising flour, unless the recipe states otherwise.

Sugar

Castor sugar is the preferred choice as it dissolves easily and creams readily with the fat. If you use granulated sugar in the creaming method, you will have to beat longer to get the sugar to dissolve, otherwise it will appear as sugar speckling on the surface of the baked cake. Dark brown sugar is a must for any cake that requires a dark colour and molasses flavour, such as gingerbread, parkin, or rich fruitcake. Sugar is vital in cake baking as it gives a soft texture to the gluten framework; it helps colour the outside as it caramelises during cooking; as well as adding sweetness to the mixture.

Fat

Fats play an important part in cake making, as illustrated in the concluding way of categorising cakes above. They are used to give a soft texture, and a good flavour, as well as improving the keeping qualities of the baked cake. If you want flavour, butter is the king, and margarine is a good queen, but proprietary cooking fats have very little flavour. However, all of them cream easily with sugar. Lard and dripping have a pungent flavour, but may be used in gingerbread or parkin, where spices can disguise their taste.

Eggs

You will have heard the saying "You can't make cakes without breaking eggs". This is because the protein in eggs, when mixed with the gluten in flour, forms the framework of the cooked cake. Also, when eggs are beaten or whisked, they entangle air, which acts as an additional raising agent. These two major properties of eggs, along with adding colour, flavour, and enrichment, highlight how vital eggs are in the cake making process.

Liquid

The liquid can be milk, water, alcohol, fruit juice, or tea. The amount required depends on the consistency of the mixture. Liquids help to bind the mixture; they assist soluble ingredients such as sugar to dissolve; they make the gluten in flour elastic; they enable baking powder to produce the gas carbon dioxide; and they provide steam, which helps the cake to rise.

Method

Cake Tin Preparation

Lightly grease the cake tin, and line it with greaseproof or silicone paper. However, if using a rubbed-in mixture or a plain cake mix, it may not be essential to line the tin.

The beauty of silicone paper is that, after use, it can be wiped clean with a piece of kitchen paper, and reused at a later date. You can also purchase baking mats that can be cut to size and used to prevent food sticking to containers. §

Cake Mixing

Assemble everything you need before you start weighing out the ingredients. Weigh or measure accurately and have all the ingredients at room temperature. Always sieve the dry ingredients before use.

With the rubbing-in method, introduce as much air as possible; sieve the flour; rub the fat into the flour using your fingertips only, and lift the mix level with the rim of the bowl; the mixture should resemble ground almonds or breadcrumbs.

When adding egg to a creamed mixture, ensure the egg is at room temperature and add it gradually, to prevent curdling or fat separation.

Try to handle the mixture as lightly as possible whenever adding the flour to an egg mixture.

Cake Baking

How do you tell when a cake is cooked?

Bake the cake at the correct temperature, as stated in the recipe. As a general rule, the richer the cake mix, or the larger the cake size, the lower the oven temperature and the longer the cooking time.

All cake recipes worth sinking your teeth into give an oven temperature and overall cooking time, so that the mixture is baked to perfection.

Here are some other signs to look for when trying to decide whether a cake is cooked or not.

◆ The cake is well risen, and evenly coloured.

◆ The cake is springy to the touch, with no impression left behind.

◆ The cake has shrunk slightly from the sides of the tin.

◆ No sound of hissing, or singing, when you listen closely to the cake.

Cooling and Storage

Allow your cake to cool and set in its tin before turning out. Usually 3 – 5 minutes is sufficient. However, gingerbread and rich fruitcakes are exceptions, and must be left until cold before removing from the tin.

When the cake has been taken out of the tin, place it on a cooling tray, but do not stand it in a draught to cool, or it may collapse.

Once the cake is cold, store it in an airtight container to prevent dehydration. A gingerbread or fruitcake should be wrapped in greaseproof paper before storage. You can leave the lining paper from baking on the cake. Do not wrap fruitcake directly in kitchen foil, which may be attacked by the acids from the fruit.

On no account should a cake be stored whilst still warm, because it will be prone to mould growth.

Great Expectations

Why don't cakes always match up to expectations?

This may be due to a number of reasons.

◆ Employed a poor recipe, with ingredient imbalance.

◆ Used too much or too little raising agent.

◆ Used too much or too little liquid, giving the wrong consistency.

◆ Insufficient or too vigorous creaming or whisking.

◆ Poor mixing of the flour into the egg mixture.

◆ Incorrect cake tin used.

◆ Wrong oven temperature used.

First Aid

Symptom: *Creamed sponge fat and sugar separated when beaten egg added.*

Diagnosis: *Either the egg was too cold, or it was added too quickly.*

Antidote: *Stir in a tablespoon of the flour from the recipe.*

Remedy: *Ensure the egg is at room temperature, and add it gradually.*

Symptom: *Baked cake has sunk in the middle.*

Diagnosis: *There are a multitude of causes:*

    – Too much raising agent, or too much liquid was used.

    – Wet fruit was used.

    – The mixture was over creamed.

    – The oven was too cool.

    – The oven door opened too soon or slammed.

    – The cake was removed from oven too soon.

    – The cake was removed from tin before set.

Antidote: *Cut out the middle and serve as a cake ring.*

Remedy: *Follow the recipe rigorously to avoid the above causes.*
Carefully measure the ingredients and dry any wet fruit before use.
If using a mixer to prepare the cake, follow the manufacturer's instructions, and do not over process the mixture.
Note the time the cake is placed in the oven. Calculate and note when the cake will be ready. If possible, set a timer alarm.

Symptom: *Baked cake has light coloured spotting on the crust.*

Diagnosis: *Raw sugar did not dissolve into the mix before baking.*

Remedy: *Check castor sugar is used, rather than granulated sugar, which takes longer to dissolve, and the mixture is beaten well.*

Symptom: *Baked fruitcake fruit ingredients all sunk to the bottom.*

Diagnosis: *Wet fruit was used.*
Mixture was too soft or slack.
Too cool an oven was used.

Remedy: *Dry fruit on kitchen paper or a clean tea towel before use.*
Check recipe quantities, and maybe reduce liquid slightly.
Check oven temperature, and maybe increase slightly.

Symptom: *Baked cake peaked or risen too high in the middle and badly cracked.*

Diagnosis: *Cooked in too hot an oven, or on too high a shelf.*

Antidote: *May be possible to slice the top off (cook's perks!).*

Remedy: *Check oven temperature, and maybe reduce slightly. Note the shelf position used and next time use a slightly lower shelf position.*

Symptom: *Baked cake sticks to tin and cannot be removed.*

Diagnosis: *Cake was left to go completely cold in tin before trying to remove.*

Antidote: *Place the cake back in the oven for a couple of minutes to warm the tin. While still hot, run a knife around outside of cake to help it release. Turn the warm cake and tin over onto a cooling rack, and cover the base of the tin with a damp cold tea towel, to help release the cake.*

Tips and Techniques of the Trade

Successful cooking is all about establishing and extending culinary skills, so that the food is dealt with efficiently and affectionately. The ability to master a technique gives a sense of achievement, and fulfilment, leading to a better understanding of food. Here I have pooled my knowledge of many tips of the catering trade to help you excel in the kitchen.

Kneaded Butter or Beurre Manié

Ingredients and Method

This uses equal quantities, about 50 g (2 oz), of flour and softened butter, blended together until thoroughly combined. It provides a useful cook's trick for quickly thickening soups, sauces, gravies, and stews, while at the same time giving them a glossy finish.

First Aid

Symptom: *Soup, sauce, gravy, or casserole is not quite thick enough.*

Diagnosis: *At the end of cooking, a dish sometimes has too much liquid.*

Antidote: *Drop pea sized pieces of the kneaded butter into the hot liquid and whisk quickly between each addition. Boil for at least 2 minutes to cook the flour and remove any floury taste.*

Faggot of Herbs or Bouquet Garni

The aim of a faggot of herbs is to infuse or impart flavour into the liquid or food they are enhancing. They are not meant to be an accompaniment, as happened to me at a dinner party, where I had a devil of a job removing the bouquet garni before the host could spot her mistake.

They are used in soups, sauces, stocks, stews, casseroles, fish dishes, or anything savoury that needs added flavour.

Ingredients and Method

Classically, fresh herbs are placed inside a square of muslin and secured with string, or the whole bunch just bound together with string like a bundle of wood. An alternative is to put the fresh herbs inside two strips of leek laid as a cross, then fold the ends of the leek strips over to enclose the herbs before tying with string like a parcel. Always leave enough string so that the faggot can be secured to the saucepan handle, and easily fished out after use.

As well as using fresh herbs, you can buy them ready made in a dry form, in a variety of shapes, sizes, and flavours, but have a go at making your own. Take a thyme sprig, a bay leaf, and some parsley stalks (use the parsley leaves in another dish). Tie them firmly with string, leaving enough string to tie to the handle of the pan. This gives a good general-purpose flavour, but if cooking fish try celery leaves, chives, and either fennel or dill.

You can vary the herbs you use according to the flavours you want to impart. Try adding 6 peppercorns to the herbs. So, go on and experiment!

Preserved Lemons

These soft-textured lemons originate from North Africa. The action of the salt over 3 – 4 weeks causes the lemons to change texture and lose their bitterness. They are ideal in pasta dishes, fish stews, couscous salads, sauces, and dressings.

Ingredients

450 g (1 lb) jar	empty sterile jar with a metal screw lid
3	unwaxed lemons
2 tablespoons	sea salt

Method

You will require a sterile jar with a metal screw lid. Place the clean empty jar and its lid on a thick wad of newspaper on a baking tray. Place in a preheated oven at Gas Mark 2 / 300°F / 150°C (130°C for fan oven) for 15 minutes.

Meanwhile, wash the lemons thoroughly, and cut two of the lemons nearly into quarters, by leaving the sections joined at one end. Place a rounded teaspoon of sea salt into the centre of each of the quartered lemons. Pack these two lemons into the sterilised jam jar.

Add a heaped tablespoon of sea salt §, and the juice of the remaining lemon to the jam jar. Top up the jar with boiling water, so that the liquid comes to the very top. Screw the lid on immediately, and leave to cool before storing in a cool place.

During the first week, you will have to shake the jar a couple of times to distribute the salt. Gradually over the following few weeks, you will see a change in colour from bright yellow fleshed lemons to a more muted yellow soft textured fruit.

Crispy Bread Croutons *

These crunchy bread cubes can be served either plain, or flavoured with your favourite spice, to accompany soups, salads, or stews. An alternative is to enjoy their crisp texture as nibbles with aperitifs.

Ingredients to serve 4 people

2 slices	thick white bread
2 tablespoons	olive oil
or 40 g (1½ oz)	unsalted melted butter

Flavour Options

1 teaspoon	curry paste *or* pesto *or* chilli paste *or* sun-dried tomato paste

Method

Preheat the oven to Gas Mark 7 / 425°F / 220°C (200°C for fan oven).

Cut the bread into even sized cubes like dice. If using one of the flavour options, blend a teaspoon of flavouring into the olive oil or melted butter. Add the diced bread to the olive oil or butter until thoroughly coated.

Place on a baking tray and bake for 5 – 8 minutes, depending on the size of the dice, until the bread is crisp and golden. Drain on kitchen paper before serving.

First Aid

Symptom: *Oven not available to make crispy bread croutons.*

Diagnosis: *An oven is not essential.*

Antidote: *Pan fry the croutons instead, until they are crispy.*

Chopping Vegetables and Herbs

Giving vegetables the chop is what skilled chefs are expert at, and with a little practice, so can you. The essentials are firm sound vegetables, a very sharp, thin bladed, easy to handle, cook's knife, and plenty of patient practice.

Finely Diced Onions

Because onions are so important in cooking, you need to know how to process them efficiently. Chopping diced onion is a worthy technique to acquire.

After cutting off the top of the onion, peel the brown outer skins, without removing the root. Leave the root intact, as this acts as a grip, and an anchor to hold all the layers of onion together. Most of the volatile oils that make you cry are also situated just above the root, so removing it would release these cry babies.

Cut the onion equally in half from the top through to the root. Lay the halves, cut side down, on a chopping board. Thinly slice both halves vertically, at right angles to the root, but without cutting through the root, so the slices are held together by the root. Then starting at the top, slice vertically across the onion, working your way along to the root. You should now have diced onion!

To avoid tears when peeling and chopping onions, there are many anecdotal suggestions. These include placing a metal spoon or piece of bread in your mouth, and placing the onion in the freezer before peeling. One solution is to peel the onion under water. That does not mean donning a wet suit. Simply place the onion in a bowl of water and peel it there. Another suggestion is to keep your mouth shut while handling onions, to prevent breathing the volatile oils. Now that would be particularly hard for me! All these tips seem plausible, but I find leaving the root on the onion the easiest to execute and remember.

Sliced or Chopped Vegetables

The trick to chopping other irregular shaped vegetables lies in understanding that you must have a flat base. Cut a thin strip from one side, so that the vegetable will sit firmly on the chopping board. Then, you can easily cut thin slices lengthways. For julienne, cut each slice into thin strips similar to matchsticks. For diced vegetables, cut across a handful of the julienne strips. Vegetables can be finely chopped using a similar technique to herbs as follows.

Finely Chopped Herbs

Before chopping any herbs, they should be washed and thoroughly dried, otherwise they will be crushed rather than chopped. Herbs ought to be chopped just before use, as they loose their flavoursome volatile oils soon after chopping. The tender herb basil is best torn rather than chopped, because it discolours easily, and looses flavour quickly.

Place the dry herbs to be chopped on a level chopping board. Hold a sharp cook's knife using both hands, one on the handle, and one on the back of the blade near the tip. While holding the tip on the board, chop the herbs with a rapid up and down movement of the handle. At the same time, sweep the handle from side to side, whilst keeping the herbs in a tidy heap.

Once chopped, use the herbs immediately, or store in a small covered pot in the fridge. If the herbs appear wet, dry them on kitchen paper before storing, otherwise they may go mouldy. Use refrigerated herbs within two days.

Alternatively, try chopping and freezing herbs into ice cubes in ice making trays, or freeze whole sprigs of herbs in freezer bags. Then, you have herbs available whenever required, but they may lose a little flavour.

Get Cracking on Eggs

Eggs should always be refrigerated soon after purchase. Keep them in their boxes, pointed ends down, and use in date stamp order. Do not store them near strong smelling foods, because eggs easily absorb aromas.

Take eggs out of the fridge half an hour before you need them, to allow them to return to room temperature.

Always wash your hands before and after handling eggshells. Discard dirty or cracked eggs, due to the risk of contamination.

To differentiate fresh eggs from stale eggs, place them in a bowl of cold water. Fresh eggs sink, and stale eggs float.

Sometimes when using eggs it is wise to sieve them to remove the chalaza, which is the membrane supporting the yolk sac within the egg white. Otherwise, the chalaza can cause white stringiness when cooked in dishes such as custard or lemon tart.

Separating White and Yolk

When separating eggs, you must take care not to get any trace of yolk into the white of the egg, otherwise its fat will inhibit the white from producing a foam. Break the white of one egg into a container, and check there is no trace of yolk, before transferring the white into a clean, grease-free, bowl. Repeat this process with the number of egg whites required.

When making meringues, it is better to use older eggs, as the whites become more viscous. In order to make the egg whites more stable, add a pinch of cream of tartar, a pinch of salt, or a squeeze of lemon juice before the whisking process.

First Aid

Symptom: *Fried or poached egg has flat, easily broken, and off centre yolk.*

Diagnosis: *The eggs are too old.*

Remedy: *Use fresh eggs to fry or poach. This will give a prominent and rounded yolk, which sits in the centre of the white.*

Symptom: *Eggs poached in a microwave oven often burst.*

Diagnosis: *The yolk explodes due to heat expansion inside.*

Remedy: *Always pierce the yolk with a fine needle before cooking, to prevent it exploding from the pressure built up within the egg.*

Symptom: *Boiled eggs sometimes burst their shells.*

Diagnosis: *Caused by the eggs being heated too rapidly. The hot air, in the pocket situated at the rounded end of the egg, has insufficient time to escape through the porous shell. Therefore, the hot air expands, and forces the shell to crack.*

Remedy: *Start the eggs cooking in cold water, and commence timing when the water is boiling.*

Symptom: *Hard-boiled eggs have a black ring around the outer edge of the yolk.*

Diagnosis: *Due to hydrogen sulphide in the white combining with traces of iron in the yolk. This happens if the eggs are over-cooked and not cooled quickly.*

Remedy: *Boil the eggs for a carefully timed 10 minutes, and immediately drain. Crack the eggshells before completely covering in cold running water. Leave to cool before removing from the water and shelling.*

Cooking With Cheese

When a cheesy taste is needed, use a strong flavoured cheese as opposed to a milder version. You will need less of the strong cheese to get the same flavour.

When grating cheese, make sure that it is chilled for one hour beforehand. Even better, freeze it for 15 minutes to firm up the fat. This makes it cleaner to grate.

Many cheeses have a high salt content, so check the flavour before adding salt to a cheesy dish.

When melting a cheese, do just that, otherwise it tends to coagulate or over-cook, releasing fat, and making the dish stringy, tough, and greasy. The cheese is then more difficult to digest.

Most cheese dishes like to be served immediately after they are cooked. To aid digestion, serve cheese with starchy foods such as pasta, potatoes, or bread. Always add mustard to a cheese dish, as this aids digestion.

Halloumi Cheese

Halloumi cheese originates from Cyprus, and is made from a combination of sheep and goats milk. It is unusual in that it does not melt readily when heated, so is ideal for barbecuing, grilling, baking, or frying. When frying, dip it in flour, shake off the surplus, and fry in hot fat until golden. Ideally, it should be eaten hot, otherwise it tends to become rubbery.

Quark Curd Cheese

Soft cheeses are used extensively in cooking to add moisture, flavour, and texture. As an alternative, try using quark, which is a low fat skimmed milk cheese. While it may not have the buttery, velvety mouth feel of calorie-laden cream cheese, its blandness readily absorbs and highlights flavours. It is a very useful substitute for soft cheese in any recipes such as cold mousses, cheese-cakes, and fools.

Cheese Fondue

The 1970s revival of melting cheese in a straight-sided cast-iron pot, over a low heat, is simplicity itself. Grate and toss a blend of two or three cheeses that ooze flavour into the pot along with a splash of sweet cider or white wine, a dollop of mustard, and a pinch of pepper. For two people use about 350 g (12 oz) mixed cheese and 150 ml (5 fl oz) cider or wine. The trick is to prevent the cheese from boiling, which causes the fat in the cheese to ooze out and form a greasy mess. Keep the heat low and gentle, and keep the contents of the pot constantly moving, by using a wooden dowel or the handle of a wooden spoon. Once the cheese and alcohol mixture has started to blend, stir until a smooth and silky consistency is achieved. On no account must the mixture boil. It is all about patience.

When ready, use colour coded skewers to dip hunks of stale French bread, large toasted croutons, or crusty farmhouse chunks into the cheesy fondue. On no account should you drink iced water while enjoying this feast. It will give you bellyache, as the water solidifies the cheese in your stomach, making you feel bloated and extremely uncomfortable. Luckily however, you can drink alcohol such as cider or wine. Hic!

Using Milk, Cream, and Yoghurt

These dairy products can be used as a single commodity, or incorporated with other foods to provide tasty results.

Milk

Fresh milk is ideal as a drink on its own, or used in a variety of dishes such as batters, sauces, custards, scones, and cakes. A splash of the white stuff will slacken any stiff mixture without being detrimental to the finished product. Even when soured it can be used, with beneficial effect, in scones or griddle cakes.

Single Cream

Single cream can be poured onto puddings, stirred into coffee, or used to enrich soups and sauces. It cannot be whipped or boiled. Soured cream and crème fraiche are similar to single cream, but somewhat thicker in texture, with a slightly acidic taste.

Whipping Cream

This is ideal for whipping, when it changes in volume and texture. Use it in sweet and savoury mousses to enlighten the texture and give a smooth mouth feel.

Double Cream

Double cream contributes creaminess to a dish, gives it volume, and adds airy bulk to trifles, mousses, and soufflés. It can be whipped or heated with care.

Clotted Cream

This is too thick to pour or whip, and can only be spooned onto dishes to bestow a touch of comfortable luxury.

Yoghurt

When used as an alternative to cream in sauces, yoghurt will give a lighter texture, with reduced fat content, but without affecting the flavour of the dish.

First Aid

Symptom: *Milk stuck to saucepan base and sides when making a sauce or custard.*

Diagnosis: *Low fat milks are prone to this, due to a lack of fat.*

Remedy: *Make the sauce in a non-stick saucepan on the hob, or use the microwave oven with a non-metallic container.*

Symptom: *Cream curdled when added to hot sauce.*

Diagnosis: *Single cream will curdle if boiled. Single or double cream will curdle if added to a high volume of acidic foods such as citrus juices, tomatoes, and vinegar.*

Remedy: *Never boil a sauce once single cream has been added without cornflour. To stabilise either single or double cream, before heating add a teaspoon of blended cornflour per 250 ml (½ pint) of cream, and bring to the boil.*

Symptom: *Single cream will not thicken when whipped.*

Diagnosis: *Cream must have at least 30 per cent fat content to produce a light foam, and single cream has only 18 per cent fat content.*

Remedy: *Use whipping cream or double cream (see below).*

Symptom: *Whipping cream refuses to thicken when whisked.*

Diagnosis: *Cream and utensils are too warm, and the cream is not viscous enough to allow its fat globules to entrap the air.*

Remedy: *Before whisking, chill the cream, bowl, and beaters in the fridge.*

Symptom: *Double cream turned into a solid mass when whipped.*

Diagnosis: *Caused by over beating or whipping.*

Remedy: *Before whipping, add a tablespoon of milk per 250 ml (½ pint) of double cream to reduce the fat percentage, and make it comparable to whipping cream.*

Symptom: *Yoghurt has a curdled appearance in a cooked sauce.*

Diagnosis: *Yoghurt is prone to splitting or curdling, especially if excessive heat is applied.*

Remedy: *Before heating, add a teaspoon of blended cornflour, or the white of an egg, per 250 ml (½ pint) of yoghurt to stabilise it.*

Traditional Custard or Crème Anglaise *

How do you achieve the perfect custard, or Crème Anglaise if you want to be posh? This is the classic sauce served warm on any hot pudding, or allowed to go cold and used as the basis for ice cream, bavarois, trifles, or a substitute pastry cream. It consists of egg yolks, sugar, vanilla pod or extract, and milk all blended together to form a smooth creamy sweet sauce.

Ingredients

4	egg yolks
25 g (1 oz)	golden castor sugar *or* granulated sugar
275 ml (10 fl oz)	full fat milk
1 pod	vanilla
or ½ teaspoon	vanilla extract

Method

The basis of the custard is egg yolks and sugar, which are whisked vigorously together in a mixing bowl.

If using a vanilla pod, cut the pod lengthways with a small sharp knife and scrape out all the seeds from inside. Place all the seeds and pod into the milk. Bring the milk to the boil, remove it from the heat, and leave to infuse for 10 minutes. Remove the vanilla pod halves.

If using vanilla extract, add it straight to the boiled milk.

The hot milk is then poured onto the egg and sugar mixture. The entire mixture is then returned to a low heat and stirred until you can trace a line with your finger on the back of a wooden spoon coated with the custard, and the custard doesn't run back through the line.

First Aid

Symptom: *Custard is too thin and watery.*

Diagnosis: *Insufficient whisking of the egg yolks and sugar.*

Remedy: *Check the ingredients and quantities used in the recipe. Whisk yolks and sugar until the mixture changes colour and consistency. The mixture should be pale and thick. You can add 1 teaspoon of custard powder or cornflour to the egg and sugar mixture to help thicken and stabilise the custard. Always use full fat milk, because skimmed or semi-skimmed milk will give you thin custard.*

Symptom: *Custard has curdled.*

Diagnosis: *Insufficient whisking of the egg yolks and sugar before adding the hot milk, or too high a heat when returned to the heat.*

Remedy: *When pouring the hot milk onto the whisked egg and sugar mixture, keep whisking. Turn the heat down slightly when returning the custard back to thicken, and stir constantly. Adding cornflour or custard powder to the egg and sugar mixture can prevent curdling, as it allows the custard to tolerate a higher temperature.*

Symptom: *Custard has too much skin on top.*

Diagnosis: *The custard was left to cool naturally and uncovered.*

Remedy: *There are several alternative remedies:*

- *Sprinkle a thin film of sugar over the surface of the hot custard and leave to cool. When ready to use, stir the sugar into the custard.*

- *Pour a thin layer of cream over the surface of the hot custard and leave to cool. When ready to use, stir the cream into the custard.*

- *Cut a piece of parchment paper to fit precisely, and lay on the surface of the hot custard. Remove the paper when ready for use.*

- *Cover the hot custard with cling film, pressing it down onto the surface. Remove the cling film when ready for use.*

Symptom: *Custard is burnt.*

Diagnosis: *Insufficient stirring whilst trying to thicken custard, or heat set too high, or saucepan base is too thin.*

Antidote: *Sieve the custard into a clean thicker based saucepan.*

Remedy: *Keep the custard moving at all times during heating. Have the heat turned down more when trying to thicken, and be a little more patient.*

Deep Fat Frying

Mention deep fat frying to me, and I think of chips, which were the first fast-food take-away I encountered as a child. The best chips are crisply cooked, with a soft fluffy interior, and no hint of greasiness. The beauty of deep fat frying is that it gives the food a crisp texture as it cooks, provided it is undertaken correctly, otherwise it will be greasy or oily.

Choose Oil Wisely

To avoid greasy tasting deep fried products, you need to choose and use your oil wisely. When heated, all oils go through three stages.

Haze Point

This is the best frying temperature, and appears as a very faint haze coming from the surface of the heated oil.

Smoke Point

If heating continues, and the haze changes to blue smoke, the smoke point has been reached. It is caused by the fat being too hot, and occurs at lower temperatures if the oil is well used or contaminated. To stop the oil smoking, either the temperature must be reduced, or the oil cooled and strained to remove food particles, or simply discarded and replaced with fresh oil.

Flash Point

If the oil is allowed to continue heating unchecked, it will reach its flash point, and may spontaneously burst into flames.

Oil Temperatures

Oil Type	Smoke Point °C	Flash Point °C
Soya oil	255	350
Vegetable oil	220	330
Groundnut oil	215	225
Corn oil	215	225
Olive oil	~200	~280
Quality dripping (lard)	~170	~300
Extra virgin olive oil	~155	~275

Best Types of Oil

For deep fat frying purposes, fats or oils must reach the ideal frying temperature of about 175°C without smoking. The food being fried will absorb the oil if it smokes at a low temperature, giving a greasy product.

Different oils reach their key points at different temperatures. You need an oil with a high smoke and flash point. This will allow you to get the best out of the oil without affecting the quality and taste of the food.

Groundnut oil has one of the highest smoke points, but beware of allergic reactions to peanuts. Corn or maize oil has similar temperature thresholds. The cheapest vegetable oils are a blend of soya, rapeseed, palm, and cottonseed oils. They also have a high smoke point, making them good value for money when deep fat frying. Olive oil has a fairly high smoke point, but is comparatively expensive.

However, the smoke point of extra virgin olive oil is much too low, and will make your food taste very oily. This highly prized and expensive oil is produced mainly for its distinctive, fruity, peppery taste, and rich green colour. The flavour is much appreciated, especially throughout the Mediterranean, where olive oil is an integral part of the diet, being used as a condiment, like salt and pepper.

Use Oil Effectively

Use oil that is recommended for deep fat frying. See the manufacturers' information printed on the container. Corn, groundnut, or blended vegetable oils are inexpensive and efficient. Follow the guidelines I have summarised below.

◆ Make sure the food to be fried is dry, as wet food causes the oil to spit.

◆ Do not overload the fryer with food. It will only lower the temperature of the oil. This will lengthen the frying time, and make the food soggy and taste greasy.

◆ If you do not have a deep fat fryer with a thermostat, test the temperature by dropping a cube of white bread into the hot oil. If it sizzles and turns dark brown within a minute, the oil is too hot. If it takes a while to colour, say 8 minutes, the oil is too cool.

◆ If the oil should smoke whilst heating there could be two causes.
The oil is too hot and burning, so turn down the temperature.
The oil is old and past its best, so discard it and use fresh oil.

◆ If the oil begins to foam, bubble, or smoke unduly, it is past its best, and should be changed once it has cooled. You will notice that the smoke point decreases with each use until it becomes unusable.

◆ Do not overheat the oil for extensive periods, as this will reduce its efficiency, and lower the smoke point. Switch off the fryer immediately after use to prolong the life of your oil.

◆ Keep the oil and fryer clean to prevent the oil becoming tainted with flavours. A careful cook should be able to use the oil up to five times. When cool, strain the oil through a sieve between each use, and wipe out the fryer with clean kitchen paper.

◆ Store the oil in a cool place, away from direct sunlight, and use within its recommended date.

Safety First

After use, a deep fat fryer retains its heat for up to 3 hours, so do not move it until completely cold.

If the oil catches fire whilst frying, do **NOT** move the fryer, do **NOT** use water, and if the blaze is out of control call the fire brigade for assistance and evacuate the house.

Otherwise, turn off the heat source, at the main supply, if you cannot reach the appliance. Cover the deep fat fryer with a fire blanket, if you have one, or a non-flammable lid or tray, to exclude the air and extinguish the flame, but beware of burning your hands, which can be wrapped in a damp cloth. Leave the fryer until completely cold before removing the fire blanket, lid, or tray as hot oil retains its heat for up to 3 hours.

First Aid

Symptom: *Deep fried onion rings and the batter come away from each other.*

Diagnosis: *Onions are too wet before coating with the batter. Any product should be dry before adding the batter.*

Remedy: *Lightly coat in seasoned flour, which will absorb any surplus moisture, before applying the batter.*

Symptom: *Deep fried fish tends to stick together when placed in the hot oil.*

Diagnosis: *Too much fish added to the oil at one time will lower the temperature and allow the batter to seal together.*

Remedy: *Reduce the amount of fish added to the fryer to smaller batches, and keep them warm uncovered in a hot oven until all the batches have been fried.*

Melting Chocolate

The best chocolate to cook with, and the easiest to melt, is cooking chocolate §.

Place a clean empty glass bowl over a saucepan of boiling water. Make sure that the water does not touch the bowl or get into the bowl. Break pieces of chocolate into the bowl.

Turn off the heat and allow the residual heat to melt the chocolate, stirring once or twice. Once completely melted use immediately. Otherwise, every time the chocolate is reheated it will get thicker and thicker.

Chocolate can be successfully melted in the microwave, but it needs careful timing. Place the broken chocolate into a microwave safe bowl. Heat it in the microwave on a high setting for 10 seconds. Check and repeat the heating, until the chocolate is just beginning to melt. The residual heat will continue to melt the remaining chocolate.

First Aid

Symptom: *Melted chocolate has become thick, gluey, or grainy.*

Diagnosis: *Usually caused by over heating or reheating.*

Antidote: *Add an equal quantity of fresh chocolate to the over heated chocolate.*

For over heated plain or milk chocolate, add a knob of butter.

For over heated white chocolate, add a splash of vegetable oil.

Prevention is Better Than Cure

Important but often overlooked aspects of catering are hygiene and safety. In this section, I offer my advice on avoiding food poisoning, the refrigeration and freezing of food, as well as cleaning, safety, and infestations in the kitchen. For more information, contact your local Environmental Health Officers, who are most helpful, and are an excellent source for booklets and training courses.

How to Avoid Food Poisoning

I do not think anyone intentionally sets out to give friends and family food poisoning, but at some stage in your life, I'm sure you will have experienced a 'funny tummy' or 'the trots'. This will last a day or perhaps two at the most, but in some cases food poisoning can have very serious consequences.

Food poisoning may be defined as an acute illness, usually of sudden onset, brought about by eating contaminated foods. The symptoms normally include one or more of the following: nausea, abdominal pain, headache, high temperature, vomiting, or diarrhoea.

The affected food may look, smell, and taste normal. Bacteria and viruses, chemicals and metals, plants, or fish can all cause food poisoning.

Here is a checklist for avoiding food poisoning.

◆ Use only the freshest foods. Do not store food for too long before using. Do not prepare food too far in advance. Make sure you have good stock rotation.

◆ Adopt and maintain high standards of personal hygiene. Wash your hands before handling any food. Always wash your hands after handling raw fish, poultry, or meat before going onto other tasks. Use hot water and soap, and dry using a clean dry towel or kitchen paper.

◆ Try to handle food as little as possible.

◆ Store high-risk food in the refrigerator at 0°C to 5°C and keep it covered.

◆ Organise your refrigerator correctly with raw foods stored at bottom and cooked foods at the top. This avoids raw foods leeching onto cooked foods and cross-contaminating them.

◆ When cooking any food, allow it to cool down completely before refrigeration, to avoid raising the fridge temperature. This can be undertaken either by placing the food in a clean sink full of ice-cold water, or by standing the food by an open window. The maximum cooling down period from cooker to refrigerator is 90 minutes.

◆ Unless the manufacturer recommends otherwise, always make sure frozen foods are thoroughly defrosted before cooking.

◆ When using leftovers, make sure the reheated food is piping hot. If possible, use a probe thermometer to check the food registers at least 180°F / 82°C before serving. If any food is not all consumed, and has been left out at room temperature more than 4 hours, throw it out; do **not** freeze or heat it again.

◆ Always cook poultry thoroughly. If you have an instant-read or meat thermometer, insert it deep into the thigh meat and check it registers 175°F / 79°C or above. Without a thermometer, you can test by piercing the thigh with a skewer or the tip of a knife, and checking that the juices run out clear, not pink with blood. Another alternative is to lift the whole cooked bird with a two-pronged fork, and tilt it so that you can check the colour of the juices that run out of the cavity into the roasting tin. They should be clear with brown bits, not pink or bloody.

◆ When using raw and cooked meat, poultry, or fish, use separate preparation boards, one for raw foods and another for cooked foods, so as to avoid cross-contamination.

◆ If there should be any doubt about the safety of any food, it is better to throw it out, rather than risk making someone ill.

Which are the High-Risk Foods?

When cooking for yourself, friends, or family, you need to know which are the high-risk foods so that you can take extra care when using them. It is the moist, high-protein foods that cause the worst problems.

◆ Cooked poultry and meats, plus their stocks.

◆ Prepared meat products such as pâté, meat pies, sausages, and burgers.

◆ Dairy produce such as milk, cream, and cream substitutes.

◆ Eggs and egg products such as mayonnaise, custards, and quiches.

◆ Shellfish and seafood.

◆ Cooked rice.

Secrets of a Successful Barbecue

Having endured months of cold, damp, dark weather, the feeling of warm rays of sunshine heralds the essence of summer, the barbecue. People either love or loathe them, or more precisely the barbecued food. Is this because it is a very informal way of eating, with no strict criteria on the number of courses nor the portion allowance, and the slow relaxed pace at which the food is cooked, served, and enjoyed? Or is it the smoky haze that permeates everything within easy reach, and can turn into an acrid blanket that smothers all in its path?

Although these factors may be momentarily considered by most people, the overriding factor as to whether you love or loathe barbecued food, is your past experiences of similar events. Being bothered with flies, wasps, and four-legged furry friends, undercooked food, cremated offerings, and the anticipated tummy problems which can occur later, all colour your perception of barbecues.

In order to alleviate some of these irritations, which can make the difference between an enjoyable event, and something to be avoided at all cost, I have produced a scheme for successful barbecuing and food safety, to supplement the checklist on avoiding food poisoning above.

◆ Maintain high standards of personal hygiene. That is, wash and dry your hands after handling raw meat and fish. Use a bucket with hot soapy water, and a clean dry towel or kitchen roll for drying your hands.

◆ All equipment and utensils used for barbecues, especially if seldom used at other times, must be thoroughly cleaned before use.

◆ Light the barbecue about half an hour before use. The charcoal should glow with a covering of thin grey ash, and all the flames should have died down, before placing food on the grill. The consequence of placing food on the grill too early, while the barbecue still looks like Dante's Inferno, is that the outside of the food will scorch black, while the centre will remain under-cooked. The coals should just smoulder, giving the food time to cook through. Keep a spray bottle of water handy to quench flames caused by fat dripping from food onto the coals. Alternatively, throw a handful of salt onto the coals to reduce the flames and smoke without cooling the coals.

◆ Ensure that any frozen food is thoroughly defrosted before barbecuing, otherwise the inside could still be frozen and will not cook through. If the barbecue is sited some distance from the kitchen, store raw meat and fish in a covered cool box, and remove food just before grilling.

◆ All food that is kept outside should be stored at least 45 cm (18") off the ground to avoid being contaminated by animals, soil, or people treading on it. Bring out little and often rather than all at the beginning. Keep cream confections in the fridge until the last minute.

◆ Keep raw and cooked foods apart at all times to avoid cross-contamination between storage and service. This is especially important when grilling foods on the barbecue.

◆ Use different equipment for handling raw food as opposed to cooked food. Try to colour code the equipment if possible. Use red handled equipment for raw food, and contrasting coloured equipment for cooked food. Make sure everyone who is involved in the cooking process understands the rules.

◆ Before serving barbecued food, check a sample to make sure it is thoroughly cooked. Cut the sample in half and check for a uniform, even colour throughout. If not, continue barbecuing until you achieve this standard. With regard to chicken, which can be a high-risk source of food poisoning, no blood should be visible when the food is pierced. The resultant liquid should be clear to yellow in colour. It is good practice to cook chicken, either whole or in pieces, in a conventional oven beforehand, and finish off on the barbecue.

◆ Always cook barbecued food to order. If you have to cook barbecued food in advance, it should be held above 63°C or cooled within 90 minutes and stored in a refrigerator. Any surplus cooked food should be safely disposed of in the waste bin at the end of the event.

◆ Provide a rubbish bin with a lid for waste, to avoid being plagued by pests.

With a little thought and attention to detail, the experience of barbecue cookery can be transformed into a stress free and successful occasion for all concerned. Let us hope that the weather next summer will allow you to put these newly found skills into practice.

Refrigeration and Freezing

To "chill out" or "be cool, real cool" are two sayings that instantly give street credibility to anyone who utters them. The same sayings apply to refrigeration and freezing, in that anyone using them discovers hidden benefits.

Refrigeration

If you care about yourself, refrigeration is for you. It saves you money, because it extends the life of foodstuffs that would perish at ambient temperatures. At the same time, it retards the growth of harmful micro-organisms, making it safer on your tummy, and better for your health.

Depending on the space available, buy the largest fridge you can afford. Do not overload it, as air has to circulate around the stored food.

To get the best out of your refrigerator, it should operate between 0°C and 5°C, and you need a fridge thermometer to monitor the situation. The fridge won't destroy any micro-organisms already present in the food, so shop wisely, buy the freshest, and store quickly.

Check the use-by dates on stored goods, and remember to follow a first in, first out policy. Raw foods should always be stored below cooked foods. This prevents drips from raw foods contaminating the cooked foods. Cover all food before placing in the fridge, to prevent cross-contamination, dehydration, and frost build-up on the cooling surfaces, which will then work inefficiently.

Do not place hot food in the fridge, because it will raise the temperature. Allow it to cool so it is easy to handle. Cooked food should come from the cooker, be cooled down, and put into the fridge within 90 minutes.

Wipe up any spills as soon as they occur, so that they do not solidify, making them harder to remove. Regularly clean the inside of the fridge with half a litre (1 pint) of warm water and a rounded teaspoon of bicarbonate of soda. Do not use detergents, as they tend to leave an aroma, which maybe absorbed by the food.

Open the fridge door as infrequently as possible. Defrost the fridge regularly, unless it does so automatically.

Frozen Food Shopping Tips

Here are a few safety tips to get the best out of purchasing your frozen foods.

◆ Make frozen foods your last purchase, just before payment.

◆ Choose clean, firm, and ice-free products with undamaged packaging.

◆ Check the best-before date, and look for long lead times.

◆ Choose frozen products stored below the load line of the shop freezer.

◆ Pack frozen foods in a cool-box or freezer-bag for transportation home.

Freezing, Storing, and Thawing Tips

All foods will freeze, but it is how they cope with thawing, and their acceptability on your palate after thawing that is the problem. Salads and vegetables such as lettuce, cucumber, and watercress, will loose their crispness and become slimy and limp. Raw whole eggs will burst their shells, and hard-boiled eggs will become rubbery. Cream containing less than 40 per cent fat will separate on freezing, and to eliminate this problem, you should whip double and whipping cream before freezing.

When freezing your own cooked or fresh foods, there are a few guidelines that you should follow:

◆ Cooked foods must be cooled completely before freezing, to avoid raising the temperature inside the freezer. Cooling should take no more than 90 minutes. This technique also helps to retain the colour, texture, and flavour of the food.

◆ Open-freeze any delicate foods such as soft fruit, cakes, and biscuits. Place the food on a tray or rack in the freezer until frozen solid. Then pack convenient amounts of the food in either plastic containers or freezer bags.

◆ Label and date stamp home-made foods to simplify their identification.

Whether bought or home produced the following tips will ensure your frozen foods are kept in the best condition:

◆ Allow sufficient storage space for cold air to circulate between items, and leave room for expansion as the food freezes.

◆ Rotate your frozen stock, with a first in, first out policy, because keeping food in the freezer for extended periods may lower its quality.

◆ Arrange foods in an orderly fashion, with similar items together, so they are easier to find. For example, reserve one compartment for meat products, one for savoury items, and another for puddings and ice creams.

◆ Beware that foods may suffer from freezer burn on the surface, due to either poor packaging, or extensive freezer storage. Freezer burn appears as a change in colour and texture, and affects the eating quality, making food dry, hard, and stringy.

◆ If you know your electricity supply is going to be suspended, turn on the fast freeze for a couple of hours before hand, and try not to open the freezer.

◆ Once you electricity has been cut off, do not open the freezer until power is restored. If the power cut lasts no more than 24 hours, all should be well.

◆ If your freezer power is off for more than 24 hours, all the contents are at risk of thawing out. Some foods, such as meat products, may be saved as long as you thaw it thoroughly, cook it well, and refreeze it after power returns. The rest of the thawed food, such as ice cream, should be discarded.

◆ Defrost foods in the regulated temperature of a fridge, or a bowl of cold water, or by using the defrost setting of a microwave oven. Do not leave the food out in a warm room, as this could increase your risk of food poisoning.

◆ Once frozen food has been thawed, do not refreeze it, unless it has been well cooked after thawing out.

Frozen Food Storage Times
The flavour and texture of thawed foods deteriorate quicker than the same foods in their fresh state. If you want to serve food that is at its best, do not exceed the storage times given below.

Dairy Produce
1 month	cream cheese
3 months	all cream, salted butter, hard and soft cheese
6 months	eggs, unsalted butter

Fruit and Vegetables
1 month	raw mushrooms
3 months	cooked mushrooms, unstoned fruit
6 months	onions, fruit pies
12 months	all other fruit and vegetables

Fish
2 months	oily fish, shellfish
3 months	white fish

Meat and Poultry
2 months	sausages
3 months	pork, tripe, offal, mince, cooked dishes (pies, stews, casseroles)
5 months	vacuum packed bacon
6 months	lamb, duck, game
8 months	beef
12 months	poultry

Bread, Cakes, and Pastry
2 weeks	risen dough
1 month	unrisen dough, yeast
2 months	sandwiches, scones
4 months	enriched bread, soft rolls
6 months	bread, breadcrumbs, croutons, cakes, pastry

Cleanliness is Next to Godliness

Like it, or loathe it, cleaning has to be tackled in one way or another. As soon as you open your eyes in the morning, it starts. Showering, scrubbing teeth, climbing into clean clothes, and swishing round the plug-hole to remove surplus bubbles and hair, are the mundane tasks undertaken by us all.

Cleaning Products

Cooking is no different. The same degree of commitment to cleaning and hygiene is required to prepare, cook, and serve food that is safe to eat. Visit the 'household cleaning' section of any supermarket, and the shelves are groaning with all manner of products, which tackle grease, grime, and bugs, whilst making a substantial hole in your wallet. The choice can be baffling and prove expensive to the novice. As a rule, look for products that are general purpose, as these cover a multitude of cleaning situations. From a cook's perspective, using products that have many uses, both cuts down on storage space, and simplifies their use.

The main food poisoning bacteria are E. coli, salmonella, listeria, and campylobacter. Antibacterial sprays, which claim to kill 99.999 per cent of such bacteria, may give you reassurance and peace of mind. When applying such sprays, follow the manufacturer's instructions. Remember to use a clean damp cloth or clean piece of kitchen roll. Also, allow the surface to air dry before you use it, otherwise the food may pick up taints from the cleaner.

Hygienic Practices

However, you should bear in mind that these sprays are no substitute for clean habits in the kitchen. If you adopt hygienic working practices and stick to them, there should be no need for antibacterial kitchen sprays. It's all about washing and drying hands and surfaces, not smoking, spitting, or coughing in the kitchen, as well as working tidily.

When I was a teenager, I went to see a cookery demonstration by a famous husband and wife duo at Sheffield City Hall. I arrived extra early and witnessed the star turn stirring a sauce with a fag hanging out of the corner of her mouth, just like Andy Capp's missus. I never saw that person in the same light again.

If you want to avoid food poisoning, and establish a clean regime, you need to embrace the following practices.

◆ Wash hands before and after preparing foods and visiting the toilet.

◆ Wash hands before and after handling raw meat and poultry.

◆ Do not smoke whilst handling or preparing food.

◆ Do not cough or spit over food.

◆ Clean and tidy as you work.

◆ Use clean dishcloths and tea towels.

If this particularly concerns you, why not enrol on a one-day hygiene course run by your local college or local council Environmental Health Office?

Cooker Cleaning

As the cooker is the powerhouse of cooking, it needs to be maintained to an acceptable level. To minimise the build up of grease and grime when cooking, wipe the cooker hob with detergent and hot water every time you use it. Don't forget the saucepan supports. This will reduce the chance of hard carbon deposits becoming established. Oven rungs or shelves can be soaked in a sink or bowl of boiling water and washing soda crystals, or you can use commercial carbon removal products that you paint on and wash off.

One tip to get maximum heat, whilst reducing cleaning, is to line your grill pan with aluminium foil, which reflects heat and catches spillages.

You need to follow manufacturers' cleaning procedures if you are to get the best out of your cooker, use it efficiently, and prolong its working life.

First Aid

Symptom: *China teapot badly stained and difficult to clean without damaging.*

Diagnosis: *Tea stains the inside, spout, and lid of well used ceramic containers.*

Remedy: *Use a container large enough to accommodate the teapot, and immerse the pot in a sterilising solution. Use baby sterilising liquid, or bleach, diluted with water according to the instructions on the bottle for sterilising strength. Alternatively, use a teaspoon of bicarbonate of soda per half litre (1 pint) of water. Leave the pot to soak overnight, then rinse well before using again for tea.*

Safety First in the Kitchen

Most accidents in the home happen in the kitchen. It is a place full of inert objects that, in the wrong hands, can take on a life of their own.

Accidents occur through ignorance, lack of concentration, curiosity, stress, and lack of culinary expertise. The most common accidents in the kitchen are burns, scalds, cuts, and falls. The most likely source of a fire in the kitchen is your deep fat fryer or chip pan – see page 87.

Protect Your Family

Take the trouble to get your family to understand the reasons why they need to be careful when in the kitchen. Never leave a child unattended in a kitchen. Keep hot liquids, kettles, and pan handles out of reach of inquisitive children.

All cleaning materials should be kept in their original containers, locked away, out of the reach of children.

Have good lighting over stairs and work areas. Flooring should be even and non-slip. Wipe up any spills at once.

Have an appropriate fire blanket or fire extinguisher, and a first aid box in the kitchen and know how to use them.

A simple first aid box should contain sterile bandages, burn dressings, adhesive plasters, cotton wool, lint, antiseptic, and scissors. Enrol in a short first aid training course.

Respect Your Equipment

All large appliances such as cookers, dishwashers, washing machines, and central heating boilers should be professionally installed and regularly maintained. Keep cookers away from corners, doors, and draughts.

Keep all equipment in good repair and use it correctly. Do not try to repair damaged equipment yourself, unless you are a professional in that discipline.

Store everything regularly used within easy reach, but keep all sharp edged or pointed utensils in a safe place. Always pick up knives and other sharp utensils by the handle.

Knives should be kept sharp, as they are easier to use and less likely to slip, because less force is needed.

Place dirty, sharp utensils that need washing somewhere safe such as behind the sink taps. Do not put them straight into the sink of hot soapy water along with the rest of the dirty crockery and cutlery. Not only is this dangerous, but also it will prematurely blunt your utensils. Always wash and dry knives and sharp utensils from the back or blunt side.

If you follow the current trend for using a catering blowtorch to get caramelised effects, treat it with the greatest caution.

My Most Reliable Recipes

It is a sad fact that not all recipes are successful. You can follow them slavishly, but through no fault of your own, sometimes they do not gel together. This is because they have not been tried and tested, or have been poorly written, perhaps omitting one vital stage. Occasionally it is caused by an imbalance of ingredients, or sloppy editing that fails to notice a typing mistake. All the following recipes are in constant use in my repertoire, and hopefully will become part of yours, so that you make them your own.

Throughout this chapter, under the heading of '**First Aid**', you will find a number of '*Symptom:*' descriptions with associated '*Diagnosis:*' and advice on corrective measures. Those headed '*Antidote:*' suggest how to rectify the problem with the current ingredients, whereas those headed '*Remedy:*' explain how to correct the problem the next time the recipe is employed.

Within this chapter, I have used a number of symbols. Many of the recipes draw upon the advice given in earlier chapters, especially the chapter '**How Do You Cook With Confidence?**'. Wherever an item is marked with the symbol § you will find further details in those chapters, and the item or technique will appear in the '**Cross Reference Index**' near the back of the book.

Sometimes in recipe ingredients you will see the tilde symbol ~ against weights and measures. This indicates that the measure is only approximate.

Budget conscious, cost efficient, recipes that lift the ordinary into the extraordinary are marked with a pound £ sign. These are dishes that have immense added value, or compare favourably with the cost of ready-prepared dishes. However, you must remember that dishes in some sections such as '**Vegetable Roots and Shoots**' are all likely to be cheaper than dishes in say the '**Poultry, Game, and Meat**' section.

Those recipes marked with an asterisk * symbol utilise only store cupboard ingredients, as explained below.

Dishes from Store Cupboard Items

In the earlier chapter, '**Are You Picking the Best Ingredients?**' I listed my essential store cupboard items. These are flour, bread, eggs, cheese, milk, butter or margarine, cooking oil, salt, pepper, sugar, and jam or marmalade. Even with such basic ingredients, and perhaps one extra commodity, you can make a surprising number of tasty dishes. They are summarised on the next page, and their full recipes can be found eelsewhere in the book, marked with an asterisk * symbol.

Cookery Crafts

You will find these recipes in the chapter '**How Do You Cook With Confidence?**'

'**Perfect Béchamel White Sauce**' is the basis for many other sauces   p64
'**Cheese Sauce**' optionally needs some Dijon mustard   p66

Delightful Dishes

The recipes for the dishes listed below are presented later in this chapter.

Dairy, Eggs, and Cheese

Cakes and Sponges

Biscuits and Scones

Breads and Doughs

See page 54 for general advice on '**Bread Making**'.

Basic Bread Loaf or Rolls

I recommend that you master this basic bread recipe using fast action yeast, and perhaps the other methods given in the earlier chapter, before attempting the fancier flavoured breads presented later in this chapter.

Ingredients for a 1 lb loaf or 12 rolls

450 g (1 lb)	strong white &/or brown bread flour §
1 level teaspoon	salt
25 g (1 oz)	lard or margarine or butter or vegetable oil
1 level teaspoon	white sugar or brown sugar or honey
10 g (½ oz)	sachet of fast / quick action easy blend yeast §
275 ml (10 fl oz)	water &/or milk – hand hot
1	beaten egg for glaze

Method

Sieve the flour and salt together with the sugar into a large mixing bowl. Rub in the fat thoroughly. Add the sugar and quick action yeast and stir well.

Add all the hand-hot liquid in one go. Mix together with your hands to make a soft, elastic dough, ensuring all the ingredients are well combined. Turn out the dough onto a clean worktop and knead for 10 – 12 minutes until smooth, elastic, and free from stickiness.

Shape the dough and place in a greased loaf tin, or divide and shape into rolls and place on a greased baking sheet. Leave somewhere warm to prove for 10 – 15 minutes until increased in size by about a third.

Bake in a hot oven at Gas Mark 7 / 425°F / 220°C (200°C for fan oven) for about 35 minutes for a loaf, or 10 – 15 minutes for rolls. Place a roasting tin of water at the bottom of the oven to improve the flavour and texture of the bread.

After about 5 minutes remove and glaze with the beaten egg, and return to the oven until golden brown and firm to the touch.

First Aid – see page 57

Flavoured Breads to Spice Up Your Life

Once you have mastered the basic technique of making bread, it is time to extend your repertoire to some fancy flavoured offerings. Try customising the basic bread recipe to suit your personal taste and making it unique to you. There is nothing more satisfying than eating food that cannot be bought anywhere, not even at those trendy food-halls and delicatessens.

Here are some simple tips to make ordinary bread extra-ordinary:

◆ Use a variety of white, wholemeal, or granary strong flours to give a taste and texture you find more agreeable.

◆ Replace the lard with olive oil to produce olive oil bread.

◆ Try one of the following flavoured breads.

Date and Walnut Tear and Share

The sweet and crunchy texture of this bread blends well with savoury soft textured dishes or simple cheeses.

You will need two 20 cm (8") sandwich tins that are greased.

Ingredients for two half-pound loaves
450 g (1 lb)	basic bread dough §
50 g (2 oz)	crushed walnuts
50 g (2 oz)	chopped dates
1 teaspoon	mixed spice

Method

Make up the bread dough as normal until just before the final proving.

Use a rolling pin to crush the walnuts in a plastic bag or inside a tea towel. Mix the crushed walnuts, chopped dates, and mixed spice into the dough. Knead until thoroughly combined.

Divide into 20 pieces, and shape into balls. Grease two sandwich tins and arrange 10 balls attractively in each tin. Leave them somewhere warm to prove for 10 – 15 minutes as usual.

Bake at Gas Mark 7 / 425°F / 220°C (200°C for fan oven) for 15 – 20 minutes. Place a roasting tin of water at the bottom of the oven to improve flavour and texture. After about 5 minutes remove and glaze with a beaten egg, and return to the oven until golden brown and firm to the touch.

Leave to cool slightly before turning out onto a wire cooling rack.

First Aid – *see also page 57*

Symptom: *Nut food allergy.*

Diagnosis: *Many people are allergic to nuts.*

Antidote: *Replace the walnuts with chopped apple or pumpkin, sunflower, or sesame seeds.*

Sun-Dried Tomato and Black Olive Round

Serve these breads with all things Mediterranean, for bags of flavour, and recollections of happy holidays, and memorable moments.

Ingredients for a 1 lb loaf
450 g (1 lb)	basic bread dough §
1 dessertspoon	sun-dried tomato paste
1 dessertspoon	tomato paste
25 g (1 oz)	sun-dried tomatoes – finely chopped §
25 g (1 oz)	black olives – roughly chopped

Method

Make up the bread dough as normal until just before the final proving.

Knead both pastes into the dough until a uniform colour is achieved. Mix in the chopped sun-dried tomatoes and black olives.

Divide the dough into 18 even sized pieces and shape into balls. Place on a large greased baking sheet so they are just touching each other. Leave somewhere warm to prove for 10 – 15 minutes as usual.

Bake at Gas Mark 7 / 425°F / 220°C (200°C for fan oven) for 15 – 20 minutes. Place a roasting tin of water at the bottom of the oven to improve flavour and texture. After about 5 minutes remove and glaze with beaten egg, and return to the oven until golden brown, firm to the touch, and sounds hollow when tapped.

Leave to cool slightly before turning out onto a wire cooling rack.

First Aid – *see also page 57*

Spicy Seedy Flat Bread

Spice up your life with this little number, which is fragrant and aromatic. It is excellent with soups, dips, and spicy foods.

You will need two 20 cm (8") sandwich tins that are greased.

Ingredients for two half-pound loaves

450 g (1 lb)	basic bread dough §
5 pods	cardamom
1 teaspoon	cumin seeds
1 teaspoon	mustard seeds
1 dessertspoon	hot curry paste

Method

Make up the bread dough as normal until just before the final proving.

Crush the cardamom pods to extract their seeds. Dry fry all the seeds until they start to pop or jump, and allow to cool. Knead the seeds and curry paste into the dough for about 10 minutes until a uniform mixture is achieved.

Grease two sandwich tins. Divide the dough into two equal portions, place one piece in each tin, and press the dough out evenly with your fingers to fit the tins. Leave somewhere warm to prove for 10 – 15 minutes as usual.

Bake at Gas Mark 7 / 425°F / 220°C (200°C for fan oven) for 15 – 20 minutes. Place a roasting tin of water at the bottom of the oven to improve flavour and texture. After about 5 minutes remove and glaze with a beaten egg, and return to the oven until well risen, light golden brown, and sounds hollow when tapped.

Leave to cool slightly before turning out onto a wire cooling rack.

First Aid

See tpage 57.

Symptom: *Spices for bread not dry fried in advance.*

Diagnosis: *Dry roasting the spices heightens flavour and releases aroma.*

Antidote: *Use the unroasted spices, but the flavour will not be as pronounced.*

Cheesy Snakes

If you want to get kids interested in cooking, get them making bread. Shaping these cheesy snakes just adds to that overall experience.

Ingredients to make 2 snakes
450 g (1 lb)	basic bread dough §
50 g (2 oz)	finely grated cheese

Decoration
	currants *or* pumpkin seeds for eyes
	tomato segments for tongues

Method

Make up the bread dough as normal, but with the addition of the grated cheese to the dry flour mixture, until you get to just before the final proving.

Divide the dough in half. Cut one half into 10 equal pieces and shape into even sized balls. On a greased baking tray, arrange the balls next to each other to resemble a curvy snake. Push two currants or seeds in one end for eyes. Repeat this with the other half of the dough.

Leave them in a warm place for 10 – 15 minutes to allow the dough to rise.

Bake at Gas Mark 7 / 425°F / 220°C (200°C for fan oven) for 10 – 15 minutes. Place a roasting tin of water at the bottom of the oven to improve the flavour and texture. After about 5 minutes remove and glaze with a beaten egg, and return to the oven until the snakes are golden brown and sound hollow when tapped.

Remove and leave to cool slightly. Make a slit in the head of both snakes and insert their tomato tongues.

First Aid – *see page 57*

Simple Pizza £

A pizza base is traditionally made from a bread dough mix. The home of pizza is Italy where a thin base is favoured, whilst Chicago USA favours a thicker base deep-pan pizza. You can't beat your own home-made pizza, because you've had hands-on experience making the dough. You've designed the topping to be tailor made. You've absorbed the pizza's aroma. Now all that's left is to enjoy yourself by eating your handy work.

Ingredients to serve 4 people

Base
225 g (8 oz)	basic bread dough §

Topping
1 tablespoon	tomato purée
225 g (8 oz)	tomatoes – sliced
	basil leaves
110 g (4 oz)	mozzarella cheese – sliced
1 dessertspoon	olive oil

Method

Make up the bread dough as normal until just before the stage of kneading. Combine the ingredients together with your hands to make a soft, elastic dough. Turn out the dough onto a clean worktop and knead briefly until it is smooth, elastic, and free from stickiness.

Roll into a 20 cm (8") or a 30 cm (12") diameter circle depending on whether you prefer a thick or a thin base. Place on a greased baking tray.

Spread the tomato purée evenly over the dough base. Add the sliced tomatoes, basil leaves, and slices of cheese, distributed evenly over the dough.

Bake at Gas Mark 7 / 425°F / 220°C (200°C for fan oven) for 15 – 20 minutes until it is well risen, golden brown, and bubbly.

Drizzle the olive oil evenly over the pizza just before serving.

First Aid – *see page 57*

Symptom: *Sweet pizza preferred to savoury pizza.*

Diagnosis: *Sweet pizza could be served as a pudding.*

Remedy: *Use the same dough base, but replace the topping with puréed fruit, fresh fruit, and cheese, then bake as normal.*

Soups Ancient and Modern

See page 59 for general guidance on making '**Basic Purée Soups**'.

Basic Savoury Vegetable Soup

This is a formula for any thickened soup, chunky or smooth, and you can tailor it to your own specific taste. "Wicked" as they say! If you want a chunky soup, remember to cut the vegetables all the same size, so they cook at the same rate, but not too big, otherwise you may look like 'Jaws' as you wrestle with the soup spoon's contents.

Ingredients to serve 3 or 4 people

40 g (1½ oz)	margarine
350 g (12 oz)	your choice of vegetable as primary ingredient
100 g (4 oz)	any mixture of leek, carrot, Swede, parsnip, onion
40 g (1½ oz)	plain flour
850 ml (1½ pt)	vegetable stock
1	bouquet garni §
	salt and pepper to taste

Method

Melt the margarine in a large saucepan. Roughly chop your primary choice of vegetable and the mixture of vegetables, and add them to the saucepan. Cook until soft but without colouring (called 'sweating').

Stir in the flour off the heat until thoroughly combined. Place the saucepan back on the heat and add the preheated vegetable stock, stirring all the time until the stock is used up.

Add the bouquet garni, cover the pan with a lid to prevent excess evaporation, and simmer the soup for about half an hour, until all the vegetables are soft and cooked. When the vegetables are cooked, remove the bouquet garni.

If you want a smooth consistency, liquidise the soup with a blender or in a food processor; otherwise, for a coarser soup, leave the vegetables as cooked.

Adjust the seasoning and consistency as necessary.

First Aid – *see page 59*

Basic Sweet Fruit Soup

I can hear you say "Sweet soups! Has Beryl lost it?" but believe me, these are worth a try, especially at the end of a meal. I've served cranberry and orange, melon and ginger, coconut and mango, apple and mint, each with an appropriate pudding.

Ingredients to serve 3 or 4 people

1	fruit bouquet garni:
	1 bay leaf, 2.5 cm (1") length of cinnamon stick,
	1 star anise *or* 6 crushed cardamom pods,
	all tied in a muslin square
40 g (1½ oz)	margarine
350 g (12 oz)	your choice of fruit as primary ingredient
100 g (4 oz)	any mixture of orange, lemon, apple, *or* pear
40 g (1½ oz)	plain flour
850 ml (1½ pt)	fruit stock of any of orange juice, cranberry juice, ginger wine, *or* coconut milk to harmonise with primary ingredient

Method

To make the bouquet garni, place the spices in the centre of the muslin square, fold over like a parcel, and secure with string, leaving enough to secure to the saucepan handle.

Melt the margarine in a large saucepan. Roughly chop your primary choice of fruit and the mixture of fruit, and add them to the saucepan. Cook until soft but without colouring (called 'sweating').

Stir in the flour off the heat until thoroughly combined. Place the saucepan back on the heat and add the preheated fruit stock, stirring all the time until the stock is used up.

Add the bouquet garni, cover the pan with a lid to prevent excess evaporation, and simmer the soup for about half an hour, until all the fruit is soft and cooked. When the fruit is cooked, remove the bouquet garni.

If you want a smooth consistency, liquidise the soup with a blender or in a food processor; otherwise, for a coarser soup, leave the fruit as cooked. Adjust the sweetness and consistency as necessary.

First Aid – *see page 59*

Instant Canned Soup

This is a standby soup, with not a fresh item in sight. The beauty of this soup is that you can substitute like mad. Use canned carrots instead of tomatoes, orange juice instead of water, lentils instead of pasta, frozen peas or beans instead of sweetcorn. As long as you have creativity, you will produce a tasty soup.

Ingredients to serve 4 to 6 people

1 tablespoon	dried onions
400 g (14 oz) can	chopped tomatoes
1 tablespoon	tomato purée
1 tablespoon	pesto
1 pinch	sugar
1 cube	vegetable stock cube
50 g (2 oz)	pasta shapes *or* spaghetti broken into even pieces
420 g (15 oz) can	mixed pulses *or* any one variety of pulses
320 g (11 oz) can	sweetcorn
	salt and pepper to taste

Method

Put the dried onions and the can of chopped tomatoes into a saucepan, plus two canfuls of water. Stir in the tomato purée, pesto, sugar, and the stock cube.

Bring the mixture to the boil. Add the pasta and simmer gently until the pasta is just cooked.

Drain and rinse the pulses and sweetcorn, and add them to the pasta mixture. Adjust the seasoning before serving.

Alternatives

You could replace the chopped tomatoes with a can of carrots, but whiz them in your food processor before making the soup.

With the carrots you can use two canfuls of orange juice instead of the water.

As an alternative for the pasta, you could substitute lentils.

In place of the sweetcorn try frozen or canned peas or beans.

First Aid – *see page 59*

Quick Mushroom Soup £

The key to quick mushroom soup is whizzing the vegetables in the food processor before cooking. This knocks valuable preparation time on the head, releases colour and flavour, as well as speeding up cooking time. The result is a soup that still has texture, but if you prefer a smoother consistency, whiz again after simmering.

Ingredients to serve 3 or 4 people

350 g (12 oz)	mushrooms
110 g (4 oz)	onion
2 cloves	garlic
25 g (1 oz)	vegetable oil
25 g (1 oz)	plain flour
850 ml (1½ pt)	milk
1	bouquet garni §

Method

Wipe the mushrooms with a damp piece of kitchen paper to remove any dirt. Do not wash in water because they will become waterlogged like a sponge.

Place the peeled and roughly chopped onion and garlic in a food processor. Add the roughly chopped mushrooms. Whiz them until evenly textured, but not too smooth.

Place a large saucepan on the heat, and add the vegetable oil and the textured vegetables. Cover with a lid and simmer for 10 minutes, until the mixture softens. Add the flour and stir well until thoroughly blended.

Stir in the milk, bring to the boil and add the bouquet garni. Simmer for 15 minutes. Adjust the seasoning and consistency if necessary. Remove the bouquet garni before serving.

First Aid – *see also page 59*

Symptom: *Mushroom soup colour looks too dark.*

Diagnosis: *Flat or field mushrooms will give the darkest colour.*

Antidote: *Add a splash of double cream to lighten the colour.*

Remedy: *Use a mixture of mushrooms to give desired flavour and colour.*

Cheese Soup

My first venture into the media was on BBC Essex local radio, through a monthly slot on its Sound Advice programme, where listeners phone in with their cookery problems. One such listener supplied this recipe, and it was the first of many from fellow enthusiasts. You could add leeks, cauliflower, or broccoli to the soup to give a little more body.

Ingredients to serve 4 people

2 small	onions – thinly sliced §
40 g (1½ oz)	butter
40 g (1½ oz)	plain flour
570 ml (1 pt)	milk
275 ml (½ pt)	vegetable stock *or* water
½ level teaspoon	salt
1 pinch	cayenne pepper
1 pinch	nutmeg
175 g (6 oz)	Cheddar cheese

Method

Fry the thinly sliced onion in the butter for a few minutes without browning. Toss in the flour and stir over a low heat for a further minute.

Add the milk and stock or water gradually, and stir until boiling. Add the seasonings, and simmer gently for five minutes.

Dice the cheese and mix into the soup off the heat, then reheat without boiling until melted. Adjust seasoning to taste. Serve hot with toast, or crispy croutons §, or warm crusty French bread.

First Aid – *see also page 59*

Symptom: *Low fat cheese substituted for regular cheese, but did not melt.*
Diagnosis: *Weight or health conscious cooks prefer low fat cheese.*
Remedy: *Do not use low fat cheese, because it does not melt successfully.*

French Onion Soup £

The secret of a good colour and flavour in this classic soup is to caramelise the onions slowly before adding the flour.

Ingredients to serve 4 people
450 g (1 lb)	shredded onions
50 g (2 oz)	butter *or* margarine *or* oil
25 g (1 oz)	plain flour
2 cloves	garlic – crushed
1 litre (2 pt)	brown stock (beef cube *or* Vegemite®)
	salt and pepper to taste
1 small	French bread stick
110 g (4 oz)	grated cheese

Method

Fry the shredded onions in the melted fat until lightly browned. Add the flour and garlic and stir well.

Add the stock, bring to the boil, and skim off the excess fat. Simmer the soup for 30 minutes. Taste and adjust seasoning.

Slice the bread stick at an angle into flutes and toast them. Top with the grated cheese and grill.

Serve the soup in earthenware soup bowls garnished with the gratinated flutes.

First Aid – *see also page 59*

Symptom: *French onion soup looks as dull as dishwater.*

Diagnosis: *Onions need to be gently coloured without burning.*

Antidote: *Add a tablespoon of black treacle to the finished soup to give it a dark colour, and readjust the flavour with seasonings.*

Chicken Soup £

I usually make this dish after using boiled chicken in another dish. That gives me fresh chicken stock, just waiting to be used. You can use a chicken stock cube if you have no stock to hand, and a raw chicken thigh sautéed with the vegetables instead of the boiled chicken. Return the chicken to the soup and season if required.

Ingredients to serve 4 people
25 g (1 oz)	vegetable oil
450 g (16 oz)	mixed chopped vegetables, such as carrot, Swede, parsnip, turnip, butternut squash, etc
200 g (8 oz)	chopped onion §

4 cloves	crushed garlic
25 g (1 oz)	flour
1 litre (2 pt)	stock from boiled chicken §
25 g (1 oz)	long grain rice
1	bouquet garni §
	salt and pepper to taste
110 g (4 oz)	frozen peas
110 g (4 oz)	finely chopped boiled chicken §
1 tablespoon	chopped chives *or* parsley §

Method

Gently fry the chopped vegetables, onion, and garlic in the vegetable oil for about 8 – 10 minutes, until soft, but do not brown. Add the flour, and stir well until combined.

Remove any grease from the top of the chicken stock, and stir the stock into the fried vegetables. Then add the rice, the bouquet garni §, and salt and pepper to taste.

Bring to the boil and simmer for 10 minutes until the rice is cooked. Add the frozen peas and chopped chicken, and simmer for another 5 minutes.

Taste and adjust the seasoning, add the fresh chopped herbs, and serve.

First Aid

See '**Basic Purée Soups**' on page 59 and the '**Boiled Chicken**' section on page 60.

Symptom: *Chicken soup has grease visible on the surface.*

Diagnosis: *Probably used chicken with skin still attached.*

Remedy: *Chicken should be stripped of its skin before use in soup.*

London Particular Pease Soup

This traditional soup is yellow in colour, and thick in consistency, just like the old London fogs, or "pea soupers" of the 19th and early 20th centuries. You can add snippets of bacon with the vegetables to give a meaty flavour. Rinse the soaked peas several times in clean water before adding to the vegetables. This reduces the risk of embarrassing bean syndrome side effects later in the day.

Ingredients to serve 4 people

225 g (8 oz)	dried yellow split peas
110 g (4 oz)	diced vegetables such as onion, carrot, Swede, leek
1 litre (2 pt)	vegetable stock
1	bouquet garni §
	salt and pepper to taste
	sliced bread

Method

Soak the split peas overnight in cold water. Rinse and drain the soaked split peas.

Place the split peas, diced vegetables, vegetable stock, and bouquet garni § into a large saucepan and bring to the boil. Boil for 10 minutes without a lid. Skim off any scum from the surface.

Cover with a lid, reduce the heat, and simmer for about half an hour until the split peas collapse and break down.

Remove the bouquet garni. Purée the soup with a blender or in a food processor to a smooth consistency.

Adjust seasoning to taste. Garnish with snippets of toasted bread or crispy croutons §.

First Aid – *see also page 59*

Symptom: *Dried split peas were not soaked overnight beforehand.*

Diagnosis: *Dried peas and beans must be soaked to hydrate them, so they become soft and edible.*

Antidote: *Put the dried peas in a large saucepan and completely cover with water. Bring to the boil, and boil for 10 minutes covered with a lid. Switch off the heat and leave the peas to soak in the hot water for about two hours to hydrate. Rinse twice in clean water, and leave to drain before use.*

Pumpkin Soup

This signals the start of autumn, when people make lanterns in time for Hallowe'en. Here is a soup that uses the flesh of the pumpkin, which is usually discarded, after the Jack 'o Lantern masterpiece has been made. The added bonus with this soup is that the pumpkin's saffron orange colours seem to glow fluorescently in the bowl, just like the hollowed-out, candle-lit monster.

Ingredients to serve 2 people

110 g (4 oz)	onion – finely chopped §
1 clove	garlic – finely chopped §
1 cm (½") stick	fresh ginger – finely chopped §
110 g (4 oz)	carrot – finely chopped §
350 g (12 oz)	pumpkin – peeled, seeded, roughly chopped
2 tablespoons	vegetable oil
1 teaspoon	ground cumin
1 teaspoon	ground coriander
1 tablespoon	plain flour
275 ml (10 fl oz)	orange juice
275 ml (10 fl oz)	water
	salt and pepper to taste

Method

Finely chop the onion, garlic, fresh ginger, and carrot. Peel, seed, and roughly chop the pumpkin.

Place all the prepared vegetables in a saucepan with the vegetable oil and simmer until soft but not brown. Add the spices and stir them in.

Off the heat, add the flour and stir until all the vegetables are well coated. Add the orange juice and water, and stir well.

Place back on the heat and stir to the boil. Allow to simmer for about half an hour.

Purée either with a blender, or in a food processor, or push through a sieve. Adjust the consistency with a little water, and adjust the seasoning.

First Aid – *see also page 59*

Symptom: *Swede used instead of pumpkin, but gave poor coloured soup.*
Diagnosis: *Swede does not have the fluorescent colour of pumpkin.*
Remedy: *Use 225 g (8 oz) of both Swede and carrot to improve the colour.*

Beetroot and Apple Soup £

What an under rated vegetable beetroot is; usually consumed pickled in vinegar, or boiled and sliced in salads. This soup extends the beetroot repertoire, highlighting its dramatic vivid colour, its sweet yet earthy taste, and its versatility.

Ingredients to serve 3 or 4 people
40 g (1½ oz)	margarine
350 g (12 oz)	beetroot (raw *or* cooked)
1	apple
110 g (4 oz)	onion
40 g (1½ oz)	plain flour
850 ml (1½ pt)	vegetable stock
1	bouquet garni §

Method
Melt the margarine in a large saucepan. Add the roughly chopped beetroot, apple, and onion. Cook until soft but without colouring the apple or onion (called 'sweating').

Stir in the flour off the heat until thoroughly combined. Place the saucepan back on the heat and add the preheated vegetable stock, stirring all the time until the stock is used up.

Add the bouquet garni, cover the pan with a lid to prevent excess evaporation, and simmer the soup for about half an hour, until all the vegetables are soft and cooked. When the vegetables are cooked, remove the bouquet garni.

If you want a smooth consistency, liquidise the cooked vegetable soup, otherwise for a coarser soup leave the vegetables as cooked. Adjust the seasoning and consistency if needed.

First Aid – *see page 59*

Pasta and Rice Dishes

'Farinaceous' is the collective word that describes pasta and rice dishes. I think of them as cost-conscious belly fillers. With the addition of a simple sauce, or a handful of tasty titbits, the mundane can become the memorable.

See the chapter **'How Do You Cook With Confidence?'** for general guidelines on cookery techniques.

Basic Plain Pasta

For main courses allow 75 g (3 oz) dry weight of any pasta per person, which will treble in weight when boiled.

Ingredients to serve 2 people
1 litre (2 pt)	boiling water
1 dessertspoon	salt
150 g (6 oz)	dry weight pasta

Method

Bring the salted water to the boil in a large saucepan with the lid on. Once boiling, add the pasta and bring back to the boil quickly. Allow it to boil uncovered for 5 minutes.

Turn off the heat, cover the saucepan with its lid, and leave for 5 minutes. Remove a piece of pasta to taste. It should be al dente or slightly under cooked. If not cooked to your liking, leave it covered for a further 5 minutes.

When satisfactory, drain and use as required, perhaps with one of the sauces below.

First Aid

Symptom: *Pasta sticks together whilst boiling in the saucepan.*

Diagnosis: *Starch released from the pasta makes it sticky.*

Remedy: *Add a tablespoon of vegetable oil per litre of water to help prevent the pasta sticking.*

Mediterranean Pasta

Here we have a taste of sunshine with heady summer aromas.

Ingredients to serve 2 people
150 g (6 oz)	dry weight pasta (spaghetti *or* macaroni *or* pasta shapes)

Sauce
110 g (4 oz)	goats cheese
2	black or green olives – chopped finely §
1 teaspoon	sun dried tomato paste
1 teaspoon	chopped parsley §
6	basil leaves
	salt and pepper

Method

Prepare the pasta as described on page 111. Meanwhile, combine all the sauce ingredients in a mixing bowl. Add the hot cooked and drained pasta, and coat well.

First Aid

Symptom: *Goats' cheese has too strong a flavour.*

Diagnosis: *Personal tastes vary.*

Antidote: *Try English goats cheese, which is usually not as strong as foreign goats cheese, or substitute any other cheese.*

Carbonara Pasta

This is like a bacon-and-egg breakfast stirred into cooked pasta.

Ingredients to serve 2 people
150 g (6 oz)   dry weight pasta (spaghetti *or* macaroni *or* pasta shapes)

Sauce
2 rashers	streaky bacon – chopped finely
2	eggs – lightly beaten
1 tablespoon	milk
	salt and pepper

Method

Prepare the pasta as described on page 111.

Dry fry the bacon in a frying pan until crispy. Lightly beat the eggs with the milk, and add to the bacon, stirring until just beginning to set. Take off the heat and add the cooked and drained pasta. Season with salt and pepper.

First Aid

Symptom: *Bacon is unsuitable for vegetarians.*

Antidote: *Replace bacon with sliced mushrooms or halved cherry tomatoes.*

Waldorf Pasta

I love the sweet yet sour taste, and the interesting combination of textures in this dish.

Ingredients to serve 2 people
150 g (6 oz)   dry weight pasta (spaghetti *or* macaroni *or* pasta shapes)

Sauce
1	Cox apple – diced §
1 stick	celery – diced §
1 tablespoon	vegetable oil
50 g (2 oz)	walnut pieces
2 tablespoons	mayonnaise
1 teaspoon	chopped parsley §
	salt and pepper

Method

Prepare the pasta as described on page 111.

Core and dice the apple and dice the celery into same sized pieces as the walnuts. Fry the diced apple and celery in the vegetable oil until just soft, and add the walnut pieces.

Take off the heat, add the mayonnaise, and add the cooked drained pasta, and the chopped parsley. Season with salt and pepper.

First Aid

Symptom: *Mayonnaise is too heavy a dressing.*

Diagnosis: *Personal taste.*

Antidote: *Use plain yoghurt or vinaigrette dressing instead.*

Minted Pea Pasta £

Frozen peas are a success story. All that flavour captured and frozen in time. This is such a simple dish, with simple ingredients, and kind on the pocket too!

Ingredients to serve 2 people

150 g (6 oz)	dry weight pasta (spaghetti *or* macaroni *or* pasta shapes)

Sauce

2	spring onions – finely chopped §
or 1	small onion – finely chopped §
1 tablespoon	vegetable oil
110 g (4 oz)	frozen peas (minted variety if possible)
150 ml (5 fl oz)	cream (single *or* whipping *or* double)
1 teaspoon	chopped mint or parsley §
	salt and pepper

Method

Prepare the pasta as described on page 111.

Fry the chopped onion in the vegetable oil until just soft. Add the peas and cream, and bring to the boil.

Season with salt and pepper. Add the chopped mint or parsley if available, and finally the cooked and drained pasta.

First Aid

See also the cream '**First Aid**' in the following pasta recipe.

Symptom: *Single cream curdles when boiled.*

Diagnosis: *Single cream is more likely to curdle than whipping or double cream.*

Remedy: *Blend half a teaspoon of cornflour with a little water, and add with the single cream before boiling.*

Tuna and Sweetcorn Pasta £

This combination is a classic sandwich filling, so why not let it make an appearance as a perfect pasta. It is simplicity to make, and slides down a treat!

Ingredients to serve 2 people

150 g (6 oz)	dry weight pasta (spaghetti *or* macaroni *or* pasta shapes)

Sauce

110 g (4 oz)	onion – finely chopped §
1 clove	garlic – crushed
1 tablespoon	vegetable oil
175 g (6 oz) tin	tuna in brine or oil – drained
110 g (4 oz)	sweetcorn (frozen *or* tinned & drained)
225 ml (8 fl oz)	single cream
	salt and pepper to taste

Method

Prepare the pasta as described on page 111.

Meanwhile, fry the finely chopped onion and crushed garlic in the vegetable oil until soft. Add the drained tuna, defrosted or drained sweetcorn, and single cream to the frying pan. Stir until hot and season to taste.

Add the cooked and drained pasta to the tuna and sweetcorn mixture. Taste and adjust the seasoning.

First Aid

See also the cream '**First Aid**' in the preceding pasta recipe.

Symptom: *Cream is too fattening.*

Diagnosis: *Need to reduce fat intake.*

Antidote: *Replace some or all of the cream with tomato juice or any other vegetable juice.*

Plenty Pasta Five

I love the play on words in the title of this dish, which sounds like twenty past five with an Italian accent. The sauce incorporates a selection of five fruit or vegetables that we are urged to consume each day, without a drop of cream.

Ingredients to serve 2 people

150 g (6 oz)	dry weight pasta (spaghetti *or* macaroni *or* pasta shapes)

Sauce

1 stick	celery – thinly sliced
2	spring onions – thinly sliced
1	Cox apple – diced
1 tablespoon	olive oil
150 ml (5 fl oz)	apple juice
110 g (4 oz)	seedless grapes – halved
110 g (4 oz)	broccoli
1 teaspoon	cornflour
75 g (3 oz)	Stilton cheese *or* any other English cheese
	pepper to taste

Method

Prepare the pasta as described on page 111. Meanwhile, cut the celery and spring onions into thin slices. Core and dice the apple. Gently fry the celery, spring onion, and apple in the olive oil for 2 – 3 minutes until soft.

Pour in the apple juice and bring the sauce mixture to the boil.

Halve the grapes, and break the broccoli florets into grape sized pieces. Add the grapes and broccoli to the sauce and simmer for 3 minutes, stirring constantly.

Mix the cornflour with a little cold water to form a smooth creamy paste. Stir the cornflour paste into the sauce to thicken it slightly, then remove from the heat.

Dice the cheese and stir it into the sauce, then season to taste. Add the cooked and drained pasta to the sauce, toss well, and serve.

First Aid

Symptom: *Cooked pasta is soft and flabby, and breaks when touched.*

Diagnosis: *Pasta is over-cooked.*

Remedy: *Time the pasta, once it has been added to the boiling salted water. The cooking time depends on the type and make of pasta. Follow the manufacturers' recommendations on the packet.*

Vegetable Lasagne £

The tip to using lasagne sheets is to pre-soak them in hot water before use. This helps the pasta to soften, and aids cutting and shaping to fit a dish. Another reason for soaking is to prevent the lasagne from absorbing liquid from the sauce as it hydrates, which leaves the dish tasting dry.

Ingredients to serve 2 people

4 sheets	lasagne

Sauce

1	onion – finely chopped §
2 cloves	garlic – crushed
1 dessertspoon	olive oil
110 g (4 oz)	Savoy cabbage *or* curly kale
110 g (4 oz)	frozen peas
225 g (8 oz)	fresh spinach
	ground nutmeg
250 g (9 oz) tub	fromage frais
2	tomatoes – sliced
2 tablespoons	Cheddar cheese *or* Parmesan cheese – grated

Method

Place the four sheets of lasagne in a shallow container, preferably in a single layer. Pour hot water over them and leave for 15 – 20 minutes to soften slightly.

In a large saucepan, gently fry the chopped onion and crushed garlic in the olive oil, until just soft.

Wash and shred the cabbage or curly kale, toss into the saucepan with the onion and garlic, add the frozen peas, cover with a lid, and sweat until soft.

Wash and drain the spinach well, add to the saucepan, and stir until just wilted.

Season and add grated nutmeg to taste. Stir in 1 tablespoon of the fromage frais.

In an ovenproof dish, evenly distribute half the vegetable mixture, topped with one thinly sliced tomato, and two sheets of the softened lasagne. Repeat this process with the remaining vegetable mixture, sliced tomato, and lasagne sheets.

Mix the grated cheese with the rest of the fromage frais, and evenly spread over the top.

Bake at Gas Mark 5 / 375°F / 190°C (170°C for fan oven) for about 20 minutes until bubbly and brown.

First Aid

Symptom: *Fromage frais is not available.*

Antidote: *Substitute other products such as double or whipping cream, or plain yoghurt mixed with a teaspoon of cornflour.*

Basic Boiled Rice

Rice is a vehicle for simple or elaborate flavours, adding overall texture and limited taste. Choose American long-grain rice for everyday, all-purpose cooking, as it is so versatile. It can be boiled, braised, steamed, or fried. There is no need to weigh it, just simply calculate that a cup of rice feeds four. The method of cooking adopted governs the amount of water required.

Ingredients to serve 4 people

1 cup ~ 225 g (8 oz)	American long grain rice
1 teaspoon	salt

Method

Bring a large saucepan of salted water to a rolling boil. Add the rice, stir once, and bring back to the boil. Boil uncovered for 10 minutes. Test to see if cooked. The rice grains should be nearly soft, but with just a small amount of bite.

Drain the rice into a large sieve. Pour fresh hot water over the rice to rinse, then drain again until free of surplus liquid. Serve into a warm dish or use as required.

First Aid

Cooked rice is a high risk food and the '**Prevention is Better Than Cure**' section on page 90 gives some sound advice on hygiene and safety.

Symptom: *Rice appears sticky or in a solid lump after boiling.*

Diagnosis: *Over-cooking or too much stirring causes rice to release its starch.*

Antidote: *Rinse well with hot water to wash away the starch, drain thoroughly, and use immediately.*

Remedy: *Only stir the rice once when it is added to the boiling water, check the rice after 10 minutes, and drain as soon as it is ready.*

Chinese Egg Fried Rice

If you have ever had a take-away Chinese meal, something like this rice dish will have passed your lips. You can tailor make the dish to suit your palate and your pocket.

Ingredients to serve 4 people

1 cup ~ 225 g (8 oz)	American long grain rice
1 teaspoon	salt
1 tablespoon	sunflower oil
1	onion – finely chopped §
2 cloves	garlic – crushed
1 small	red or yellow pepper – thinly sliced §
110 g (4 oz)	button mushrooms – sliced §
110 g (4 oz)	frozen peas
2 large	eggs – beaten
1 teaspoon	Chinese five-spice powder

Method

Boil the rice as described previously. Meanwhile, in a large frying pan or wok, fry the chopped onion in the sunflower oil, until just soft. Add the crushed garlic, sliced pepper, sliced button mushrooms, and the peas. Stir for approximately 2 minutes.

Mix the five-spice powder into the beaten eggs, and pour into the fried vegetable mixture. Stir until the egg just begins to set, then toss in the cooked rice. Combine well until thoroughly heated through.

First Aid

Symptom: *Chinese five spice powder is not available.*

Diagnosis: *It is usually found in supermarkets and Chinese food shops.*

Antidote: *Substitute ground ginger or ground cinnamon.*

Bacon or Mushroom Risotto £

When making risotto, as a rule of thumb, use twice the amount of water as the quantity of rice. If like me, you like a moist creamy risotto, add a slug of cream or yoghurt just before serving.

Ingredients to serve 4 people

	2 tablespoons	vegetable oil
	175 g (6 oz)	onion – finely chopped §
	2 cloves	garlic – crushed
	4 rashers	streaky bacon – chopped
or	110 g (4 oz)	mushrooms – sliced
	225 g (8 oz)	American long grain rice
	3 tablespoons	tomato purée
	570 ml (1 pt)	hot water
		salt and pepper to taste

Method

Heat the vegetable oil in a frying pan. Add the chopped onion, crushed garlic, and chopped bacon, or sliced mushrooms. Stir until slightly brown, then stir in the rice and coat well.

Dissolve the tomato purée in the hot water and pour over the rice mixture.

Bring the mixture to the boil. Stir gently, reduce the heat to a simmer, and cover with a lid. Simmer for about 20 minutes until the rice is tender, and all the liquid has been absorbed.

Season to taste. Serve with a crisp green salad.

First Aid

Symptom: *Tomato flavour in all things Italian is monotonous.*

Diagnosis: *Personal taste.*

Antidote: *Omit the tomato purée, and stir in a handful of your favourite herb with the finely grated zest of a lime.*

Symptom: *Risotto is not moist and creamy.*

Diagnosis: *Cooked with insufficient water.*

Antidote: *Add a slug of cream or yoghurt just before serving.*

Lentils and Rice

Cheap eats, that's how I view this dish, but with a little ingenuity, you can turn it into posh nosh.

Ingredients to serve 4 people

175 g (6 oz)	green or orange lentils
175 g (6 oz)	basmati rice
~600 ml (~1 pt)	vegetable stock *or* water
2 large	onions – chopped §
2 cloves	garlic – crushed
3 tablespoons	vegetable oil
	salt and pepper to taste

Method

Wash the lentils and rice separately.

Boil the lentils in a saucepan, with about 600 ml (1 pt) of vegetable stock or water, for 15 minutes until just tender but not soft, and remove from the heat.

Fry the chopped onions and crushed garlic in the vegetable oil until soft. Add the onions and garlic to the lentils, and stir in the rice until blended.

Place the mixture back on the heat and bring to the boil, then reduce to a simmer. Cover the saucepan with a tightly fitting lid, and leave to simmer for 20 – 25 minutes until the rice and lentils are cooked. More vegetable stock or water may need to be added if the liquid is absorbed too quickly.

Adjust seasoning to taste before serving.

To spice up this simple dish into posh nosh you can add one of the following:

◆ Chopped ginger and coriander.

◆ Chopped sun dried tomato and black olives.

◆ Spring onions and chopped preserved lemons §.

You can use this dish as a meal on its own served with a green or mixed salad, or as the base for a vegetarian shepherd's pie, or a filling for pasties, or a topping for baked potatoes.

First Aid

Symptom: *Lentils and other pulses tend to produce too much flatulence.*

Diagnosis: *Natural tendency of pulses.*

Antidote: *Soak the pulses in water for an hour or two, then rinse twice in fresh clean water before cooking.*

Vegetable Roots and Shoots

See the earlier chapter **'Are You Picking the Best Ingredients?'** for general advice.

Potato Cakes £

These flattened balls of potato are ideal for party food, because you can add different flavours, thereby altering their taste and appeal.

Take a square of cheese, surround it with prepared potato mixed with finely chopped spring onion, dip in beaten egg, coat in sesame seeds, and deep fry. What you have is a wonderful enhancement to the simple potato cakes described below.

Ingredients to serve 6 to 8 people

700 g (1½ lb)	even-sized floury potatoes such as King Edward, Cara, *or* Maris Piper
1 tablespoon	chopped fresh parsley §
or 1 teaspoon	dried parsley
	salt and pepper to taste
3 tablespoons	vegetable oil

Method

If possible, choose even sized potatoes, so that they will cook evenly. Wash the potatoes, but do **NOT** peel them.

Place them in a saucepan, cover completely with water, and boil them for about 10 – 15 minutes, until just soft when tested by inserting a sharp knife. Drain off the water, and leave until cool enough to handle.

Peel the potatoes. Use a coarse hand grater to grate the potatoes into a large bowl. Add the parsley, salt and pepper, and mix together well.

Using floured hands, divide the mixture into 6 – 8 even sized pieces, and roll into balls. Flatten each ball slightly, and chill for at least 1 hour until required.

Shallow fry the potato cakes in hot vegetable oil until golden brown on both sides.

First Aid

Symptom: *Potatoes are gluey after grating.*

Diagnosis: *Probably grated using a food processor.*

Remedy: *Use a coarse hand grater to reduce the chance of gluey potatoes.*

Bubble and Squeak Cakes £

The first rule in the kitchen is: don't throw anything away. So leftover vegetables, meat, fish, or poultry minced finely, and added to cooked potatoes, will double their quality.

The second rule in the kitchen, if you have on occasion broken the first rule, is keep quiet about it.

Ingredients to serve 4 people

450 g (1 lb)	even sized floury potatoes such as King Edwards, Cara, *or* Maris Piper
225 g (8 oz)	left-over cooked vegetables such as sprouts, cabbage, carrots, peas, beans, *or* onions
	salt and pepper to taste

Method

If possible, choose even-sized potatoes, so that they will cook evenly. Wash the potatoes, but do **NOT** peel them.

Place the potatoes in a saucepan, cover completely with water, and boil them for about 10 – 15 minutes, until just soft when tested by inserting a sharp knife. Drain off the water, and leave the potatoes until cool enough to handle.

Peel the potatoes. Use a coarse hand grater to grate the potatoes into a large bowl. (Do not be tempted to use a food processor grater, as it makes the potato very gluey.)

Roughly chop the left-over cooked vegetables, add to the potatoes, season well, and mix thoroughly. While the mixture is still warm, place tablespoons of the mixture onto a floured surface, and shape into flattened ball shape cakes. Chill the cakes until firm and keep refrigerated until needed.

Fry the bubble and squeak cakes in hot fat, until golden brown on both sides.

First Aid

See the '**First Aid**' section of '**Potato Cakes**' above.

Symptom: *Bubble and squeak cakes disintegrate when handled or fried.*

Diagnosis: *Vegetables and potatoes need to be the same consistency.*

Remedy: *Chop the vegetables more finely. Blend well with the potatoes and shape into cakes while the potatoes are still warm. Chill until firm before frying.*

Potato and Cheese Bake £

When I think of this dish, I think of my childhood. We used to watch my dad eat this dish with relish, while we had just potatoes cooked in milk. Now, I can eat potato and cheese bake whenever I like with just as much pleasure.

Ingredients to serve 2 people

700 g (1½ lb)	potatoes
	vegetable oil
	salt and pepper to taste
110 g (4 oz)	Cheddar cheese – finely grated
110 g (4 oz)	onion – finely chopped §
50 g (2 oz)	margarine

Method

Peel, wash, and thoroughly dry the potatoes. Then cut the potatoes evenly into 0.5 cm (¼") thick slices. Do not rewash the potatoes.

Oil a 1 litre (2 pint) casserole dish, then salt and pepper the dish.

Lay some of the sliced potatoes, to cover the base of the dish, with each slice overlapping the next. After one layer of potatoes, add a layer of finely grated cheese, finely chopped onion, blobs of margarine, and salt and pepper to taste.

Continue adding alternate layers of potatoes, then cheese and onion, finishing off with a layer of potatoes, and some extra blobs of margarine.

Bake at the top of your oven at Gas Mark 6 / 400°F / 200°C (180°C for fan oven) for 1¼ – 1½ hours. During baking, occasionally press the potatoes down. When cooked, the potatoes should be soft and slightly brown.

Serve with a tomato and cucumber salad.

First Aid

Symptom: *Potatoes discoloured with blackened edges after baking.*

Diagnosis: *Sliced potatoes left too long before baking.*

Remedy: *As soon as the dish is assembled bake it immediately.*

Vegetable Charlotte £

Autumnal colours with harmonising flavours are what first drew me to this dish. We used to serve this charlotte regularly in the restaurant, and if I had a pound for every time I was asked for the recipe, I would be worth a bob or two by now.

Ingredients to serve 6 people

700 g (1½ lb)	root vegetables such as any combination of carrot, Swede, turnip, parsnip, *or* celeriac
110 g (4 oz)	onion
1 tablespoon	vegetable oil
50 g (2 oz)	breadcrumbs *&/or* cheese *&/or* seeds

Method

Wash and peel, then grate the root vegetables and the onion. Place the grated vegetables and onion in a saucepan with the vegetable oil. Cover with a lid and cook on a medium heat for about 8 – 10 minutes until soft. Stir occasionally to prevent burning.

Distribute evenly in an ovenproof dish. Sprinkle the top evenly with the breadcrumb, &/or cheese, &/or seed mixture. Grill until brown and crispy. Reheat in a microwave oven before serving if necessary.

First Aid

Symptom: *Charlotte topping burnt whilst grilling.*

Diagnosis: *Need to watch the grill carefully, as the topping readily burns.*

Antidote: *Remove the burnt topping carefully with a spoon, reapply fresh topping, and grill again.*

Veggie Burger £

Who would have thought that a few grated basic vegetables, and the cheapest of protein packed nuts, mixed with seasonings, would produce such a healthy, tasty, and money saving dish. I sometimes coat the burgers in sesame seeds or dry polenta to give them a different texture.

Ingredients to serve 1 or 2 people

175 g (6 oz)	one carrot
175 g (6 oz)	one parsnip
110 g (4 oz)	one small onion
1 clove	garlic
50 g (2 oz)	cheapest raw peanuts *or* other nuts of your choice
1 slice	bread
1 teaspoon	tomato purée *or* curry paste
½ teaspoon	mixed herbs
	salt and pepper to taste

Method

Coarsely grate the vegetables. Crush the garlic. Finely chop the nuts. Grate or finely chop the bread.

Mix all the ingredients thoroughly, and shape into balls with floured hands. Slightly flatten each ball into burger shaped cakes. Leave on a floured plate in the refrigerator for about 2 hours until firm.

Bake at top of the oven at Gas Mark 4 / 350°F / 180°C (160°C for fan oven) for about 20 minutes.

Serve with a crisp salad or coleslaw.

First Aid

Symptom: *Nut food allergy.*

Diagnosis: *Many people are allergic to nuts.*

Antidote: *Replace the nuts with seeds of your choice.*

Deep Fried Cauliflower £

This dish gives a crunchy texture to the cauliflower, and is definitely worth getting the deep fat fryer out. You can substitute peeled parsnips, onion rings, broccoli florets, or small whole mushrooms for the cauliflower.

Ingredients to serve 4 people

8 florets	even-sized florets of raw cauliflower
110 g (4 oz)	self-raising flour
1 pinch	salt and pepper
125 ml (5 fl oz)	cold water

Method

Cut even sized florets from a raw cauliflower, so they will fry evenly.

The batter should not be made until about 10 minutes before it is used, in order to get the best effect from the self-raising flour.

Sieve the flour and seasonings into a bowl. Make a hollow in the centre of the flour, and using a nylon whisk, slowly add the water, gradually working in the flour. When all the water is added, beat the mixture until it becomes smooth and lump free. The batter should have the consistency of double cream.

Using a deep fat fryer §, heat the oil to 345°F / 175°C. Coat the cauliflower florets in the batter, then carefully place each piece into the hot oil. Fry until lightly golden brown. Drain well on kitchen paper, before serving immediately.

First Aid

See the '**Deep Fat Frying**' section on page 86.

Symptom: *Battered cauliflower pieces stick together in one mass in the fryer.*

Diagnosis: *Over-crowding of the deep frying basket.*

Remedy: *Reduce the number of pieces fried at the same time, and place each piece in the oil away from the others.*

Jerusalem Artichokes Gratin with Whole Grain Mustard

The beauty of this dish is that you can substitute any vegetable as the main ingredient; now there's versatility! Watch out for Jerusalem artichokes though, as they have a tendency to come back and haunt you in the smelly way, later in the day. They have a lovely nutty taste though!

You will need a 1 litre (1½ pt) ovenproof dish.

Ingredients to serve 6 people

900 g (2 lb)	Jerusalem artichokes *or*
	substitute celeriac, parsnip, Swede, *or* turnip
half	lemon
275 ml (10 fl oz)	double cream
1 dessertspoon	whole grain mustard (optional) *or*
	substitute creamed horseradish *or* grated cheese
	salt and pepper to taste
50 g (2 oz)	Parmesan *or* strong cheddar cheese – grated
50 g (2 oz)	breadcrumbs *or* oatmeal

Method

Preheat the oven to Gas Mark 7 / 425°F / 220°C (200°C for fan oven).

Wash, peel, and slice the artichokes or other vegetable to 0.5 cm (¼") thickness.

Extract the juice and rind of the half lemon, and mix with the double cream, the mustard (or substitute), and the salt and pepper.

Add the sliced vegetables, coat well, and pour into a 1 litre (1½ pt) ovenproof dish. Cover the dish with foil and bake in the oven for about 30 minutes.

Remove the foil and sprinkle evenly with the mixed grated cheese and breadcrumbs or oats. Return to the oven for another 15 – 20 minutes, until the vegetables are completely tender, and the topping is golden brown.

First Aid

Symptom: *Cream boiled over the baking dish in the oven.*

Diagnosis: *Dish too small for the contents.*

Remedy: *Use a dish that is only half to three-quarters filled by the contents. If the contents fill the dish more than this, there is a tendency for the filling to overflow, so place the dish on a baking tray.*

Pepper and Tomato Charlotte

Traditionally, charlotte is a sweet dish using bread, but here it is a breadcrumb topping on a savoury base. The base could comprise any mixture of cooked vegetables, lightly dusted with breadcrumbs and grated cheese. This gives a golden coat to the colourful vegetables.

Ingredients to serve 4 to 6 people

110 g (4 oz)	onion – finely chopped §
2 cloves	garlic – crushed
1 tablespoon	olive oil
225 g (8 oz)	tomatoes – quartered
450 g (16 oz)	peppers
	salt and pepper to taste
1 bunch	basil leaves – torn
75 g (3 oz)	breadcrumbs
50 g (2 oz)	Parmesan cheese – grated

Method

Finely chop the onion, crush the garlic, and add to a frying pan with the oil. Fry until just soft but not brown, then add the quartered tomatoes, cover with a lid, and simmer until the tomatoes collapse.

Meanwhile, cut the peppers in half, and remove the stem, core, and seeds. Lightly oil the outside of the peppers, and place them cut side down on an oiled baking tray.

Bake at Gas Mark 6 / 400°F / 200°C (180°C for fan oven) on the top shelf, for about 30 minutes, until just charred. Once charred, remove the peppers from the oven, completely cover with cling film, and allow to cool slightly. This allows the skins to be easily peeled away from the flesh.

Using scissors, snip pieces of the peppers into the tomato mixture. Pour any remaining pepper juice into the tomatoes and season to taste. Stir in the torn basil leaves. Transfer the mixture to a 1 litre (2 pint) ovenproof dish.

Mix the breadcrumbs with the grated cheese, and sprinkle evenly over the tomato and pepper mix. Bake at Gas Mark 5 / 375°F / 190°C (170°C for fan oven) for 15 – 20 minutes until bubbly and golden brown.

First Aid

Symptom: *Breadcrumbs and cheese are not a desirable topping.*

Diagnosis: *Many alternatives are available.*

Antidote: *Cover with mashed or sliced cooked potato; or sprinkle with oats, or crushed Cornflakes, or mixed seeds.*

Tomatoes Baked with Basil

This is a savoury crumble, where tomatoes, spring onions, and basil leaves are the filling. An ideal dish when tomatoes are at their peak, and kind on the pocket into the bargain.

Ingredients to serve 4 people

Tomato Filling

750 g (1½ lb)	tomatoes
1 bunch	spring onions
2 tablespoons	fresh basil leaves
	salt and black pepper
1 teaspoon	granulated sugar

Crumble Topping

110 g (4 oz)	self-raising flour
50 g (2 oz)	margarine
25 g (1 oz)	mixed chopped nuts &/or mixed seeds
1 tablespoon	fresh basil leaves

Method

Wash and thinly slice the tomatoes and spring onions. Lightly grease a 1 litre (2 pint) casserole dish and layer with the sliced tomatoes, spring onions, roughly torn basil leaves, and seasonings.

Rub the margarine into the flour until the mixture resembles ground almonds. Add the nuts or seeds, and roughly torn basil leaves to the crumble mix.

Cover the tomato filling with the crumble topping evenly distributed.

Bake at Gas Mark 5 / 375°F / 190°C (170°C for fan oven) for 20 – 25 minutes, until golden brown and bubbly.

First Aid

Symptom: *Fresh tomatoes are too expensive.*

Diagnosis: *Outside the home-grown season of July to September, tomatoes will be more expensive.*

Antidote: *Use tinned tomatoes and thicken slightly with cornflour. The flavour will be better than insipid air-freighted imports.*

Stuffed Mushrooms £

Try to obtain even sized mushrooms, so there is no squabbling over who gets which one, when it comes to dishing them up. These make an impressive hot starter at a dinner party or as a main course for vegetarians.

Ingredients to serve 4 people

4 large flat	mushrooms
1 dessertspoon	vegetable oil
	salt and pepper to taste
225 g (8 oz)	leeks
50 g (2 oz)	fresh green beans (*or* frozen peas)
110 g (4 oz)	cream cheese with herbs and garlic
75 g (3 oz)	ready-made puff pastry
	egg wash

Method

Wipe the mushrooms clean with damp kitchen paper. Do not wash in water, because they will become waterlogged like a sponge. Rub the mushrooms with vegetable oil, and season with salt and pepper.

Wash the leeks and green beans, and cut them into small dice. Gently fry the prepared leeks and beans (or peas) in a little vegetable oil until just soft. Allow the vegetables to cool before mixing with the cream cheese, and seasoning the stuffing to taste. Distribute the stuffing evenly among the upturned mushrooms.

Cut the pastry into four equal pieces, and roll each piece into a circle so it will cover one mushroom. Use a lattice cutter, or make diagonal 0.5 cm (¼") cuts in the pastry, to form a lattice effect. Brush with egg wash, and place the pastry on each mushroom, egg washed side down. Brush the top of the pastry with egg wash and leave in the refrigerator until required.

Bake at Gas Mark 5 / 375°F / 190°C (170°C for fan oven) for 15 – 20 minutes, until golden brown.

First Aid

Symptom: *Mushrooms appeared too soft when cooked.*

Diagnosis: *Filling was not retained within the mushrooms.*

Remedy: *Choose large firm-walled mushrooms, rather than flatter loose-gilled varieties.*

Crispy Roast Parsnips

The coating of breadcrumbs intensifies the crunchiness of roast parsnips. I sometimes add grated Parmesan cheese to the breadcrumbs, or use dried polenta as a coating for extra flavour and texture.

Ingredients to serve 6 people

700 g (1½ lb)	parsnips
75 g (3 oz)	breadcrumbs
3 tablespoons	vegetable oil

Method

Wash and peel the parsnips, and cut them into even sized wedges. Place in a saucepan, barely cover with water, and boil for 5 minutes.

Drain well, and whilst still hot, roll the parsnips in the breadcrumbs. Place them on a baking tray, and when cool, refrigerate until required.

Roast the parsnips in the vegetable oil in the oven at Gas Mark 6 / 400°F / 200°C (190°C for fan oven) for about 45 minutes until golden brown and crispy.

First Aid

Symptom: *Parsnips are not a favourite vegetable.*

Diagnosis: *Other root vegetables can be substituted.*

Antidote: *Try carrots, wedges of swede, celeriac, or turnips.*

Stir Fried Sprouts £

I can honestly say that I hated Brussels sprouts. Little balls of wind that taste like soggy pickled onions on a bad day.

But I have completely changed my mind since I've started stir frying them. I have no more sogginess or wind problems. Stir-fried sprouts; today is a good day!

Ingredients to serve 6 people

700 g (1½ lb)	sprouts
3 rashers	streaky bacon (optional)
1 tablespoon	vegetable oil

Method

Lightly wash the sprouts, and remove any outside leaves that are discoloured. Using a sharp knife, finely slice the sprouts as thinly as possible.

Cut the streaky bacon into short thin strips. Heat the vegetable oil in a large frying pan or wok and add the bacon.

Stir until the bacon starts to colour and cook, then add the sprouts and stir them quickly for about 3 – 5 minutes until the sprouts are cooked, which is just soft, and light green in colour.

First Aid

Symptom: *Sprouts appeared blackened and tasted burnt.*

Diagnosis: *Over-cooking is the problem.*

Remedy: *Lightly toss the sprouts in oil, keeping them moving all the time. They should slightly lighten colour, and appear just soft in texture.*

Sweet and Sour Red Cabbage

What you have to remember about red cabbage is that it doesn't like being cooked in water. It turns blue at the very thought. So if you want to keep its vibrant colour, cook it in an acid such as citrus juice, apple juice (which contains malic acid), or soft wine vinegar in preference to the harsher malt vinegar.

Ingredients to serve 6 people

2 tablespoons	vegetable oil
1	red onion – finely chopped §
1 clove	garlic – crushed (optional)
450 g (16 oz)	red cabbage – finely shredded
1	eating apple – diced
110 g (4 oz)	fresh cranberries
50 g (2 oz)	granulated sugar
50 ml (2 fl oz)	red wine vinegar
50 ml (2 fl oz)	orange juice *or* cranberry juice
½ teaspoon	ground cinnamon
1 teaspoon	cornflour
	salt and pepper to taste

Method

Heat the oil in a large saucepan. Add the finely chopped red onion and crushed garlic, and fry for 2 – 3 minutes, until soft but not brown.

Add the finely shredded red cabbage, diced eating apple, and the remaining ingredients, except for the cornflour, salt and pepper.

Cover the pan with a lid and gently braise on the stove for 20 – 25 minutes.

or

Transfer the ingredients to a casserole dish, cover with a lid, and braise in the middle shelf of the oven at Gas Mark 4 / 350°F / 180°C (160°C for fan oven) for about 45 minutes. Braise until the cabbage is tender.

Mix the cornflour with cold water to form a thin paste, and add to the braised vegetables. Bring to the boil until the juices thicken; adjust seasoning to taste.

First Aid

Symptom: *Fresh cranberries are not available anywhere.*

Diagnosis: *Seasonal cranberries add tartness as well as vibrant colour.*

Antidote: *Substitute dried or frozen cranberries, or another tart and colourful fresh, dried, frozen, or canned fruit such as Morello cherries.*

Pumpkin and Leek Bake

The idea of roasting vegetables, then topping them with breadcrumbs and grated cheese, or seeds and nuts, is a simple one, but very effective.

Ingredients to serve 4 to 6 people

900 g (2 lb)	pumpkin
2	leeks
2	carrots
1	onion
2 tablespoons	olive oil
½ teaspoon	ground nutmeg
	salt and pepper to taste
110 g (4 oz)	breadcrumbs
25 g (1 oz)	grated cheese

Method

Peel and seed the pumpkin, and cut into about 1 cm (½") cubes. Slit the leeks lengthways, trim and wash, then cut into 5 cm (2") lengths. Peel the carrots and onion, and cut into about 1 cm (½") cubes.

Place the vegetables on a roasting tray, drizzle over with the olive oil, and sprinkle with ground nutmeg.

Roast in a preheated oven at Gas Mark 5 / 375°F / 190°C (170°C for fan oven) for 30 to 40 minutes until tender.

Place the roasted vegetables in a serving dish and sprinkle with salt and pepper. Cover with breadcrumbs and grated cheese.

Bake at Gas Mark 4 / 350°F / 180°C (160°C for fan oven) for about 20 minutes, until golden brown.

First Aid

Symptom: *Oven is not available, so vegetables cannot be baked.*

Diagnosis: *Need to consider different methods of cooking.*

Antidote: *Steam or pan-fry the vegetables until they are soft. To crisp the topping, grill instead of baking.*

Underground Hot-Pot £

There is something subterranean about this little number. A dish for a cold winter's evening, served with horseradish dumplings or your favourite flavoured mashed potatoes.

Ingredients to serve 4 people

3 tablespoons	vegetable oil
225 g (8 oz)	onions – sliced
2 cloves	garlic – crushed (optional)
1 dessertspoon	plain flour
1 dessertspoon	paprika pepper
1 pinch	cayenne pepper
400 g (15 oz) tin	chopped tomatoes
2 teaspoons	tomato purée
275 ml (10 fl oz)	hot water
225 g (8 oz)	carrots
225 g (8 oz)	parsnips
225 g (8 oz)	Swede
2 sticks	celery
1	bunch mixed herbs *or* bouquet garni §
	salt and pepper to taste

Method

Heat the oil in a large flameproof casserole dish. Add the sliced onions and crushed garlic, and fry until soft but not brown.

Stir in the flour, the paprika pepper, and the cayenne pepper. When the onions and garlic are well coated with the mixture, stir in the chopped tomatoes, tomato purée, and hot water. Bring the sauce up to the boil, stirring constantly.

Cut the carrots, parsnips, Swede, and celery into large even sized chunks and add to the casserole dish with the herbs or bouquet garni, and salt and pepper.

Cover with a lid and braise in a preheated oven at Gas Mark 4 / 350°F / 180°C (160°C for fan oven) for 30 – 45 minutes until the vegetables are soft. Test them by piercing the vegetables with the tip of a knife.

Remove the bunch of herbs or bouquet garni before serving.

First Aid

Symptom: *Curried hot-pot would be nice, but I don't know how to make it.*

Diagnosis: *Curry has a wider range of spices and more flavour.*

Antidote: *Substitute curry paste for the paprika pepper, mustard seeds for the cayenne pepper, and coconut milk for the tinned chopped tomatoes.*

Fish and Shellfish

One of my favourite aromas is of fish and chips being cooked. Immediately I have whiffed that fragrant essence, I become hungry. When I was growing up in Sheffield, there was a take away 'Fish and Chip Shop' on every street corner, open twice a day, sometimes six days a week.

With popular fish, such as cod and haddock becoming over-fished, fish suppliers will have to search further afield or deeper down, in order to satisfy demand, but without disaffecting quality and taste.

See the chapter '**Are You Picking the Best Ingredients?**' for my general tips to '**Find the Freshest Fruits of the Sea**'.

Deep Fried Fish

Here is a quick and easy recipe for deep fried fish, which should be cooked in clean fresh oil, using either sun-flower, rape-seed, ground-nut, or lard. Try not to use the oil more than a couple of times (strained between use) as high heat breaks down the molecules in the oil, causing it to deteriorate. Over-heating over a long period will accelerate this condition.

Ingredients to serve 1 person

~200 g (~7 oz)	fillet of cod *or* haddock
25 g (1 oz)	seasoned flour
50 g (2 oz)	self-raising flour
	salt and pepper
4 tablespoons	cold water

Method

Dry the fish thoroughly using kitchen paper then coat in seasoned flour.

Using a deep fat fryer §, heat the oil to 345°F / 175°C. In a bowl, mix the self-raising flour and seasonings with the water, to form a creamy batter, just before frying.

Dip the fish in the batter until well coated. Fry the battered fish in the hot fat for about 5 – 8 minutes, depending on the thickness of the fillet, until golden brown and floating on top of the oil. Remove and drain on crumpled kitchen paper. Serve with lemon wedges, tartare sauce, tomato ketchup, and malt vinegar.

First Aid

See the '**Deep Fat Frying**' section on page 86.

Symptom: *Deep fried fish tasted greasy.*

Diagnosis: *Temperature of frying oil too low, possibly due to overloading the fryer.*

Remedy: *Fry fish at about 175°C. Add fish in small batches and keep them warm uncovered in a hot oven.*

Marinated Herrings £

Not much cooking is involved in this dish, except for boiling the cider vinegar. Make sure that the herrings, or any fish you wish to marinate, are completely covered with the boiled vinegar, and use the freshest of fish.

You will need a large shallow ovenproof non-metal dish.

Ingredients to serve 4 starters or 2 main courses

2 large	herrings
1	Spanish onion
1	eating apple
275 ml (10 fl oz)	cider vinegar

Method

Place the descaled, filleted, and washed herrings, flesh side uppermost, in a shallow, ovenproof dish. The dish should **not** be metal, and should be just large enough to accommodate the rest of the ingredients.

Thinly slice the onion and apple, and place evenly over the filleted herrings. Bring the cider vinegar to a rolling boil and immediately pour over the herring, onion, and apple, making sure the ingredients are well covered.

Leave to cool completely, then cover the dish in cling film, and transfer it to the refrigerator. Leave to marinate for at least two hours in the fridge. Turn the fish at least once; making sure that it is completely covered in the marinade.

After marinating, serve the herrings with fresh crunchy bread. For a main course, serve them with salad and new potatoes. This dish will keep in the refrigerator for up to three days, provided it remains covered in cling film.

First Aid

See the marinating '**First Aid**' on page 152.

Symptom: *Herrings are not available.*

Diagnosis: *Erratic fish supplies are caused by weather conditions, seasonal availability, supply and demand.*

Antidote: *Use any other oily fish such as salmon, sprats, sardines, or mackerel, but ensure they are the freshest possible.*

Dressed Crab

Usually, when you purchase freshly cooked crabs, they are already dressed, but if you should be able to buy a live crab, this is what you do. The flavour of fresh crab is up there with lobster. It's a very distinctive taste.

Ingredients to dress 1 medium crab

~1 kg (~2¼ lb)	fresh crab *or* cooked crab
	salt and pepper to taste
	lemon juice
	white breadcrumbs
	mayonnaise
1	hard boiled egg
	chopped parsley §

Method

Cook Fresh Crab

Place a 1 kg (2¼ lb) medium crab in a saucepan covered with cold water, and bring to the boil. When boiling allow 10 minutes per ½ kg (1 lb) of crab. When cooked, remove the crab from the water, and leave to cool completely. Do not over-cook, otherwise the meat will be tough.

Prepare Cooked Crab

Place the crab on its back, with its legs in the air, and the head furthest away from you. Start by removing the legs nearest to you, by holding each individual leg, and twisting it in towards the body. Proceed until all the legs, including both large claws, have been removed.

Place your hands on the shell, either side of the dislocated leg sockets, and put your thumbs under the tail flap. Using your thumbs, push the soft under-body upwards, until the body breaks away from the shell. This will come away in one piece.

Turn the crab round so that its head is facing you. With your thumbs, press down on the mouthpiece (situated just below the eyes) and push forwards, so that the mouth and stomach come away in one piece. Discard this.

Remove Brown Meat

Using a spoon, remove the soft brown meat inside the main shell, and place it in a basin, leaving the shell case clean.

Using the handle of a knife, tap sharply along the "false line" which runs around the shell. This looks like a brown line painted about 1 cm (½") from the edge of the shell. The surplus shell should come away neatly, leaving the cavity more open to accommodate the dressed crabmeat later.

Scrub the outside of the shell, dry with kitchen paper, and rub over with a little cooking oil.

Remove White Meat

From the soft under-body remove the "dead men's fingers" which appear as grey wet fingers encasing one side of the under-body. Discard these "dead men's fingers" because they are inedible.

Cut the body in half, and using a skewer, scoop out the white meat from the leg sockets, and place in a second basin.

Remove the meat from the claws, by twisting off the first joint, and scooping out the meat. Tap sharply around the broadest part of the claw, with the back of a knife, and break open. Remove the white meat from both sides of the cartilage, and place in the second basin. Proceed with the remaining legs, until you have removed all the white meat.

The brown and white meat is now ready to use as required.

Dress Prepared Crab

Cream the brown meat, adding salt, pepper, and lemon juice to taste. Add sufficient fine white breadcrumbs to stiffen the brown crabmeat. Place the brown meat at each side of the cleaned shell, and level the mixture with a fork.

Flake the white meat, adding salt, pepper, and a little mayonnaise to moisten. Place the white meat in the centre of the shell, between the brown meat, and level with a fork.

Hard boil an egg, and remove the shell. Chop the egg white finely, and sieve the yolk. Place a fine line of chopped egg white along both edges of the brown meat where it meets the white meat. Next to the egg white, place a fine line of sieved yolk along both edges of the white meat.

Finally, place a line of chopped parsley next to both lines of egg yolk.

First Aid

Symptom: *Crab has too much brown meat for my liking.*

Diagnosis: *Female crabs have smaller claws than male crabs, and therefore less white meat and more brown meat.*

Remedy: *Buy male crabs, which are easily identified by their larger claws, and narrower tail flaps.*

Fish Satés with Spicy Peanut Sauce

Firm fleshed fish is what you want when barbecuing on bamboo skewers. The flesh needs to be able to stand up to fierce heat without falling apart.

You need eight 15 cm (6") bamboo skewers soaked in cold water for about 1 hour.

Ingredients to serve 4 people

450 g (1 lb)	monkfish fillet, swordfish, turbot, *or* John Dory

Marinade

3 large cloves	garlic
1 cm (½") stick	fresh ginger
½ teaspoon	turmeric powder
3 tablespoons	Thai fish sauce *or* light soy sauce *or* anchovy essence
1 tablespoon	lime juice
1 teaspoon	muscovado sugar
½ teaspoon	cayenne pepper
2 tablespoons	vegetable oil

Spicy Peanut Sauce

2 tablespoon	sunflower oil
2	shallots
or 25 g (1 oz)	onion
2 cloves	garlic
1	red finger chilli
½ teaspoon	cayenne pepper
40 g (1½ oz)	roasted peanuts
40 g (1½ oz)	crunchy peanut butter
1 tablespoon	lime juice
1 tablespoon	muscovado sugar
½ teaspoon	salt
175 ml (6 fl oz)	coconut milk

Method

Marinate Fish

If using swordfish, turbot, or John Dory cut the fish into 2 cm (¾") pieces. Finely chop the garlic and fresh ginger. Freshly squeeze the lime juice. Place the pieces of fish in a glass bowl with all the marinade ingredients. Mix well together. Leave to marinate for 20 minutes.

Prepare Spicy Peanut Sauce

Heat the sunflower oil in a frying pan or wok. Finely chop the shallots or onion, and crush the garlic. De-seed and chop the chilli. Add the prepared vegetables and cayenne pepper to the pan, and fry them for about 5 – 7 minutes until soft and lightly golden in colour.

Place the roasted peanuts in food processor and whiz until finely chopped, or chop by hand. Freshly squeeze the lime juice. Stir the chopped peanuts into the pan of fried mixture, and add the remaining sauce ingredients.

Simmer gently for about 5 minutes until thickened slightly. Keep warm until required.

Barbecue Fish Satés

Thread the fish pieces onto the soaked bamboo skewers. Place the skewered fish onto the preheated barbecue §, and barbecue them for about 8 – 10 minutes, turning them over halfway through cooking. Serve with the spicy peanut sauce.

First Aid

See the marinating '**First Aid**' on page 152.

Symptom:	*Shellfish is preferred to fish.*
Diagnosis:	*Various raw shellfish can be substituted for raw fish.*
Antidote:	*Use raw shell-on or peeled prawns, or raw scallops wrapped in bacon.*

Salmon Fishcakes

These are fishcakes that are 100% fish. Now there's a novelty! Usually fishcakes are padded out with mashed potatoes or a thick white sauce. In Yorkshire, fishcakes consist of a thin slice of raw fish sandwiched between two thick slices of raw potato. The whole lot is dipped in batter before being deep fried.

Ingredients to serve 4 people

400 g (1 lb)	salmon fillets – boneless and skinless
1 tablespoon	egg white
1 pinch	salt and pepper to taste

Options

Choose **one** of the following:

1 dessertspoon	freshly chopped herbs § – parsley *or* dill
or 1 teaspoon	chopped gherkins *or* capers
or ½ teaspoon	dried chilli flakes

Method

Place the salmon in the food processor and whiz until the salmon is in small pieces but still has some texture. Add the egg white and seasonings, plus one of the options if desired, and whiz until combined.

Remove the mixture from the machine and divide into 4 equal portions. Mould each portion into a flattened disc and chill for at least 1 hour.

Shallow fry in hot fat until slightly brown on both sides.

First Aid

Symptom: *Food processor is not available.*

Diagnosis: *Food processor blends and chops the fish most efficiently.*

Antidote: *Chop the fish finely by hand, and combine with the other ingredients in a mixing bowl.*

Salmon Pizza

This is a pizza where the base is salmon instead of dough, and the topping is whatever flavour you like. If you have a problem getting children to eat fish, try this tasty alternative to the traditional bread-based variety.

Ingredients to serve 1 person

75 g (3 oz)	salmon
1	sliced tomato
1	sliced mushroom
50 g (2 oz)	grated cheese

Method

Place the piece of salmon in the freezer for half an hour to just firm up. Take a sharp knife and cut across the salmon, like slicing bread, into 0.5 cm (¼") thin slices. Chill until required.

Arrange the salmon slices to form a circle on a greased baking sheet, making sure there are no gaps. Top with sliced tomatoes and mushrooms, and some grated cheese, or choose your own topping.

Bake at Gas Mark 5 / 375°F / 190°C (170°C for fan oven) for 10 – 15 minutes, until the cheese is bubbly and golden brown.

First Aid

Symptom: *Oven is not available for baking pizza.*

Diagnosis: *An oven is not essential, so consider alternatives.*

Antidote: *Place the assembled pizza under the grill, or assemble the pizza on a microwave safe shallow dish or plate and use a microwave oven.*

Quick Fried Salmon

This is the quickest way to fry salmon, and is so economical into the bargain. Fresh salmon is as cheap as chips these days, but that's because it's farmed. When I was a lass, salmon was expensive and wild!

Ingredients to serve 1 person

75 g (3 oz)	salmon

Method

Place the piece of salmon in the freezer for half an hour to just firm up. Take a sharp knife and cut across the salmon, like slicing bread, into 0.5 cm (¼") thin slices. Chill until required.

Shallow fry the salmon slices in hot fat for about 2 minutes until just changing colour. Turn over and similarly fry the other side, for another 2 minutes.

Serve with a green salad and your favourite mayonnaise.

First Aid

Symptom: *Salmon disintegrates when lifted out of the frying pan.*

Diagnosis: *Probably over-cooked.*

Remedy: *Fry for a little less time, watch the flesh change colour, immediately turn over, watch other side change colour, and remove quickly.*

Smoked Haddock or Mackerel and Potato Pasties £

A small amount of fish stretches a long way here, but with bags of flavour. These are a real treat served with a gutsy salsa or mushy peas spiked with mint.

Ingredients to serve 4 people

450 g (16 oz)	ready-made shortcrust *or* puff pastry
225 g (8 oz)	peeled weight potatoes
225 g (8 oz)	naturally smoked haddock *or* cooked smoked mackerel
2	spring onions
1 tablespoon	chopped parsley *or* chive §
	salt and pepper to taste
	egg to glaze

Method

Divide the pastry into four even sized portions, and roll out each into a circle.

Cut the peeled potatoes into 1 cm (½") dice, flake the fish, and chop the onions and herbs. Mix these ingredients together and season.

Share the fish mixture evenly between each pastry circle. Brush the rim of each pastry circle with beaten egg. Draw them up to enclose the filling. Pinch the pastry edges together to prevent the filling from escaping. Brush the outside of the pastry with the beaten egg wash to glaze.

Bake at Gas Mark 6 / 400°F / 200°C (180°C for fan oven) on the middle shelf of the oven for 25 – 30 minutes until golden brown.

First Aid

Symptom: *Filling bursts from the pasty when baked.*

Diagnosis: *Either too much filling, or pastry edges not well sealed.*

Remedy: *Reduce the amount of filling, and make sure the pastry edges are well coated with egg wash and firmly pinched together.*

Stuffed Herrings £

Any oily fish can be substituted for the humble herring. I sometimes fillet the herrings before stuffing them, as my better half doesn't like fiddling with bones.

Ingredients to serve main course for 4 people

4 large	herrings

Stuffing

1 small	onion
or 2	shallots
225 g (8 oz)	cooking apple
1 tablespoon	vegetable oil
1 tablespoon	chopped chives §
1 dessertspoon	horseradish sauce
75 g (3 oz)	fresh breadcrumbs
	salt and pepper to taste

Method

Remove the scales, gut, and wash the herrings. Finely chop the onion or shallots. Peel, core, and grate the cooking apple.

Prepare the stuffing by gently frying the onion or shallots, and the apple, until they are soft, and then add the rest of the ingredients until well combined.

Place the washed herrings in a lightly greased, shallow, ovenproof dish. Using a dessertspoon, place the stuffing into the cavity created by the removal of the guts. Ensure that the stuffing is evenly distributed between the herrings. Place four tablespoons of cold water into the dish, before covering the dish with baking foil.

Bake at Gas Mark 4 / 350°F / 180°C (160°C for fan oven) for 20 – 25 minutes on the middle shelf, until the eyes are opaque, and the skin peels away easily.

First Aid

Symptom: *Herrings and other oily fish give me indigestion.*

Antidote: *Use small whiting, which are white fish, instead.*

Fish on a Dish

This is a visually attractive and very tasty dish, using whatever fish or seafood you can find at its freshest. The fish is laid on ovenproof saucers, eared dishes, or large ramekins, with pick and mix flavourings, then topped with cheese pastry, before being baked. After baking, the dish is turned out upside down onto the serving plate, so it looks stunning. Here, I am using fresh tiger prawns, but I've used all manner of fish combinations in the past.

You will need four lightly oiled individual ovenproof dishes or plates.

Ingredients to serve 4 people

20	fresh tiger prawns – peeled
1 tablespoon	salted capers – thoroughly rinsed
1	preserved lemon § – thinly sliced
110 g (4 oz)	onion – sliced
1 tablespoon	olive oil
	salt and pepper to taste

Pastry Topping

225 g (8 oz)	self-raising flour – sieved
110 g (4 oz)	butter
75 g (3 oz)	Parmesan cheese – grated
4 tablespoons	cold water

Method

First, prepare the pastry topping. Sieve the flour and rub in the butter. Grate and stir in the cheese. Add the water and form into a pastry dough. Chill for half an hour.

Meanwhile, peel the prawns, rinse the capers thoroughly, and thinly slice the lemon and onion. Fry the sliced onion in the olive oil until soft but not coloured. Leave to cool, and season with salt and pepper.

Lightly oil four dishes. Lay five peeled prawns on one dish, like the spokes of a wheel, with the tails toward the centre. Add a quarter of the rinsed capers, lemon slices, and fried onion. Repeat the process with the other three dishes and the rest of the ingredients.

Retrieve the chilled pastry and divide into four even pieces. Roll out each piece into a circle so that it just covers and encloses the ingredients on each dish.

Bake at Gas Mark 6 / 400°F / 200°C (180°C for fan oven) for 15 – 20 minutes, until golden brown. Turn out the dishes upside down on the serving plates, so that the pastry is at the bottom with the prawns on top. Enjoy with a green salad or stuffed tomatoes.

First Aid

Symptom: *Preserved lemons have not been prepared in advance.*

Diagnosis: *Preserved lemons are a tasty addition to many dishes.*

Antidote: *Substitute another vegetable such as mushrooms or asparagus.*

Remedy: *Preserve lemons as described in preceding chapter.*

Poultry, Game, and Meat

See the earlier chapter '**Are You Picking the Best Ingredients?**' for general advice on buying poultry, game, and meat. See page 60 for guidance on cooking '**Succulent Roast Meat**'.

On a food safety note, after handling raw poultry, immediately wash your hands and any equipment involved, before moving on to another task.

Japanese Chicken £

The marinade for this dish can be used with any meat, fish, or vegetable to give pungency. If that is all you want, it is a quick in and out dunking job. However, if it is tenderness you are after, meat needs to be left dunked overnight for the marinade to do its work. Fish and vegetables do not need this because they do not have muscular fibres.

You will need an ovenproof, but non-metallic dish, so that it won't taint the marinade.

Ingredients to serve 4 people
8 pieces	chicken – mixture of drumsticks and thighs

Marinade
25 ml (1 fl oz)	lemon juice
50 ml (2 fl oz)	Japanese sake (rice wine)
50 ml (2 fl oz)	Japanese soy sauce
110 g (4 oz)	onion – finely chopped §
2 cloves	garlic – crushed
2 tablespoons	pickled ginger – finely chopped §
2 teaspoons	honey

Method

Place all the marinade ingredients, in an ovenproof and non-metallic dish, and thoroughly mix them together.

Coat the chicken pieces all over with the marinade. Cover and leave to marinate for at least 1 hour, but preferably overnight, in the refrigerator. Turn the chicken occasionally to make sure the meat is well coated.

Remove the chicken marinade from the fridge 1 hour before cooking, to allow it to return to room temperature. Decant the marinade into a saucepan.

Bake the chicken pieces uncovered in the dish at Gas Mark 4 / 350°F / 180°C (160°C for fan oven) for 45 minutes. Baste the chicken occasionally with the marinade.

To make a delicious sauce, place all the remaining marinade in the saucepan along with 150 ml (5 fl oz) of dry ginger ale, and bring to the boil.

Mix a couple of teaspoons of cornflour with a little cold water, and stir until smooth. Add to the hot marinade, and mix well. Taste and adjust the seasoning.

First Aid

See the marinating '**First Aid**' on page 152.

Symptom: *Japanese sake or rice wine cannot be found in the shops.*

Diagnosis: *These should be found in larger supermarkets or oriental food stores.*

Remedy: *If you still cannot find any sake, substitute dry sherry.*

Symptom: *Pickled ginger cannot be found in the shops.*

Diagnosis: *This bright pink, vacuum-packed ginger should be in large supermarkets or oriental food stores.*

Remedy: *If you still cannot find any pickled ginger, substitute fresh ginger, and store any remaining sliced fresh ginger in white wine vinegar in a sterilised jar, to use at a later date.*

Yoghurt Spiced Chicken £

The beauty of this dish is that the ingredients are readily available. There is no long list of exotic fresh and dried spices, that you use once and then confine to the back of the cupboard; only to re-emerge, past their use-by date and diminished in flavour and aroma.

You will need a non-metallic dish, so that it won't taint the marinade.

Ingredients to serve 4 people

8 pieces	chicken – mixture of drumsticks and thighs
	juice of a lime

Marinade

110 g (4 oz)	onion – roughly chopped
2 cloves	garlic – crushed
5 cm (2") length	fresh ginger – peeled and finely chopped §
1 tablespoon	red *or* green Thai curry paste
125 ml (5 fl oz)	yoghurt

Method

With the point of a knife, slit the meatiest parts of each chicken piece, and immediately coat in the lime juice.

Place the marinade ingredients in a food processor and whiz until you get a thick, smooth paste. Turn the mixture out into a non-metallic dish.

Coat the chicken pieces all over with the marinade. Then cover and leave to marinate for at least 2 hours, but preferably overnight, in the refrigerator. Turn the chicken occasionally to make sure the meat is well coated.

Remove the chicken marinade from the fridge 1 hour before cooking, to allow it to return to room temperature.

Remove from the marinade, and place the coated chicken pieces uncovered on a baking tray at the top of the oven.

Bake at Gas Mark 8 / 450°F / 230°C (210°C for fan oven) for 25 – 30 minutes until golden brown.

First Aid

See the marinating '**First Aid**' on page 152.

Symptom: *Thai curry paste is not as potent after it has been stored for a while.*

Diagnosis: *Thai curry paste is sold in 90 g (3.5 oz) jars at large supermarkets and can easily deteriorate, because you only need small amounts for each dish.*

Remedy: *Once opened, cover the contents with a thin film of vegetable oil, to extend its shelf life, so you can enjoy it for longer.*

Chicken Supreme with Rocket Pesto

Chicken breast meat is the easiest of meat to cook, and you can purchase it in a variety of forms, either with or without skin, or sliced ready for stir frying, or with the wing bone still attached. It is ideal for the nervous cook because the meat is already portioned, it needs very little further preparation before cooking, and the juices run clear when cooked.

Ingredients to serve 4 people

4 supremes	chicken (breast fillets with wing bone attached)

Rocket Pesto

75 g (3 oz)	quark §
25 g (1 oz)	Parmesan cheese – grated
1 clove	garlic – crushed
75 g (3 oz)	rocket leaves *or* watercress
25 g (1 oz)	pistachio nuts – shelled
½ level teaspoon	Maldon sea salt §

Method

Loosen the skin covering each chicken breast, so that it forms a pocket.

Place the pesto ingredients in a food processor and whiz until smooth. Divide the rocket pesto to stuff each chicken breast evenly. Gently reform the skin over the stuffing and chicken for each supreme. Lightly coat the skin in olive oil and place uncovered on a greased baking tray.

Bake at Gas Mark 6 / 400°F / 200°C (180°C for fan oven) for 25 – 30 minutes.

Leave to rest for 5 minutes before serving with new potatoes and roasted Mediterranean vegetables.

First Aid

Symptom: *Rocket or watercress is not available in the shops.*

Diagnosis: *Seasonal lack of supply.*

Antidote: *Substitute another flavoursome vegetable such as spinach or red pepper.*

Turkey Escalope with Sweetcorn and Pancetta

Turkey escalopes are a versatile alternative to chicken recipes. Using this basic technique, you can stuff the thin pieces of breast meat with any filling of your choice. For example you could use Mediterranean flavours such as sun-dried tomatoes, black olives and feta cheese, or a more traditional taste like cranberries, red onion, and walnuts.

Ingredients to serve 4 people

4 escalopes	turkey (breast fillets)
	salt and pepper
8 slices	pancetta *or* thinly sliced dry cured bacon §
12 spears	baby sweetcorn
1 tablespoon	olive oil
25 g (1 oz)	butter

Method

Place one turkey escalope between 2 sheets of cling film, and beat with a rolling pin to flatten slightly. Repeat with the remaining turkey escalopes.

Lightly season one escalope and place on top of two adjacent slices of pancetta. Arrange three sweetcorn spears across one end of the escalope. Roll up the escalope to enclose the sweetcorn with the pancetta wrapped round the outside of the roll. Repeat this process with the remaining turkey escalopes. Chill until required.

Pan fry the escalopes in olive oil and butter until evenly golden brown all over. Then bake on a baking tray at Gas Mark 5 / 375°F / 190°C (170°C for fan oven) for about 15 minutes.

First Aid

Symptom: *Pancetta and dry cured bacon are not available or too expensive.*

Diagnosis: *Pancetta and dry cured bacon is costly to produce.*

Remedy: *Substitute streaky bacon rashers with the rind removed. To make each rasher thinner, lay a rasher on a work surface, hold one end, and stroke the bacon with a knife, like buttering bread, while pulling the rasher taut. Repeat with each rasher.*

Guinea Fowl Stuffed with Garlic and Lemon

I often described guinea fowl to my restaurant customers as educated chicken, or chicken that had gone to college to taste right! It has a more pronounced flavour than chicken, but with a similar texture. So, go on, get educated, and be more refined like guinea fowl.

Ingredients to serve 4 to 6 people

~1.6 kg (~3.5 lb)	whole oven ready guinea fowl
	salt and pepper
1 unwaxed	lemon
6 cloves	garlic – unpeeled
50 g (2 oz)	butter – softened
1 small sprig	fresh bay leaves
3 whole bulbs	garlic
1 tablespoon	olive oil

Method

Remove any excess fat from the cavity of the guinea fowl and season inside. Using your index and middle fingers, loosen the skin away from the breast and legs, taking care not to break the skin.

Grate the lemon for its zest. Then halve and squeeze out the juice. Place the 6 unpeeled garlic cloves in a saucepan with water to just cover them, simmer for 6 minutes, and drain. Snip the root end of each clove and squeeze out the contents into a bowl. Add the softened butter, lemon zest, and half the lemon juice. Mix thoroughly.

Gently ease the flavoured butter under the skin of the guinea fowl breast and legs until they are evenly covered. Carefully press the loosened skin back into its original position.

Place the sprig of bay leaves and halved lemon skins in the guinea fowl cavity. Tie the legs together and place the guinea fowl on a trivet in a roasting tin §. Cut the garlic bulbs in half, coat with the olive oil, and lay them on the trivet with the fowl.

Roast at Gas Mark 5 / 375°F / 190°C (170°C for fan oven) as for a chicken § (20 minutes per lb + 20 minutes extra) until the thickest part of the guinea fowl leg produces clear juices when pierced with a skewer. Allow 10 – 25 minutes resting time before carving.

After roasting, add the other half of the lemon juice to the juices in the roasting tin to form a jus or gravy.

First Aid *– see also page 61*

Symptom:	*Butter is too laden with fat for weight watchers.*
Diagnosis:	*Butter has the best flavour, but is not essential.*
Antidote:	*Simply substitute quark §, which is a skimmed milk curd cheese.*

Venison Steak with Port Sauce

If you have never eaten venison, you've missed a treat. It is dense textured, high protein meat, which is low in fat, but with bags of flavour. Venison benefits from lightness of frying, otherwise, since it is so low in natural fat, it is easy to over-cook and become dry.

Ingredients to serve 4 people

Port Sauce

25 g (1 oz)	butter
1 small	onion – finely chopped §
1 clove	garlic – crushed
10 berries	juniper berries – crushed
1 teaspoon	thyme
10 g (½ oz)	plain flour
150 ml (5 fl oz)	port
150 ml (5 fl oz)	orange juice
1 teaspoon	dark brown sugar
1 tablespoon	red wine vinegar
	salt and pepper

Venison Steaks

175 g (6 oz) x 4	venison steaks
2 tablespoons	olive oil

Method

Port Sauce

Lightly fry the chopped onion and crushed garlic in the butter. When just soft, add the crushed juniper berries and thyme. Stir in the flour until completely absorbed. Add the port and orange juice, stirring constantly, and bring to the boil. Then, add the sugar, vinegar, and seasoning to taste. Simmer for 5 minutes.

Venison Steaks

Heat a dry frying pan until hot, but do not add any oil. Brush the venison steaks with the olive oil, and place in the dry pan. This technique reduces the amount of spattering when shallow frying. Fry for 3 – 4 minutes on each side depending on their thickness. To enjoy the steaks at their most succulent, they should still be a little pink in the middle.

Serve with braised red cabbage, mustard creamed potatoes, and the port sauce.

First Aid

Symptom: *Port sauce is not suitable for teetotallers.*

Diagnosis: *Port gives depth of flavour, but is not essential.*

Remedy: *Substitute cranberry, blackcurrant, or red grape juice.*

Roast Venison

This dish could not be simpler. Roasting the meat in a roasting bag § or oiled foil prevents it drying out excessively. Venison is one of those meats that should be served slightly pink, when it is meltingly tender. Over-cooking makes it tough, due to its lack of natural fat or marbling through the meat. All roast meat and poultry should be rested before carving, to allow the meat juices that bubble up to the surface during roasting to subside, and be absorbed back into the meat fibres.

Ingredients to serve 6 people

~1½ kg (~3 lb)	boneless haunch or saddle of venison
1 tablespoon	olive oil

Sauce

150 ml (5 fl oz)	sediment from the roast venison
1 tablespoon	redcurrant jelly *or* cranberry jelly
150 ml (5 fl oz)	full bodied red wine – cabernet *or* shiraz
2 teaspoons	cornflour
	salt and pepper to taste
75 ml (3 fl oz)	double cream or crème fraiche

Method

Heat a dry frying pan until very hot, but do not add any oil. Brush the surface of the venison with the oil and place in the hot pan. This technique reduces the amount of spattering when shallow frying.

Quickly seal the entire surface of the venison by turning in the pan. This should take about 5 minutes. The surface colour will change when sealed.

Place in a roasting bag § or wrap in oiled foil and roast at Gas Mark 5 / 375°F / 190°C (170°C for fan oven) for 15 minutes per lb, which you must calculate.

Remove the joint from the oven, drain off the sediment for the sauce, and leave the joint covered, to rest for 20 – 25 minutes before carving.

Sauce

Meanwhile, use the sediment from the roast venison to make a sauce. Dissolve the jelly in the sediment, add the wine, and bring to the boil.

Mix the cornflour with just enough cold water to form a thin creamy paste. Stir into the hot liquid, bring back to the boil, and season well.

Stir in the cream just before serving and carving the venison into slices.

First Aid – *see also page 61*

Symptom: *Dry frying to seal the venison creates too much mess.*

Diagnosis: *This is the best way to seal in flavour, but not essential.*

Antidote: *Can omit the dry frying process altogether, but will result in reduced flavour and colour.*

Venison and Cranberry Pie

This is the upper-crust version of a pork pie. The flavour is rich and meaty with a touch of tartness from the cranberries. If you don't like the use of fruit with meat, substitute caramelised onions in place of the cranberries.

You will need a 20 cm (8") flan ring that is greased.

Ingredients to serve 4 to 6 people

225 g (8 oz)	potato pastry §

Filling

225 g (8 oz)	pork *or* venison sausage-meat
110 g (4 oz)	onion – finely chopped §
1 tablespoon	redcurrant jelly *or* cranberry jelly
1 tablespoon	chopped parsley §
	salt and pepper
350 g (12 oz)	venison haunch steak
25 g (1 oz)	butter
225 g (8 oz)	cranberries
1	egg to glaze

Method

Prepare the potato pastry, and leave to become completely cold.

Prepare the filling by mixing the sausage-meat, chopped onion, jelly, parsley, and seasonings in a large bowl until thoroughly combined.

Heat a frying pan. Brush the venison steak with the butter and seal in the pan. Leave to cool, and season each side of the steak.

Divide the potato pastry into two portions, one twice the size of the other.

Using the larger portion, roll out into a circle to line a 20 cm (8") flan ring. Grease the flan ring and line with the pastry, making sure there are no gaps, and cut off any surplus pastry. Fill the centre of the pie with the sausage-meat filling, then the cranberries, and lastly the venison steak.

Roll out the remaining smaller portion of pastry into a circle to cover the pie. Wet the pastry before placing on the pie to form a pastry lid. Glaze with the beaten egg. Make a small hole in the middle of the pastry lid to allow the steam to escape.

Bake at Gas Mark 7 / 425°F / 220°C (200°C for fan oven) for 20 minutes, remove the metal flan ring, and return to the oven for 20 minutes, until golden brown.

Serve either hot or cold.

First Aid

Symptom: *Venison is unavailable or disliked.*

Diagnosis: *With most dishes you can replace like with like.*

Antidote: *Substitute any variety of meat, but it must be a tender cut from a similar part of the animal.*

Casseroles and Hot-Pots

See page 62 for general advice on '**Braised Casseroles**'. For all these recipes you will need an ovenproof casserole dish §.

Mediterranean Chicken £

This is one of these one-pot wonders, where the meat and vegetables are already married together. Just serve with garlic bread, buttered noodles, or creamy mashed potatoes.

Ingredients to serve 4 people

1½ kg (3 lb)	chicken – cut into joints
1 tablespoon	vegetable oil
225 g (8 oz)	onion – chopped §
2 cloves	garlic – crushed
1	red pepper
1	aubergine
1	courgette
400 g (15 oz) tin	chopped tomatoes
1 teaspoon	chopped basil in oil
50 g (2 oz)	black olives

Method

Cut the chicken into joints. Heat the oil in an ovenproof casserole dish, and brown the chicken pieces all over.

Meanwhile, chop the onion and crush the garlic. De-seed the red pepper, and cut the pepper, aubergine, and courgette into even sized pieces.

Temporarily, remove the chicken pieces from the casserole. Add the onion, garlic, pepper, and aubergine to the casserole and fry for 5 minutes. Then add the courgette and chopped tomatoes.

Return the chicken pieces to the casserole, cover with a lid, and braise in the oven at Gas Mark 5 / 375°F / 190°C (170°C for fan oven) for about 1 hour.

Stir in the basil oil and black olives, return to the oven for half an hour. Adjust taste and consistency before serving.

First Aid – *see also page 62*

Symptom: *Fried chicken joints are too fattening.*

Diagnosis: *Weight watchers prefer a reduced calorie version of this dish.*

Antidote: *Remove all the skin and fat from the chicken pieces, and without any frying, place all the ingredients in the casserole dish straight into the oven.*

Cowboy Hot-Pot

This is loosely based on the traditional French cassoulet, which originates in the Languedoc region, but with smoky, spicy flavours.

Ingredients to serve 4 people

225 g (8 oz)	dried haricot beans
1 kg (2 lb)	boned and rolled shoulder of pork with skin on
1 tablespoon	olive oil
225 g (8 oz)	onion – chopped §
2 cloves	garlic – crushed
2 sticks	celery – sliced
175 g (6 oz)	spicy sausage: chorizo *or* black pudding *or* salami
1 teaspoon	dry mustard powder
2 tablespoons	black treacle
2 tablespoons	red wine vinegar
2 tablespoons	dark muscovado sugar
2 tablespoons	tomato purée

Method

Soak the haricot beans overnight in cold water. Rinse twice in clean water, and leave to drain.

Seal the shoulder of pork in the hot oil in an ovenproof casserole dish. Meanwhile, chop the onion, crush the garlic, and slice the celery.

Temporarily, remove the pork from the casserole. Add the onion, garlic, and celery to the casserole, and soften the vegetables without browning. Slice the sausage of your choice and add to the casserole with the rest of the ingredients. Stir thoroughly and add sufficient water just to cover the haricot beans.

Sit the pork on top of the haricot beans, cover with a lid, and braise in the oven at Gas Mark 4 / 350°F / 180°C (160°C for fan oven) for about 4 hours. Check after about 3 hours that the haricot beans are not drying out, and add more water if required.

Remove the casserole to allow the pork to rest for about 15 minutes before slicing and serving the pork on top of the beans, vegetables, and sausage.

First Aid – *see also page 62*

Symptom:	*Dried haricot beans were not soaked overnight beforehand.*
Diagnosis:	*Dried peas and beans must be soaked to hydrate them, so they become soft and edible.*
Antidote:	*Put the dried pulses in a large saucepan and completely cover with water. Bring to the boil, and boil for 10 minutes covered with a lid. Switch off the heat and leave the pulses to soak in the hot water for about two hours to hydrate. Rinse twice in clean water, and leave to drain before use.*

Lamb with Yoghurt and Mint

A fresh, clean-tasting lamb dish, which utilises the first of the garden mint along-side English lamb in the late Spring.

Ingredients to serve 4 people

700 g (1½ lb)	neck fillet *or* shoulder of lamb

Marinade

1 tablespoon	olive oil
2 tablespoons	whole grain mustard
2 tablespoons	dry cider

Casserole

225 g (8 oz)	onion – chopped §
2 cloves	garlic – crushed
1 tablespoon	vegetable oil
2 tablespoons	plain flour
570 ml (1 pt)	dry cider
1	bouquet garni §
16 leaves	fresh mint
1 tablespoon	mint sauce
150 ml (5 fl oz)	plain yoghurt
1 level teaspoon	cornflour

Method

Trim all excess fat from the lamb, and cut into even sized chunks. In a large glass or earthenware container, mix the three marinade ingredients, add the chunks of lamb, and leave to marinate for at least 8 hours, but preferably overnight.

Chop the onion, crush the garlic, and fry in the vegetable oil until soft. Add the marinated lamb chunks, and seal them thoroughly. Add any remaining marinade, and stir in the plain flour until smooth.

Add the dry cider and the bouquet garni, cover with a lid, and braise in the oven at Gas Mark 4 / 350°F / 180°C (160°C for fan oven) for about 2 hours.

Once tender, remove the bouquet garni, and stir in the fresh mint leaves, the mint sauce, and the yoghurt already mixed with the cornflour. Adjust the taste and consistency before serving.

First Aid

See page 62 and the marinating '**First Aid**' section on page 152.

Symptom: *Lamb has not been marinated in advance.*

Diagnosis: *Marinating softens the texture and adds flavour.*

Antidote: *Marinate the lamb while preparing the other ingredients, even if only for 10 minutes, and braise the casserole a little longer than usual.*

Lancashire Legend or Hot-Pot

Fancy – a Yorkshire woman promoting a Lancashire dish. Quick – phone a doctor! This was the first fast-food dish, which the Lancastrians took to the races wrapped in a blanket. How stingy can you get? If Yorkshire folk had thought of it though, I'd have to say it was thrifty. Even I have to admit it is a bit of a legend, or as one diner in our restaurant once said "a Lancashire Leg End"!

Ingredients to serve 4 people

1 kg (2 lb)	best end &/or middle neck of lamb
or 800 g (1¾ lb)	boned shoulder of lamb
3 tablespoons	vegetable oil
225 g (8 oz)	roughly chopped onion
1 tablespoon	plain flour
570 ml (1 pt)	hot water
1 tablespoon	Worcestershire sauce
1 tablespoon	mint sauce
	salt and pepper to taste
3	bay leaves
1 kg (2 lb)	peeled potatoes

Method

Dice the lamb. In a large frying pan of hot vegetable oil, seal the diced lamb until brown all over. Transfer the drained meat to an ovenproof casserole dish.

Fry the roughly chopped onions in the same frying pan until golden in colour. Add the plain flour, stirring until all the fat has been absorbed. Gradually add the hot water, stirring constantly. Add the Worcestershire sauce, mint sauce, and salt and pepper to taste.

Pour the liquid over the lamb, and place the bay leaves amongst the meat. Cut the potatoes into 1 cm (½") slices, and arrange on top of the diced lamb in an even overlapping fashion.

Cover the casserole dish with a lid, and braise on the middle shelf of the oven at Gas Mark 3 / 325°F / 170°C (150°C for fan oven) for 1¼ – 1½ hours.

Remove the lid from the dish, and braise for a further 30 – 45 minutes, until the meat is tender and the potatoes are browned and crispy at the edges. Move the dish to the top of the oven, or increase the heat for the last 15 minutes.

First Aid – *see also page 62*

Symptom: *Meat is still chewy when cooked for the recommended time.*

Diagnosis: *Recommended cooking time is only a guide, and depends on the cut, age, and storage of the meat.*

Antidote: *Put the dish back in the oven for another half an hour at the same temperature before testing again.*

Beef in Stout with Horseradish Dumplings

If you are a red meat eater, get your chops round this substantial dish. The dumplings have white breadcrumbs added, instead of the traditional all flour variety, to give a lighter touch.

Ingredients to serve 4 people

700 g (1½ lb)	braising beef
225 g (8 oz)	thinly sliced onion
3 tablespoons	vegetable oil
1 tablespoon	seasoned plain flour
2 sticks	celery
2 teaspoons	paprika
1 tablespoon	black treacle
440 ml (16 fl oz) can	stout
1	bouquet garni §

Horseradish Dumplings

110 g (4 oz)	soft white breadcrumbs
110 g (4 oz)	self-raising flour
50 g (2 oz)	suet
	salt and pepper to taste
1 tablespoon	fresh grated horseradish *or* hot horseradish sauce
	cold water to bind

Method

Cut the beef into even sized chunks, so that they will cook evenly.

In a flameproof casserole dish, fry the thinly sliced onion in 1 tablespoon of the vegetable oil, until soft but not coloured. Temporarily remove the fried onion slices. Heat the remaining vegetable oil in the same dish. Coat the beef chunks in the seasoned flour, and quickly seal in the hot oil.

Slice the celery and add to the dish, together with the fried onion, and paprika, and stir until well combined. Stir in the black treacle and a can of stout.

Bring to the boil, add the bouquet garni, cover with a lid, and braise in the oven at Gas Mark 4 / 350°F / 180°C (160°C for fan oven) for about 2 hours.

After about 1½ hours, prepare the dumplings. First, mix all the dry ingredients together, stir in the horseradish, and add the cold water to form a soft dough. Shape the dough into eight balls with damp hands to avoid sticking.

Remove the casserole from the oven, check the meat is tender, and adjust the seasoning and consistency if required. Remember to remove the bouquet garni.

Distribute the prepared dumpling balls on top of the braised beef, and return the uncovered dish to the oven for 20 – 25 minutes, until the dumplings are golden brown, well risen, and firm to touch.

First Aid – *see also page 62*

Symptom: *Horseradish is not a popular flavour.*

Diagnosis: *Leave it out.*

Antidote: *Serve plain dumplings or add another flavour such as mixed herbs, mustard, or chopped onion.*

Beef in Walnut, Chilli, and Chocolate Sauce

Although this may sound a strange combination of flavours, most people will have enjoyed a chilli beef at some time, such as chilli con carne. This just takes that idea a stage further, by adding the bitter cocoa taste, and giving a deep mahogany colour to the finished dish, popular in Mexican and South American cooking. The walnuts add an interestingly different texture.

Ingredients to serve 4 people

700 g (1½ lb)	braising beef
225 g (8 oz)	onion
3 cloves	garlic
1 to 3	fresh chillies (depending on your taste)
2 tablespoons	vegetable oil
1 tablespoon	cocoa powder
570 ml (1 pt)	tomato juice
275 ml (10 fl oz)	hot water
110 g (4 oz)	walnut halves *or* walnut pieces

Method

Cut the beef into even-sized chunks, so that they will cook evenly.

Peel the onion and garlic, roughly chop the onion, and slice the chillies. Place all these vegetables in a food processor and whiz until smooth.

Heat the oil in a flameproof casserole, and seal the chunks of beef until they are well coloured. Add the puréed onion mix, and stir well. Sprinkle in the cocoa powder and stir well to thoroughly combine with the mixture.

Add the tomato juice and hot water, cover with a lid, and braise at Gas Mark 4 / 350°F / 180°C (160°C for fan oven) for 2 – 2½ hours, until the beef is tender. Add the walnuts for the last 10 minutes.

Before serving, adjust the taste, seasoning, and consistency if required.

First Aid – *see also page 62*

Symptom: *Fresh chillies are not available.*

Diagnosis: *Can use dried whole chillies, or powdered chillies.*

Antidote: *Reduce the quantity of whole chillies by half, or use a teaspoon of powdered chillies.*

Venison Casserole

Venison is perceived by many as luxury meat at a luxury price. But because the meat fibres are tightly packed, it is a dense meat, and you need less of it per person. Perhaps 75 – 150 g (3 – 5 oz) per serving. It is extremely low in fat, and is seen as healthy meat. Hunt out independent producers, to discuss your requirements, and start cooking venison with this flavoursome dish.

Ingredients to serve 4 to 6 people

1 kg (2 lb)	shoulder *or* casserole of venison
2 tablespoons	vegetable oil
2 tablespoons	plain flour

1 dessertspoon	tomato purée
570 ml (1 pt)	beef stock *or* red wine
	salt and pepper
2	bay leaves
1 bunch	thyme *&/or* parsley stalks
110 g (4 oz)	button onions
110 g (4 oz)	button mushrooms
225 g (8 oz)	streaky bacon – cut into strips

Marinade

275 ml (10 fl oz)	red wine
2 tablespoons	olive oil
2 tablespoons	red wine vinegar
4 cloves	crushed garlic
110 g (4 oz)	chopped onions §
6 to 9	crushed juniper berries

Method

Mix up all the marinade ingredients in a non-metallic container. Cut and trim the venison into good sized pieces about 5 cm (2") square, and leave in the marinade for at least one day. It will keep marinated much longer.

Drain the meat and seal in a frying pan of hot vegetable oil. Drain the meat and transfer to an ovenproof casserole dish.

Add the flour to the frying pan stirring well. Add the tomato purée, marinade, and beef stock or red wine, and season well.

Pour the liquid over the meat, add the herbs, cover with a lid, and braise in the oven at Gas Mark 4 / 350°F / 180°C (160°C for fan oven) for one hour until tender. Toss the onions, mushrooms, and bacon in a hot frying pan, and add to the casserole about halfway through cooking. Adjust the seasoning before serving.

First Aid – *see also page 62*

Symptom: *Meat takes on a stronger metallic taste the longer it is marinated.*

Diagnosis: *Acids in the marinade attack metallic dishes, especially aluminium, which will appear brighter below the level of the marinade.*

Remedy: *Do not use aluminium or other metallic containers for marinades.*

Dairy, Eggs, and Cheese

See guidelines on producing a '**Baked Egg Custard**' on page 66 and a '**Perfect Béchamel White Sauce**' on page 64.

Poached Eggs on Toast £ *

If you want to test someone's understanding of the cookery process, get him or her to poach a couple of eggs. This is a cheap and quick method adopted by knowledgeable restaurateurs, to identify immediately if the chef is a charlatan.

Firstly, the eggs should be absolutely fresh; the fresher the better; so that they retain their shape and are cohesive in the acidulated poaching water.

The poaching pan selection is also important. It should be shallow for ease of access, with a wide base to cook several eggs at once, and have a fitted lid. Something similar to a frying pan is ideal. The water level should be three-quarters of the way up the pan, so that each egg is submerged and therefore poached evenly.

Having given you all this technical information, if you follow the advice below, you will poach eggs that may get you a job as a chef.

Ingredients to serve 1 person

5 tablespoons	white wine vinegar
2 fresh	eggs – at room temperature
2 slices	buttered toast

Method

Three-quarters fill a frying pan with water and bring to the boil. Add the white wine vinegar and bring back to the simmer.

Carefully break the eggs into the water, cover with a lid, and simmer for just one timed minute, then turn off the heat. Leave to stand still and covered for another 4 minutes.

Remove the lid, and gently lift the eggs out of the water using a strainer. Drain well before placing on buttered toast.

First Aid

Symptom: *Poached white of egg breaks into little pieces throughout the water.*

Diagnosis: *Stale eggs are not as cohesive as fresh eggs.*

Remedy: *Use the freshest eggs possible, at room temperature, and add white wine vinegar to the water before poaching.*

Symptom: *Poached egg yolk breaks into the water when lifted from the pan.*

Diagnosis: *The egg has stuck to the base of the pan.*

Remedy: *Ensure there is enough water in the pan to allow the eggs to float while poaching, and remove them very carefully.*

Egg Croquettes £ *

These contain a chopped egg mixture bound together with a thick white sauce, known as a panada, and deep-fried in a crispy coating. The chopped parsley adds colour and flavour, but can be omitted if you have none readily to hand.

Ingredients to serve 2 people

Binding White Sauce §

25 g (1 oz)	margarine
25 g (1 oz)	flour
150 ml (5 fl oz)	milk

Egg Filling

4	hard boiled eggs
1 tablespoon	chopped parsley §
	salt and pepper

Crispy Coating

75 g (3 oz)	seasoned flour
1 medium	beaten egg
75 g (3 oz)	breadcrumbs

Method

Make the binding or panada white sauce as normal §.

To the white sauce, add the finely chopped hard-boiled eggs, chopped parsley, salt and pepper. Spread the mixture onto a lightly floured plate. Leave until cold and set.

Cut the egg mixture into four equal sized pieces. Shape each piece into a short thick sausage or small flat cake with a little flour.

Coat the shaped pieces, first in flour, then beaten egg, and finally breadcrumbs. Make sure they are completely covered. Repeat if necessary, refrigerating between times, until thoroughly coated. Refrigerate for at least 1 hour before deep fat frying §.

Deep-fry the croquettes in fat at 180°C / 360°F until just golden brown. Drain on kitchen paper.

First Aid

See the '**Deep Fat Frying**' section on page 86.

Symptom: *White sauce is too runny and soft to hold the chopped egg.*

Diagnosis: *Either the flour has not cooked out completely, or the recipe is unbalanced due to incorrect weighing.*

Antidote: *Place the sauce back on the heat, bring to the boil, and simmer for 5 minutes while stirring constantly, to cook all the flour. If still runny, then add pea-sized pieces of kneaded butter § to the sauce, stir until thoroughly combined, and repeat until suitably thickened.*

Symptom: *Egg croquettes burst once in the hot oil.*

Diagnosis: *Poor or insufficient coating of the egg filling.*

Antidote: *Discard the burst croquettes. Coat any uncooked croquettes again in more flour, beaten egg, and breadcrumbs until fully coated, and freeze before frying.*

Symptom: *Egg croquettes misshapen with no two the same.*

Diagnosis: *Over handling of the mixture.*

Remedy: *Handle lightly, once cut into portions, coat in flour, and refrigerate for about an hour until firm, before coating with egg and breadcrumbs.*

Cheese Pudding £ *

You can jazz up this cheesy egg custard by adding sliced mushrooms, tomatoes, onions, bacon, peas, or spicy sausages, but the store cupboard version requires only the basic ingredients.

You will need a half litre (1 pint) ovenproof dish.

Ingredients to serve 2 people

Coating
25 g (1 oz)	melted butter
50 g (2 oz)	strong Cheddar *or* Parmesan cheese – grated

Savoury Egg Custard §
275 ml (10 fl oz)	milk
25 g (1 oz)	butter
50 g (2 oz)	white breadcrumbs
3 medium	eggs
1 teaspoon	English mustard (optional)
	salt and pepper
75 g (3 oz)	strong flavoured Cheddar cheese – grated

Method

Coating
Grease an ovenproof dish with melted butter and coat with grated cheese.

Savoury Egg Custard §
Pour the milk into a saucepan and bring to the boil, then take off the heat. Add the butter and breadcrumbs, and leave to soak for about half an hour.

Separate the yolks from the whites of the eggs §.

Add the yolks, mustard, and seasoning to the milk mixture and stir thoroughly. Fold the grated cheese into the mixture.

Whisk up the egg whites until stiff. Blend a tablespoon of the stiff whites into the cheesy mixture to soften it. Fold in the remaining stiff whites, and pour into the coated ovenproof dish.

Place the dish in a roasting tin half full of hot water.

Bake at Gas Mark 4 / 350°F / 180°C (160°C for fan oven) for 30 – 35 minutes until well risen, golden brown, and set. Serve immediately.

First Aid – *see also page 67*

Symptom: *Cheese pudding lacks flavour.*

Diagnosis: *Mild flavoured cheese used.*

Remedy: *Try a stronger flavoured cheese and add a little more seasoning to suit your palate.*

Savoury Bread and Butter Pudding £ *

When you mention bread and butter pudding, people think of the sweet variety, but this savoury offering gives a traditional dish a new twist. Try mixing Marmite®, mustard, curry paste, or sun-dried tomato paste with the butter, before spreading it on the bread, to give bite to the pudding!

You will need a greased 1 litre (2 pint) oblong ovenproof dish.

Ingredients to serve 4 people

4 slices	bread
	butter
75 g (3 oz)	grated cheese
570 ml (1 pt)	baked egg custard – savoury mixture §

Method

Butter four slices of bread. Cut each slice diagonally in half and in half again. Evenly coat each triangle of buttered bread with grated cheese.

Grease an oblong baking dish and layer the cheesy triangles over the base. Pour the savoury egg custard mixture over the cheesy triangles.

Place the dish in a roasting tin half full of hot water.

Bake at Gas Mark 4 / 350°F / 180°C (160°C for fan oven) for 30 – 40 minutes until well risen, golden brown, and just firm.

First Aid – *see also page 67*

Symptom: *Egg custard is not set after baking savoury pudding.*

Diagnosis: *Insufficient cooking due to a low temperature or too little time.*

Antidote: *Return the dish to the oven for 10 minutes or until just set.*

Symptom: *Pudding is black and burnt on top after baking.*

Diagnosis: *Baked at too high a temperature or for too long.*

Antidote: *Remove the burnt bits, then cover with a cheese sauce §.*

Sweet or Savoury Omelettes £ *

The plus point of making omelettes is that they are quick to prepare and cook, but you need a lightness of touch to master the art. They also allow you to utilise any surplus cooked vegetables, fish, meat, or poultry either within the omelette mix, or as a filling, or even an accompaniment.

Remember that **you** must wait for the omelette, rather than the other way round. You need to be ready to eat before you start, so that, once cooked, you can enjoy the omelette at its peak – soft, fluffy, and moist.

I prefer to use large free-range eggs, because they give a better colour to the omelette, but any eggs will do.

Ingredients to serve 1 person

2 large	eggs
1 pinch	salt and pepper – for savoury omelette
or 1 good pinch	sugar – for sweet omelette
10 g (½ oz)	oil *or* butter

Method

Break the eggs into a bowl, add the seasonings or sugar, and beat with a fork until no streaks of egg white are visible.

Heat an omelette pan §, and when hot, add the oil or butter. Swirl the pan to coat the base evenly with the fat. Do **not** allow the fat to smoke.

Pour the beaten egg into the pan and stir gently with a fork or wooden spatula. Draw the set sides of the egg to the middle, and let the wet centre run to the sides. After about a minute, stop stirring as soon as the egg has set. Cook it for a further minute, while gently shaking the pan, to colour the omelette base lightly, but retaining a creamy top.

Remove the pan from the heat. Make sure the outside edges of the omelette are loose, by running the fork or spatula around between the omelette and the edge of the pan.

Tilt the pan away from you and use the fork or spatula to fold the third of the omelette nearest the handle into the centre. Fold the opposite third over on top of the first, so that the omelette resembles a cigar shape. Turn out onto a warm plate with the folded sides underneath. Serve immediately.

First Aid

Symptom: *Omelette looks more like scrambled egg and appears very lumpy.*

Diagnosis: *The egg mixture has been stirred too much.*

Antidote: *All you can do is serve it as scrambled egg.*

Remedy: *The egg mixture must be stirred and shaken quickly and evenly across the base of the pan. Stop stirring as soon as the egg starts to set. Over stirring will result in scrambled egg. Gently shake the pan for a minute to crisp the base.*

Symptom: *Omelette tastes tough and rubbery.*

Diagnosis: *Over-cooking or long slow cooking of the egg mixture.*

Antidote: *Cut the omelette into strips and serve with stir-fried vegetables.*

Remedy: *The omelette pan should be hot enough to set the egg mixture almost as soon as it is poured into the pan. An omelette should only take about two minutes from entering the pan to being served.*

Sweet or Savoury Griddle Cakes £ *

Every chef has a handful of basic recipes that they can turn to, knowing that with limited resources, they can produce something different each time they are used. This is one of those standby recipes, where the skeleton consists of flour, egg, and milk. Then you can dress it up anyway you want. Here I have added cheese, but any cooked vegetables, fish, meat, or poultry will suffice. If it is a quick pudding you're after, add chopped fresh fruit, dried fruit, or nuts and spices to the mixture.

Ingredients to serve 2 people

110 g (4 oz)	self-raising flour
50 g (2 oz)	grated cheese
1 large	egg
75 ml (3 fl oz)	milk
25 g (1 oz)	diced cheese
	salt and pepper to taste
1 tablespoon	olive *or* vegetable oil

Method

In a bowl, mix the flour, grated cheese, egg, and milk into a batter. Add the diced cheese and seasonings.

Heat a frying pan and add the oil.

Drop dessertspoons of the mixture into the hot fat. Leave to sizzle until they form a crispy base. Then turn each griddle cake over and sizzle its other side until crispy.

Serve and eat immediately.

First Aid

Symptom: *Griddle cakes are greasy or stuck together.*

Diagnosis: *The oil was not hot enough, possibly due to too many cakes in the pan, which will lower the temperature.*

Antidote: *Ensure the oil is hot. Tip the pan slightly and the oil should run in tiny waves or ribs. Fry no more than four griddle cakes at one time.*

Sweet or Savoury Gypsy Toast £ *

This is one of the items I cooked on my first encounter with the media, namely BBC Essex Radio. I like to serve it for breakfast or lunch with home-made green tomato chutney. If you want to give it a sweet twist, replace the cheese and onion with jam, or marmalade, or your favourite sandwich filling, and serve with traditional custard §.

Ingredients to serve 1 person

2 slices	your favourite bread
25 g (1 oz)	butter *or* margarine

Filling

75 g (3 oz)	Cheddar cheese
	onion rings (optional)

Coating

1	beaten egg
25 g (1 oz)	breadcrumbs *or* sesame seeds
1 tablespoon	vegetable oil

Method

Evenly spread the sliced bread with the butter or margarine. Cut the cheese into slices and arrange to cover one slice of the bread. Optionally, lay the onion rings over the cheese. Place the other slice of bread on top to form a sandwich.

Beat the egg and dip the sandwich in the egg to coat both sides of the bread. Then dip it in the breadcrumbs or sesame seeds to cover both sides of the sandwich thoroughly.

Shallow fry the sandwich in hot vegetable oil until golden brown on both sides.

Serve with a crisp mixed salad or home-made chutney.

First Aid

Symptom: *Gypsy toast sandwich fell apart whilst frying.*

Diagnosis: *Sandwich was not stuck together properly.*

Remedy: *Make sure the sandwich is lined up accurately just before dipping in beaten egg, and ensure it is completely coated in egg and seeds.*

Bread and Jam Pudding £ *

Although this is only nursery food of jam sandwiches set in a sweet and lightly set egg custard, it is yummy! All you need is a jug full of hot vanilla custard. Heaven!

You will need a greased 1 litre (2 pint) oblong ovenproof dish.

Ingredients to serve 4 people

4 slices	bread
	butter and jam
570 ml (1 pt)	baked egg custard – sweet mixture §

Method

Make up two bread and jam sandwiches. Cut each sandwich diagonally in half and then in half again.

Grease an oblong baking dish and layer the sandwich triangles over the base. Pour the sweet egg custard mixture over the sandwiches.

Place the dish in a roasting tin half full of hot water.

Bake at Gas Mark 4 / 350°F / 180°C (160°C for fan oven) for 35 – 45 minutes until well risen, golden brown, and just firm.

Serve with home-made traditional custard §.

First Aid – see also page 67

Symptom: *Egg custard fails to set properly.*

Diagnosis: *Insufficient cooking due to a low temperature or too little time.*

Antidote: *Return the dish to the oven for 10 minutes or until just set.*

Burnt Cream or Crème Brûlée *

This cold pudding is associated with Trinity College, Cambridge, and so is sometimes known as Trinity Cream. A 19th century Fellow of the college, who had studied there for many years, bestowed the recipe to the college, where its crest was impressed into the caramel with a branding iron. The French have also adopted the recipe and dubbed it Crème Brûlée, but it is unclear whether the dish was created first in Britain or France.

Ingredients to serve 4 people

570 ml (1 pt)	baked egg custard – sweet mixture §
1 dessertspoon	icing sugar

Method

Pour the egg custard mixture into four ramekin dishes or individual ovenproof dishes. Bake the egg custard §, leave to cool, and refrigerate as normal.

When required, sprinkle icing sugar as evenly as possible over the custard in each dish. The more even, the better the final result.

Grill the dishes until the icing sugar just melts and turns a caramel colour. Wait until they have cooled slightly before serving.

First Aid – *see also page 67*

Symptom: *Caramel coating is uneven on top of burnt cream egg custard.*

Diagnosis: *Uneven application of sugar coating.*

Remedy: *Apply the icing sugar to the egg custard using a miniature dredger or a tea strainer. Ensure it is as even as possible with a generous coating.*

Symptom: *Caramel coating is soft and tacky when served.*

Diagnosis: *The sugar coating was applied too early, or was grilled too early.*

Antidote: *Carefully lift off the caramel, coat in fresh sugar, and caramelise again.*

Remedy: *The sugar coating must be applied just before grilling. The coating may be caramelised up to 4 hours before serving; but the thinner the coating the sooner it is likely to revert to soft sugar.*

Symptom: *Grill not suitable to caramelise a sugar coating.*

Diagnosis: *A good substitute is a small catering blowtorch as seen in the hands of many television chefs to obtain quick caramel results.*

Remedy: *Small blowtorches are available from catering suppliers and cook shops. Beware of safety when using the blowtorch, as it produces a 1500°C flame. So we are talking seriously hot. Do not use a DIY blowtorch, which is designed for stripping paint, and is not safe for use on food.*

Baked Egg Custard Tart *

When you undertake this recipe, you are aiming for a soft set custard, encased in a feather light pastry, and dusted with grated nutmeg.

Ingredients to serve 4 to 6 people

175 g (6 oz)	sugar pastry §
or 20 cm (8")	circular ready-made sweet pastry case
275 ml (10 fl oz)	baked egg custard – sweet mixture §
	grated nutmeg (optional)

Method

Make a 20 cm (8") circular sweet pastry case, using sugar pastry and a flan ring. Before baking brush the pastry shell with egg white, and only bake for about 10 minutes until the pastry is just firm. Alternatively, you can buy a ready-made sweet pastry case.

Make up and pour the sweet baked egg custard mixture into the pastry case. For an authentic finish, sprinkle the top with grated nutmeg.

Bake at Gas Mark 5 / 375°F / 190°C (170°C for fan oven) for 25 – 35 minutes until the custard is just set. Serve cold.

First Aid – *see also page 67*

Symptom: *Pastry flan shell leaks the filling while baking.*

Diagnosis: *Pastry shell cracked, although this may not be visible.*

Remedy: *Brush the inside of the shell with egg white and bake blind for about 10 minutes to just set and seal the pastry.*

Symptom: *Pastry flan shell bubbles and blisters after baking with the filling.*

Diagnosis: *Pocket of air trapped under the pastry surface.*

Remedy: *When lining the flan ring ensure the pastry lies flat, especially in the corners, so that no air is trapped.*

Symptom: *Pastry flan shrinks during baking.*

Diagnosis: *Pastry over-stretched while lining the flan ring.*

Remedy: *Pastry should be rested half an hour before use. Roll out to 5 cm (2") larger than the flan ring, and carefully fit into position.*

Queen of Puddings *

Traditionally, this is a lightly set, sweet custard, textured with breadcrumbs spread with jam, and topped with a crispy meringue. But piping the meringue in a lattice shape creates more interest, and filling the lattice holes with jam gives a jewel-like appearance to this queen of puddings.

You will need a greased half litre (1 pint) ovenproof dish.

Ingredients to serve 2 people

50 g (2 oz)	stale cake crumbs *or* breadcrumbs
275 ml (10 fl oz)	baked egg custard – sweet mixture §

Meringue § Lattice

2 large	egg whites
1 pinch	salt
110 g (4 oz)	castor sugar
2 tablespoons	raspberry jam

Method

Evenly distribute the stale cake crumbs or breadcrumbs over the bottom of a greased ovenproof dish.

Make up and pour the sweet baked egg custard mixture over the crumbs. Leave to stand and soak for 15 minutes.

Place the dish in a roasting tin half full of hot water.

Bake at Gas Mark 4 / 350°F / 180°C (160°C for fan oven) for 25 – 30 minutes until just set.

Meringue § Lattice

Place the egg whites in a bowl with a pinch of salt and whisk until it forms stiff glossy peaks. Add half the sugar and whisk until stiff. Fold in remaining sugar.

Pipe the meringue mixture onto the baked egg custard to form a lattice.

Return to the oven for about 15 minutes to just set the meringue.

Pipe raspberry jam into the meringue lattice holes.

First Aid – *see also page 67*

Symptom:	*Piping bag is not available to pipe meringue or jam.*
Diagnosis:	*A good substitute is a clean polythene food or sandwich bag.*
Antidote:	*Place the meringue or jam in the plastic bag, snip off the corner, and use just like a piping bag. Alternatively, simply drop teaspoonfuls of the meringue over the egg custard to give an attractive bobble effect. Be creative and enjoy yourself.*
Symptom:	*Meringue mixture is sloppy and won't hold its shape.*
Diagnosis:	*Either grease has got into the utensils, or the egg whites insufficiently whisked, or left too long before piping onto the egg custard.*
Remedy:	*All utensils must be grease-free. Wash and dry them thoroughly with a clean tea towel. Ensure the egg whites are free of egg yolk, which also contains fat. Whisk the egg whites thoroughly. Once the meringue has been made, it should be used immediately; otherwise it will become unstable and revert to a liquid.*

Savoury Tarts and Pastries

See page 70 onwards for guidelines on '**Potato Pastry**' and '**Shortcrust Pastry**' and '**Baking Blind**'.

Stilton, Pear, and Walnut Quiche

Stilton cheese served with fresh pear and walnuts is a classic end to a meal. Fill a pastry case with this trio, bound in egg yolks and cream, and you may have another classic.

You will need a 20 cm (8") flan ring.

Ingredients to serve 4 people

110 g (4 oz)	shortcrust pastry §

Filling

1	just-ripe pear – William *or* Rocha *or* Comice
110 g (4 oz)	Stilton cheese
2	spring onions
50 g (2 oz)	walnut halves
4	egg yolks
150 ml (5 fl oz)	double cream
1 dessertspoon	chopped parsley §
	salt and pepper to taste

Method

Prepare the shortcrust pastry, and roll out to line a 20 cm (8") flan ring. Bake blind in a preheated oven at Gas Mark 6 / 400°F / 200°C (180°C for fan oven) for about 10 minutes, until just firm. Remove and allow the pastry to cool.

Dice the pear, cut the cheese into small dice, and chop the spring onions. Place the diced pear, diced cheese, chopped spring onions, and walnut halves evenly in the pastry flan. Mix the egg yolks, double cream, and seasonings together, and pour over the filling.

Bake at Gas Mark 4 / 350°F / 180°C (160°C for fan oven) for 35 – 45 minutes, until the centre of the filling is just set.

Alternative Fillings

Try these delicious alternative fillings for your quiche.

◆ Leek, bacon, and Cheshire cheese.

◆ Grapes, celery, and Brie.

◆ Smoked mackerel or naturally smoked haddock, peas, and chive.

◆ Roasted peppers, red onion, and goat's cheese.

First Aid – *see also page 71*

Symptom: *Quiche pastry case is cracked, before adding the filling.*

Diagnosis: *The pastry was over-stretched, or the flan ring was lined poorly.*

Antidote: *Egg wash a spare piece of raw pastry and patch the crack. Fill and bake the quiche as usual and the patch will bake with the filling.*

Asparagus Quiche

The vibrant colour of asparagus shouts, "Eat me! Eat me!", and this is one way of enjoying this succulent vegetable.

You will need a 20 cm (8") flan ring.

Ingredients to serve 4 people

110 g (4 oz)	shortcrust pastry §

Filling

225 g (8 oz)	fresh asparagus
3	spring onions – chopped §
50 g (2 oz)	Parmesan cheese – grated
2 large	eggs
275 ml (10 fl oz)	milk *or* double cream
1 teaspoon	chopped parsley §
	salt and pepper to taste

Method

Prepare the shortcrust pastry, and roll out to line a 20 cm (8") flan ring. Bake blind in a preheated oven at Gas Mark 6 / 400°F / 200°C (180°C for fan oven) for about 10 minutes, until just firm. Remove and leave the pastry to cool.

Prepare the asparagus by snapping off its woody base. To do this, hold the asparagus stalk in both hands, as near the base as possible, and use your thumbs to push against the tough bottom stalk until it snaps off. Cut into 5 cm (2") lengths.

Sprinkle the asparagus, chopped spring onions, and grated cheese over the partly cooked pastry flan. Beat the eggs, milk or cream, and seasonings together, and pour over the asparagus mixture.

Bake at Gas Mark 4 / 350°F / 180°C (160°C for fan oven) for 35 – 45 minutes, until the centre of the filling is set, and the entire filling is golden brown, and puffy.

First Aid *– see also page 71*

Symptom: *Asparagus is tough and stringy.*

Diagnosis: *The asparagus is not in its flush of youth.*

Remedy: *Steam or microwave the asparagus for about 5 minutes, until just tender, before adding to the quiche.*

Pumpkin and Cheese Tart

The fluorescent orange pumpkin flesh blends well with the smoky bacon and cheeses. If you are vegetarian, replace the bacon with a couple of smoked garlic cloves.

You will need a 20 cm (8") flan tin.

Ingredients to serve 4 people

110 g (4 oz)	shortcrust pastry §

Filling

1	onion – peeled and thinly sliced
3 thin rashers	rind-less smoked bacon – chopped
25 g (1 oz)	pumpkin seeds
50 g (2 oz)	grated Gruyere cheese
50 g (2 oz)	grated Parmesan cheese
110 g (4 oz)	pumpkin purée
½ teaspoon	grated nutmeg
2 large	eggs
150 ml (5 fl oz)	milk
	fresh ground pepper to taste

Method

Prepare the shortcrust pastry, and roll out to line a 20 cm (8") flan tin. Bake blind in a preheated oven at Gas Mark 6 / 400°F / 200°C (180°C for fan oven) for about 12 minutes, until just firm. Remove and allow the pastry to cool.

Gently fry the sliced onion and chopped bacon until the onions are soft.

Arrange the onion and bacon in the pastry case, and add the pumpkin seeds.

Mix together the grated cheeses, add the remainder of the ingredients, and pour into the pastry case.

Bake at Gas Mark 4 / 350°F / 180°C (160°C for fan oven) for 35 – 45 minutes, until the filling is set.

First Aid *– see also page 71*

Symptom: *Pumpkin is not available in the shops.*
Diagnosis: *Seasonal supply.*
Antidote: *Substitute puréed squash, softened leeks, onions, or mushrooms.*

Bacon, Apple, and Cheese Plait

I was first introduced to this dish at the local college, where I taught catering students. I like the combination of sweet and savoury flavours encased in feather light pastry.

Ingredients to serve 4 people

110 g (4 oz)	onion – finely chopped §
110 g (4 oz)	cooking apple *or* eating apple – finely chopped §
225 g (8 oz)	bacon – roughly chopped
50 g (2 oz)	breadcrumbs
50 g (2 oz)	grated Cheddar cheese
1 teaspoon	mixed herbs *or* chopped parsley §
4 leaves	freshly shredded sage (optional)
1 teaspoon	ready made English mustard
	salt and pepper to taste
225 g (8 oz)	ready-made puff pastry *or* shortcrust pastry

Method

Finely chop the onion and apple. Roughly chop the bacon. Grate the cheese. Place all the ingredients, except the pastry, into a large mixing bowl, and combine the filling thoroughly. Season with salt and pepper to taste.

Roll out the pastry into a rectangle about 30 cm x 20 cm (12" x 8").

Spread the filling evenly in the centre of the pastry rectangle, leaving some bare pastry on all sides.

Use a sharp knife to cut the bare pastry into twelve 2.5 cm (1") fingers along both the longer edges. Brush all the bare pastry with water.

Fold the uncut shorter pastry edges over the filling top and bottom.

Take the top left-hand pastry finger and fold over the filling at a slight angle. Take the top right-hand pastry finger and fold over the top left-hand pastry finger at an angle. Repeat alternately left and right, similar to plaiting hair, with all of the other pastry fingers.

Brush the plait with a little beaten egg, and place on a baking sheet on the middle shelf of the oven.

Bake at Gas Mark 6 / 400°F / 200°C (180°C for fan oven) for 30 – 40 minutes, until golden brown, well risen, and firm to the touch.

First Aid

Symptom: *Pastry plait does not cover the entire filling.*
Diagnosis: *Essential to cover the filling to prevent spillage.*

Remedy: *Roll the pastry rectangle a little larger, and ensure the filling only occupies the centre third of the pastry before plaiting.*

Sausage-Meat Pie £

I think of this as poor man's pork pie, but with its fine ingredients it's up there with the best, and you know exactly what's in it!

You will need a 20 cm (8") flan ring.

Ingredients to serve 4 people

225 g (8 oz)	potato pastry §

Filling

450 g (16 oz)	sausage-meat
110 g (4 oz)	onion – finely chopped §
1 tablespoon	chopped parsley § (preferably fresh)
1 teaspoon	dried mixed herbs
	salt and pepper to taste

Method

Prepare the potato pastry, and leave to become completely cold.

Prepare the filling by mixing the sausage-meat, finely chopped onion, herbs, and seasonings in a large bowl until thoroughly combined.

Divide the potato pastry into two portions, one twice the size of the other.

Using the larger portion, roll out into a circle to line a 20 cm (8") flan ring. Grease the flan ring and line with the pastry, making sure there are no gaps.

Place the mixed filling into the flan ring and spread out evenly.

Roll out the remaining smaller portion of pastry into a circle to cover the flan. Wet the pastry before placing on the pie to form a pastry lid. Make a small hole in the middle of the pastry lid to allow the steam to escape.

Bake in the oven at Gas Mark 6 / 400°F / 200°C (180°C for fan oven) on the middle shelf for 40 – 45 minutes, until golden brown and well risen.

First Aid – *see also page 70*

Symptom: *Sausage-meat pie is not moist enough.*

Remedy: *Add wilted spinach, or finely shredded watercress, or mushrooms, or tomatoes for extra moisture.*

Cornish Pasties £

Cubed beef and root vegetables are the traditional filling for these oval-shaped pasties. The story goes that the devil never crossed the River Tamar into Cornwall for fear of the Cornish woman's habit of putting anything and everything into a pasty. I've put one of my favourite combinations together to give a moist filling.

Ingredients to serve 4 people
225 g (8 oz) — potato pastry §

Filling
225 g (8 oz) — minced beef
110 g (4 oz) — onion – finely chopped §
half a can — baked beans (optional)
225 g (8 oz) — peeled weight potatoes
— salt and pepper to taste
1 — egg to glaze

Method
Prepare the potato pastry, and leave to become completely cold.

Dry fry the minced beef, and add the chopped onion. Stir until the beef is brown, and the onion is soft. Drain off any surplus fat, and leave to cool. Add half a can of baked beans if desired.

Cut the peeled potatoes into 1 cm (½") dice, and mix with the beef, onion, and beans, then season well.

Divide the potato pastry into four equal portions, and roll out each into a circle. Share the potato, beef, onion and beans filling evenly between each pastry circle.

Beat the egg, and brush egg wash around the edge of each pastry circle. Draw up each pastry circle into a traditional pasty shape to enclose the filling, and pinch the pastry edges together to prevent the filling from escaping. Brush the outside of the pastry with egg wash to glaze.

Bake in the oven at Gas Mark 6 / 400°F / 200°C (180°C for fan oven) on the middle shelf for 25 – 30 minutes, until golden brown.

First Aid – *see also page 70*

Symptom: *Pasty filling is too soft and moist to enclose with pastry drawn up each side.*

Antidote: *Move the filling to one half of the pastry circle, and fold the other half of the pastry over the filling to form a half moon shape, and seal with egg wash.*

Cheese and Onion Pasties £
These are a vegetarian alternative to the traditional Cornish pasties. You can add whatever vegetable you like to the grated cheese and onion mixture.

Ingredients to serve 4 people
225 g (8 oz) — potato pastry §

Filling
225 g (8 oz) — peeled weight potatoes
110 g (4 oz) — grated Cheddar cheese *or* a cheese of your choice
110 g (4 oz) — onion – finely chopped §
1 tablespoon — chopped fresh parsley *or* chive §
— salt and pepper to taste
1 — egg to glaze

Method

Prepare the potato pastry, and leave to become completely cold.

Cut the peeled potatoes into 1 cm (½") dice, and mix with the grated cheese, finely chopped onion, herbs and seasonings.

Divide the potato pastry into four equal portions, and roll out each into a circle. Share the potato, cheese, and onion filling evenly between each pastry circle.

Beat the egg, and brush egg wash around the edge of each pastry circle. Draw up each pastry circle into a traditional pasty shape to enclose the filling, and pinch the pastry edges together to prevent the filling from escaping. Brush the outside of the pastry with egg wash to glaze.

Bake in the oven at Gas Mark 6 / 400°F / 200°C (180°C for fan oven) on the middle shelf for 25 – 30 minutes, until golden brown.

First Aid – *see also page 70*

Symptom: *Pasties need to be prepared well in advance of consumption.*

Diagnosis: *Pasties can be frozen in either the uncooked or cooked state.*

Antidote: *Place the prepared pasties on cling film on a baking sheet and open freeze them until solid. Wrap the frozen pasties in freezer bags or place in a box. They will keep in the freezer for 1 month if uncooked, or for 3 months if they were cooked.*

Meat and Potato Pie £

This is a traditional dish from the North of England, eking out a little meat with potatoes, and topping the whole lot with a pastry crust. Serve with lashings of relish, or Worcester sauce, as Southerners would know it. Pure heaven!

You will need a 23 cm (9") ovenproof casserole dish.

Ingredients to serve 4 people

225 g (8 oz)	shortcrust pastry §

Filling

350 g (12 oz)	braising steak *or* stewing steak
110 g (4 oz)	onion – finely chopped §
1	bunch mixed herbs *or* bouquet garni §
1 cube	beef stock cube
570 ml (1 pt)	water *or* beer *or* red wine
450 g (1 lb)	peeled weight potatoes
	salt and pepper to taste

Method

Preheat the oven to Gas Mark 5 / 375°F / 190°C (170°C for fan oven).

Prepare the meat by removing all the visible fat and gristle, and cutting into even sized pieces, about the size of a chestnut, to ensure even cooking.

Place the meat in a casserole dish, with the chopped onion, and bouquet garni. Dissolve the stock cube in the water, beer, or wine, and pour into the dish.

Cover with a lid. Place on the middle shelf of the oven. Braise for 1 – 2 hours (depending on the cut of meat) until tender. Taste a piece of the meat to check.

Meanwhile, prepare the shortcrust pastry, and chill for at least half an hour.

Peel the potatoes, and cut into even sized pieces about the same as the meat. Boil the potatoes in a saucepan for only 5 minutes. They should stay slightly hard. Drain the potatoes well. Add them to the cooked meat. Remove the bouquet garni. Adjust the seasoning. Allow to cool completely.

Place the meat and potato mixture into a 23 cm (9") oval dish. Roll out the pastry to fit the dish. Place the dish on a baking tray, to catch any excess juices. Bake on the top shelf of the oven at Gas Mark 6 / 400°F / 200°C (180°C for fan oven) for 25 – 30 minutes, until the crust is golden brown, and firm to touch.

First Aid – *see also page 71*

Symptom:	*Fresh red meat is not available or is too expensive.*
Antidote:	*Use tinned meat such as corned beef or ham.*

Sweet Tarts and Pastries

See page 70 onwards for guidelines on '**Baking Sugar Pastry**' and on '**Baking Blind**'.

Syrup and Walnut Tart

This is a cross between the traditional English treacle tart, and the popular American pecan pie. Like all creative cooking, I have taken the treacle filling of the English tart, and added some walnuts, so it takes on the texture of America's favourite pie.

You will need a 20 cm (8") flan ring.

Ingredients to serve 8 people
175 g (6 oz)	sugar pastry §

Filling
110 g (4 oz)	melted butter
50 g (2 oz)	soft brown sugar
110 g (4 oz)	golden syrup
3 large	eggs
1	lemon – zest and juice
225 g (8 oz)	walnut halves

Method

Prepare the sugar pastry, and roll out to line a 20 cm (8") flan ring. Bake blind in a preheated oven at Gas Mark 6 / 400°F / 200°C (180°C for fan oven) for about 10 minutes, until just firm. Remove and allow the pastry to cool.

To prepare the filling, add the sugar and syrup to the melted butter. Lightly beat the eggs, and add to the sugar mixture, with the lemon zest and juice.

Arrange the walnut halves evenly over the base of the flan ring. Pour the sugar and egg mixture over the walnuts.

Bake at Gas Mark 4 / 350°F / 180°C (160°C for fan oven) for 30 – 45 minutes, until set. Remove and leave to cool completely.

Serve cold with Greek yoghurt or clotted cream.

First Aid *– see also page 76.*

Symptom: *Tart syrup filling not set after recommended cooking time and temperature.*

Diagnosis: *Different ovens cook at slightly different temperatures.*

Antidote: *Allow a slightly longer cooking time, and ensure the tart is baked on the middle shelf of conventional ovens.*

Remedy: *Check the oven temperature against an oven thermometer.*

Figgy Pie

The homely sounding name persuaded me to try this recipe, and I wasn't disappointed with the sweet lemony tasting figs and crunchy hazelnuts. Yummy! You will need a 20 cm (8") flan ring.

Ingredients to serve 8 people
225 g (8 oz)	sugar pastry §

Filling
50 g (2 oz)	butter
1 large	lemon – zest and juice
75 g (3 oz)	soft brown sugar
110 ml (4 fl oz)	water
50 ml (2 fl oz)	brandy
225 g (8 oz)	figs – finely chopped §
1 tablespoon	plain flour
1 teaspoon	ground cinnamon
50 g (2 oz)	chopped hazelnuts
1	beaten egg to glaze

Method

Prepare the sugar pastry, wrap in cling film, and chill for at least half an hour.

Meanwhile prepare the filling. Place the butter, lemon zest and juice, sugar, water, and brandy into a saucepan. Stir the mixture, on a low heat, until the sugar is completely dissolved, and makes no grating sound.

Add the chopped figs, flour, and cinnamon. Stir to combine, then bring the mixture to the boil, stirring constantly until thick. Finally, add the chopped nuts. Allow the filling to cool completely before assembling the pie.

Divide the sugar pastry into two portions, one twice the size of the other.

Roll out the larger portion into a circle, and line a 20 cm (8") flan ring. Evenly distribute the cold filling over the base of the pastry flan.

Roll out the smaller portion of pastry into a circle to cover the filling.

Brush the top of the pastry with beaten egg, and bake on the middle shelf of oven at Gas Mark 6 / 400°F / 200°C (180°C for fan oven) for 30 – 40 minutes, until golden brown and firm.

First Aid – *see also page 76*

Symptom: *Pastry is too soft to handle and roll out.*

Diagnosis: *Pastry handled too much or overworked.*

Antidote: *Chill the pastry for at least half an hour to firm up. Flour the work surface and rolling pin, and handle the pastry lightly. If excessively wet, roll the pastry ball in flour before rolling out.*

Remedy: *Check that correct amount of ingredients used.*

Lemon Tart

This is a tartly tart; really sharp tasting and creamy smooth in texture. I have tried other citrus fruit in place of lemons, but always return to the original. You will need a 20 cm (8") flan ring.

Ingredients to serve 6 people

175 g (6 oz)	sugar pastry §

Filling

175 g (6 oz)	castor sugar
2	lemons zest
150 ml (5 fl oz)	lemon juice
110 ml (4 fl oz)	orange juice
50 g (2 oz)	melted butter
4 large	eggs
50 ml (2 fl oz)	double cream

Method

Prepare the sugar pastry, and roll out to line a 20 cm (8") flan ring. Bake blind in a preheated oven at Gas Mark 6 / 400°F / 200°C (180°C for fan oven) for about 10 minutes, until just firm. Remove and allow the pastry case to cool.

Mix the sugar, lemon zest, fruit juices, and melted butter in saucepan, on a low heat, until the sugar has completely dissolved, and makes no grating sound.

Beat the eggs, and to remove their chalaza, pass them through a nylon sieve, into the fruit juice mixture. Finally, add the double cream. Heat the mixture, while stirring constantly, until just becoming thick, but **DO NOT BOIL**.

Pour the filling into the baked pastry case, and bake on a tray in the oven at Gas Mark 5 / 375°F / 190°C (170°C for fan oven) for 20 – 30 minutes until just set.

Leave to cool on the tray before moving to the refrigerator until required.

First Aid – *see also page 76*

Symptom: *Lemon tart filling turns to a scrambled egg appearance.*

Diagnosis: *Too much heat applied to the lemon filling.*

Antidote: *Sieve the scrambled filling mixture, and stir well before pouring into pastry case to bake.*

Apple and Cheese Pie

This combination of sweet and savoury flavours under one piecrust reminds me of that North Country saying, "An apple pie without some cheese, is like a kiss without a squeeze". It was the norm in the West Riding, where I originated, that the cheese was placed under the piecrust.

Another acceptable taste is to serve cheese with fruitcake. At Christmas, cold Christmas pudding was served with Wensleydale cheese. In true Yorkshire fashion, nothing was wasted.

You will need a 20 cm (8") plate or flan ring

Ingredients to serve 6 people

225 g (8 oz)	sugar pastry §

Filling

450 g (1 lb)	cooking apples *or* cooking and eating apples
110 g (4 oz)	Wensleydale cheese

Method

Prepare the sugar pastry, wrap in cling film, and chill for at least half an hour.

Divide the sugar pastry into two portions, one twice the size of the other.

Roll out the larger portion into a circle, and line a 20 cm (8") plate or flan ring. Peal and thinly slice the apples, and distribute evenly over the pastry base. Thinly slice the cheese, and distribute evenly over the sliced apples.

Roll out the smaller portion of pastry into a circle to cover the filling. Brush the pastry with cold water, place on top of the filling wet side down, and seal down well. Make a small hole in the top of the pie to allow steam to escape.

Bake at Gas Mark 5 / 375°F / 190°C (170°C for fan oven) for 15 minutes. Then, reduce to Gas Mark 4 / 350°F / 180°C (160°C for fan oven) for a further 30 – 45 minutes, until golden brown and firm.

First Aid – see also page 76

Symptom: *Individual tarts required instead of one large tart.*

Diagnosis: *Individual professional baking rings are expensive.*

Remedy: *Buy the smallest available tins of baked beans, eat the beans, remove the ends of the tins, and use as small baking rings.*

Richmond Maids of Honour

I love the pedigree that comes with these little moist morsels, invented by the pastry-cook to Catherine of Aragon, the first wife of Henry VIII. The story goes that Henry encountered a group of Maids of Honour, one being Anne Boleyn, whilst strolling through the grounds of Hampton Court. Henry was offered one of the cakes the maids were eating, and declared the cakes delicious. When he enquired the name of the cakes, he was told they had no name, so he decreed them Maids of Honour.

Now the story thickens, for the Maids of Honour recipe was a closely guarded secret for over 200 years, until the reign of George II. It was at this time that a local businessman named Burdekin, gleaned the recipe from one of the ladies to the court. He immediately set up shop in Richmond upon Thames, and for generations the Burdekin family lived well on making and selling Richmond Maids of Honour.

You will need 16 greased patty tins.

Ingredients to make 16 cakes

225 g (8 oz)	curd *or* cottage cheese – sieved
75 g (3 oz)	castor sugar
50 g (2 oz)	currants
	grated rind of lemon
10 g (½ oz)	almonds – chopped and blanched
1 large	egg – beaten
2 teaspoons	brandy
10 g (½ oz)	butter – melted
225 g (8 oz)	ready-made puff pastry *or* shortcrust pastry §

Method

Mix all the ingredients together, except the pastry, until well combined to form the curd filling.

Roll out the pastry 3 mm ($^1/_8$"*) thick and cut into circles using a pastry cutter. Line 16 greased patty tins with the pastry. Half fill each one with the curd mixture.

Bake at Gas Mark 5 / 375°F / 190°C (170°C for fan oven) for 20 – 25 minutes, until golden brown.

First Aid

Symptom: *Currants and other dried fruit are not to my liking.*

Diagnosis: *Dried fruit are rarely essential in recipes.*

Antidote: *Leave out the dried fruit.*

Mince Pies

The aroma of spicy sweet mincemeat filled pastry pies baking is one of my favourite smells. It heralds the preparations for Christmas and the tradition of eating one mince pie per day for the 12 twelve days of Christmas. This ensures health and happiness for the following 12 months.

You will need greased bun tins for about 12 pies.

Ingredients to make about 12 pies

225 g (8 oz)	sugar pastry §

Filling

450 g (1 lb) jar	mincemeat

Method

Prepare the sugar pastry, wrap in cling film, and chill for at least half an hour.

Roll out half the pastry to 3 mm ($^1/_8$") thick and use an 8 cm (3") fluted cutter to cut out the pie bases. Grease some bun tins, and line with the pie bases. Put a teaspoon of mincemeat into each base.

Roll out the other half of pastry to 3 mm ($^1/_8$") thick and use a 6 cm (2½") fluted cutter to cut out the pie lids. Lightly wet the underside of each lid with water before sealing onto the bases. Lightly prick each lid to allow steam to escape.

Bake at Gas Mark 5 / 375°F / 190°C (170°C for fan oven) on the middle shelf of the oven for 20 – 25 minutes, until golden brown, and firm to touch.

Leave to cool slightly before removing from the tin.

First Aid – *see also page 76*

Symptom: *Mince pie filling bubbles over and sticks the pies to the tin.*

Diagnosis: *Too much filling used, or poorly sealed pie lids.*

Remedy: *Only add a teaspoon of filling to each pie, make sure the lids are wet before sealing down, and prick them to allow steam to escape.*

Puddings Galore

See the earlier chapters '**Are You Picking the Best Ingredients?**' and '**How Do You Cook With Confidence?**' for general advice and guidance.

Coconut Mousse

Quark is a skimmed milk curd cheese that is virtually fat-free. In large supermarkets, it is usually in the chiller cabinet with the cottage cheeses. It has a bland taste and therefore readily absorbs other flavours, either sweet or savoury, without becoming cloying.

Ingredients to serve 4 people

1 sachet	gelatine granules – from 6 sachet 70 g (3 oz) pack
50 ml (2 fl oz)	hot water
250 g (9 oz) tub	quark skimmed milk cheese §
110 g (4 oz)	granulated sugar
425 g (15 oz) can	coconut milk
150 ml (5 fl oz)	double cream (optional)

Method

Sprinkle the gelatine evenly over the surface of the hot water in a small bowl. Help the gelatine to dissolve by stirring for about 5 minutes.

Place the quark, sugar, and coconut milk in a food processor and whiz for about one minute until combined. Add the dissolved gelatine and whiz for another minute until combined.

Optionally, whip the double cream until floppy and fold gently into the mixture.

Pour the mixture into individual moulds or glasses and refrigerate to set for about 2 hours.

First Aid
See the '**Soft Fruit Jelly**' gelatine '**First Aid**' below.

Symptom: *Gelatine goes stringy in the water.*

Diagnosis: *Water has gone too cold before the gelatine fully dissolves.*

Antidote: *Place the bowl in a saucepan of hot water, so the water comes half-way up the bowl, and simmer for about 2 minutes until the gelatine dissolves.*

Symptom: *Food processor is not available.*

Diagnosis: *A food processor is quick, but not essential.*

Antidote: *Mix the quark and sugar in a mixing bowl, gradually blend in the coconut milk, and finally the dissolved gelatine.*

Cranberry, Pear, and Pecan Pudding

This pudding works equally well with blackcurrants, apples, and hazelnuts as the topping. The sponge base is quick to make and light in texture. If you divide the mixture between dariole moulds, you can bake and serve them as individual fruit puddings. Otherwise, you will need a 1 litre (2 pint) oval baking dish.

Ingredients to serve 6 to 8 people

2	ripe Conference *or* William pears
225 g (8 oz)	fresh *or* frozen cranberries
110 g (4 oz)	pecan halves
1 tablespoon	granulated sugar

Sponge

50 g (2 oz)	melted butter
3 large	beaten eggs
110 g (4 oz)	self-raising flour
50 g (2 oz)	castor sugar

Method

Wash and dice the pears. Wash and pick over the cranberries. Mix the pears, cranberries, and pecans with the tablespoon of granulated sugar.

Place the mixture in buttered dariole moulds, or a large oval baking dish.

Mix the melted butter, beaten eggs, flour, and castor sugar into a smooth batter. Pour the batter over the fruit and nut mixture.

Bake at Gas Mark 3 / 325°F / 170°C (150°C for fan oven) for either 15 – 20 minutes with dariole moulds, or 45 – 50 minutes with a large dish, until well risen and golden brown.

Turn out upside down like a traditional sponge pudding.

First Aid

Symptom: *Cranberry juice discolours the sponge pudding.*

Diagnosis: *Sponge tends to be a little soggy next to the fruit.*

Remedy: *Arrange only half the fruit in the base of the dish and save the rest for a topping.*

Quick Tiramisu

I think this Italian dish is similar to the English Tipsy Cake, with sponge soaked in alcohol, then covered in whipped cream. Mixing ready-made custard and mascarpone cheese with the cream gives it more body, but you could just use them in separate layers to give the pudding a striped effect.

You will need a 1 litre (2 pint) rectangular dish.

Ingredients to serve 8 people

2 tablespoons	coffee powder *or* granules
4 tablespoons	demerara sugar
275 ml (10 fl oz)	boiling water
4 tablespoons	brandy
~200 g (~7 oz) pack	sponge fingers
425 g (15 oz) can	ready-made custard
250 g (9 oz) tub	mascarpone cheese
275 ml (10 fl oz)	double cream
2 bars	chocolate flake
	cocoa powder for dusting

Method

Mix the coffee and sugar with the boiling water until dissolved. Add the brandy and leave to cool in a shallow dish.

Dip the sponge fingers in the coffee solution until soaked.

In a bowl, mix the custard and mascarpone using an electric whisk. Whip the cream and fold into the custard mixture.

In a large rectangular dish, spread 4 tablespoons of the creamy mixture evenly over the bottom. Cover with half the soaked sponge fingers and sprinkle with one chocolate flake bar. Repeat this process with the creamy mixture, and the remaining sponge fingers and chocolate flake. Cover with the remaining creamy mixture and dust with cocoa powder.

First Aid

Symptom: *Mascarpone cheese is not available or unsuitable.*

Diagnosis: *Used to add body and additional flavour.*

Antidote: *Substitute Italian ricotta, or quark skimmed milk cheese for a sharper taste.*

Raspberry Ripple Cream

If you want to use fresh raspberries, mash about half the quantity with a fork, to release their juices, and give the dish a marbled effect. Alternatively, freeze the raspberries for about one hour, and use as described in the recipe. This will rupture their cell walls, release the raspberry juice, and colour the cream mixture. You can substitute any other fresh soft fruit, similarly slightly crushed, according to availability.

Ingredients to serve 4 people

6 tablespoons	Greek yoghurt
2 tablespoons	clear honey
275 ml (10 fl oz)	double cream – whipped
25 g (1 oz)	fine oatmeal – lightly toasted
225 g (8 oz)	frozen raspberries – slightly thawed
	fresh raspberries for decoration

Method

Stir the yoghurt and honey into the whipped cream. Add the cold toasted oatmeal and stir until thoroughly combined. Gently fold in the partly thawed raspberries. Taste and adjust if required.

Spoon the mixture into glasses and leave to stand in the fridge for at least 1 hour, but ideally overnight.

Sprinkle with fresh raspberries just before serving.

First Aid

Symptom: *Porridge oatmeal is only available in the jumbo variety.*

Diagnosis: *Oats add body and texture to the dish, and the fine oatmeal more readily absorbs the other ingredients.*

Antidote: *Lightly toast the jumbo oats, then whiz in a food processor to obtain a finer texture.*

Lemon Pavlova

This dish contains raw egg §, so to avoid the risk of salmonella, look for packs of chilled pasteurised eggs in the chiller cabinet of your supermarket. Alternatively, you can use 'Lion' brand eggs produced by hens vaccinated against salmonella.

Ingredients to serve 8 people

Meringue §

4 large	egg whites
1 pinch	salt
225 g (8 oz)	castor sugar
2 level teaspoons	cornflour
1 teaspoon	white vinegar
¼ teaspoon	vanilla extract

Lemon Filling

4 large	egg yolks §
110 g (4 oz)	castor sugar
1 teaspoon	lemon rind
2 tablespoons	lemon juice
225 g (8 oz)	double cream

Method

Meringue §

Place the egg whites in a large bowl with a pinch of salt and whisk until it forms stiff glossy peaks.

Blend the sugar and cornflour together. Add 1 tablespoon of this mixture at a time to the whisked eggs, and beat between each addition. This should take 5 – 10 minutes. Once all the mixture is combined, stir in the white vinegar and vanilla extract.

Cover two baking trays with silicone paper. Lightly spread or pipe the meringue mixture to form a 22 cm (9") circle on each tray

Bake at Gas Mark 2 / 300°F / 150°C (130°C for fan oven) for about 1 hour until the meringues are dry to the touch and peel away from the silicone paper. Leave to cool completely.

Lemon Filling

Place the egg yolks and sugar in a bowl over a pan of hot water (the bowl must not touch the hot water) and whisk until creamy and the thickness of mayonnaise. Add the lemon rind and juice, and whisk again. Leave to cool completely.

Whip the cream until thick and gently fold into the lemon mixture until thoroughly combined.

Assembly

Place one meringue on a serving dish, and cover with the lemon filling. Place the other meringue on top of the filling. Dust with cocoa powder just before serving.

First Aid

Symptom: *Lemon Pavlova filling is too runny to spoon onto meringue.*

Diagnosis: *Too much lemon juice used.*

Antidote: *Spread meringues with lemon curd, and serve the runny lemon filling as an accompanying sauce. For a lighter filling whip up half a pint of cream, and fold in a tablespoon of lemon curd.*

Bags of Gold

You will have to prepare the filling and laces before frying off the pancakes; otherwise, the pancakes will not draw up easily, as they will have gone cold and set.

The pancake batter will benefit from being made a day in advance, to allow the starch granules to swell and become more adhesive. This produces a thinner batter, which yields more pancakes. Yippee! Yorkshire shrift strikes again.

Ingredients to serve 6 to 8 people

Pancake Batter §

110 g (4 oz)	plain flour
1 pinch	salt
2 large	eggs
150 ml (5 fl oz)	milk
150 ml (5 fl oz)	water

Laces and Filling

4 large	oranges – washed
2 dessertspoons	castor sugar
1 level teaspoon	cornflour
1 dessertspoon	cold water

Method

Batter

Sieve the flour and salt into a mixing bowl. Break the eggs into the flour and add the milk. Beat the mixture into a smooth thick batter, gradually adding all the water. Pour the batter into a jug and leave in the refrigerator overnight to relax.

Laces

Using a channelling knife § or vegetable peeler, remove the rind from the oranges in thin 15 cm (6") long strips, and keep covered in cling film to prevent drying out. These will form the laces to tie up the pancake bags of gold.

Filling

Use a sharp knife to remove the pith from the oranges, by slicing off the top and bottom of each orange and cutting down the sides. Segment the oranges into a bowl.

Drain off the orange juice into a small saucepan, add the castor sugar, and bring to the boil. Mix the cornflour with the water until smooth and then add to the orange juice off the heat. Return to the heat, and stir to the boil until thickened.

Add the thickened orange juice to the fresh orange segments, and leave to cool.

Pancakes §

Lightly oil a frying pan and allow it to get hot. A faint blue haze should appear just above the surface of the frying pan.

Pour in just enough pancake batter to thinly coat the surface of the frying pan. Allow the pancake to set around its edge. Flip the pancake over with a flick of the wrist, or using a palette knife or round-ended knife, and lightly cook the other side.

Turn onto a plate and spoon a small amount of the orange filling into the centre of the pancake, then draw up the pancake into a bag like a money pouch. Using the orange rind, tie the pancake bag around its neck to hold it in place.

Repeat the process with the remainder of the pancake batter and orange filling. If any filling remains, it can be served as a sauce with the bags of gold.

First Aid – *see also page 69*

Symptom: *Orange rind laces to tie pancakes are very difficult to create.*

Diagnosis: *Practice makes perfect.*

Antidote: *With the channelling knife §, start at one end of the orange and cut into the rind, then draw the knife around the orange peeling off a zesty ribbon.*

Remedy: *Alternatively, use a long leaf of chive for each lace.*

Chocolate, Rum and Raisin Cheesecake

Cheesecakes went out of fashion for a while, but let's hope this recipe brings them back onto dinner tables again. It is a rich, distinctively flavoured cheesecake that requires nothing more than an appetite to enjoy it. You can replace the quark with curd or cream cheese, but quark will give a lighter mousse. It is found in the chiller cabinets of large supermarkets.

You will need a greased 22 cm (9") flan dish or tin with a loose base.

Ingredients to serve 6 to 8 people

Base

150 g (5 oz)	digestive biscuits
75 g (3 oz)	butter
50 g (2 oz)	demerara sugar

Topping

40 g (1½ oz)	raisins
25 ml (1 fl oz)	rum
2	eggs – separated into whites and yolks §
50 g (2 oz)	caster sugar
1 teaspoon	instant coffee
5 tablespoons	boiling water
1 sachet	gelatine granules – from 6 sachet 70 g (3 oz) pack
50 g (2 oz)	plain chocolate §
250 g (9 oz) tub	quark §
150 ml (5 fl oz)	double cream
2 tablespoons	milk

Method

Soak the raisins in the rum, preferably overnight.

Base

Crush the biscuits between sheets of greaseproof paper until fine crumbs. Melt the butter in a saucepan, and stir in the crumbs and sugar on a gentle heat until well blended. Press the base into a greased flan dish or tin with a loose base. Refrigerate to harden well.

Topping

Mix the egg yolks, caster sugar, and coffee dissolved in 2 tablespoons of boiling water in the top of a double saucepan, or a bowl placed over boiling water. Stir steadily until the mixture clings to the back of a wooden spoon.

Dissolve the gelatine thoroughly in 3 tablespoons of boiling water, stir into the topping mixture, and remove from the heat.

Melt the chocolate § in a bowl placed over boiling water. Stir until smooth and blend into the topping mixture. Leave to cool.

Beat the quark, and when the topping is cool, stir it gradually into the quark. Whisk the cream with the milk to soft peaks and fold into the topping. Whisk the egg whites until stiff but not brittle and fold into the topping. Stir the rum-soaked raisins into the topping mixture. Pour the topping into the flan dish or tin and refrigerate until firmly set.

Decorate with piped whipped cream and chocolate flakes or crystallised flowers and leaves. Vary the flavour with sweet sherry instead of rum, or omit the raisins and double the quantity of chocolate.

First Aid

See the '**Coconut Mousse**' gelatine '**First Aid**' on page 175, and the '**Soft Fruit Jelly**' gelatine '**First Aid**' on page 188.

Symptom: *Gelatine and chocolate mixture set solid in the bowl.*

Diagnosis: *Mixture left unattended for too long.*

Antidote: *Place the bowl of chocolate mixture over a pan of simmering water, but without touching the water, until the sides of the mixture start to melt, and stir until all the mixture is of even consistency.*

Chocolate Truffle Cake

I have seen this type of pudding in the freezer cabinet of my local supermarket, but now you can make this yummy, calorie-laden cake for yourself. I have made it both with and without the sponge base. If you decide to omit the sponge, you must put the truffle mixture into the refrigerator to firm slightly, before pouring into the mould. Another tip is to use chocolate with a high percentage of cocoa solids; otherwise it won't set with the cream.

You will need a 22 cm (9") round loose-bottomed cake tin.

Ingredients to make a 9" cake

2 tablespoons	granulated sugar
50 ml (2 fl oz)	water
50 ml (2 fl oz)	dark rum
450 g (1 lb)	cooking chocolate § (minimum 50% cocoa solids)
570 ml (1 pt)	whipping cream
22 cm (9") round	chocolate sponge base
25 g (1 oz)	cocoa powder

Method

Boil the sugar in the water until to form a thin syrup, and add the dark rum.

Meanwhile, melt the chocolate § in a large bowl over a saucepan of simmering water, ensuring the water does not touch the bowl.

Lightly whip the cream until floppy and just holding its shape.

Place the sponge base into a loose-bottomed round cake tin. Brush the sponge base with the rum syrup.

Pour the whipped cream into the melted chocolate and lightly blend together. Pour the mixture over the sponge base and set in the refrigerator until firm.

Just before serving, remove the cake from the tin and dust with cocoa powder.

First Aid

Symptom: *Chocolate and cream unevenly mixed before pouring into base.*

Diagnosis: *Probably added the chocolate to the cream instead of vice versa.*

Antidote: *Place the bowl of chocolate and cream over a pan of simmering water, but without touching the water, until the mixture starts to blend together. Remove from the heat and stir constantly until a uniform colour is obtained.*

Strawberry Hearts

What sells this dish is its simplicity; good quality shortbread, strawberry jam, and fresh strawberries, but not a dollop of cream in sight!

Ingredients to serve 6 people

Biscuits

150 g (6 oz)	plain flour
100 g (4 oz)	butter
50 g (2 oz)	castor sugar

Topping

2 tablespoons	good quality strawberry jam
225 g (8 oz)	fresh strawberries
	icing sugar for dusting

Method

Either buy six shortbread biscuits, or make your own biscuits as follows.

Sieve the flour, and rub in the butter, until it looks like breadcrumbs. Add the castor sugar, and rub in until the mixture forms a ball.

Roll out onto a floured surface. The mixture should be 3 mm ($^1/_8$") thick. Using a heart shaped cutter, stamp out six biscuits, and place on a greased baking sheet.

Bake at Gas Mark 5 / 375°F / 190°C (170°C for fan oven) for 10 – 15 minutes, until pale beige in colour.

Leave to cool slightly, before carefully removing from the baking sheet. Allow to cool completely, before spreading the biscuits with strawberry jam.

Hull the fresh strawberries, and slice them evenly. Starting from the outside edge, overlap the sliced strawberries onto the biscuits, working towards the middle in a spiral.

Lightly dust with icing sugar just before serving.

First Aid

Symptom: *Shortbread hearts are soft and soggy when served*

Diagnosis: *Either the shortbread was not cooked sufficiently, or assembled too far in advance.*

Remedy: *Bake the shortbread biscuits a little longer, so that they are crispy when broken in half. Do not assemble until just before serving.*

Fresh Fruit Dishes

See the earlier chapter '**Are You Picking the Best Ingredients?**' for general advice on finding the '**Pick of the Bunch of Fruit and Vegetables**'.

Rhubarb Upside Down Scone

The beauty of this dish is that it has that wow factor when you turn it out onto a serving plate. What you see are pieces of rhubarb standing on end, like old-fashioned cobbles, held in place by a soft textured scone base. Use the first of the season 'Champagne rhubarb', which has pale pink stalks, yellow tufted leaves, and the sweetest of flavours, and you will need no further sweetening. Otherwise, you will require the granulated sugar mentioned in the ingredients for the fruit.

Ingredients to serve 6 people

450 g (1 lb)	rhubarb
25 g (1 oz)	granulated sugar

Scone

225 g (8 oz)	self-raising flour
1 teaspoon	baking powder
1 teaspoon	cinnamon powder
1 teaspoon	ground ginger
50 g (2 oz)	granulated sugar
75 ml (3 fl oz)	plain low fat yoghurt
50 ml (2 fl oz)	skimmed milk

Method

Wash and trim the rhubarb, and cut into even sized 2.5 cm (1") pieces. Arrange them evenly on end in a circular 20 cm (8") sponge tin, and lightly sprinkle the sugar over the rhubarb.

Sieve the flour, baking powder, and spices into a large mixing bowl and stir in the sugar. Add the yoghurt and milk to form a soft, elastic scone dough.

Knead the dough lightly until just combined and shape it to the size of the circular sponge tin. Place the scone dough on top of the rhubarb.

Bake at Gas Mark 7 / 425°F / 220°C (200°C for fan oven) at the top of the oven for 30 – 40 minutes, until it is well risen, golden brown, and sounds hollow when tapped on top.

Leave to cool slightly before turning out scone side down onto a plate.

First Aid

Symptom: *Rhubarb stuck to the base of the tin after baking.*

Remedy: *Line base of tin with silicone paper to ease removal.*

Clementines with Rubies

This is a winter dish, when both fruits are readily available. Being light and juicy, it is an ideal pudding after a heavy meal. I usually segment the clementines, but you can serve them whole or sliced as you prefer.

Ingredients to serve 4 people

8 uniform size	clementines
150 ml (5 fl oz)	water
110 g (4 oz)	granulated sugar
2 tablespoons	Grand Marnier® *or* Dubonnet® (optional)
1	pomegranate

Method

Peel and segment the clementines, and carefully remove all the white pith. Place the clementine segments in a serving bowl.

Boil the water and sugar in a saucepan, stirring occasionally, until a thick syrupy mixture is obtained. The syrup should have the consistency of cough linctus.

Remove from the heat, and add the liqueur if desired. Pour the syrup over the clementine segments, and leave to cool.

Peel and separate the pomegranate, carefully removing all the membranes. Stir the pomegranate fruit pods (rubies) into the clementine mixture and serve.

First Aid

Symptom: *Clementines are messy to prepare and sometimes unavailable.*

Diagnosis: *Other types of fruit are acceptable.*

Antidote: *Use halved kumquats with the skin on, or stoned and peeled lychees.*

Banana Rumba

Banana and rum are a marriage made in heaven, providing you like both ingredients. If you want to serve this dish later rather than sooner, then add a little lemon juice, otherwise the bananas will eventually discolour.

Ingredients to serve 4 people

2 large ripe	bananas
2 tablespoons	dark rum
1 tablespoon	brown sugar
275 ml (10 fl oz)	double cream
	cocoa powder

Method

Mash the bananas with the rum and sugar until the mixture is smooth.

Whip the double cream until it is just floppy.

Add the banana mixture to the whipped cream and mix thoroughly.

Serve in long tall glasses, and dust with cocoa powder. Alternatively, you could serve in chocolate cup cases.

First Aid

Symptom: *Bananas are too hard, and difficult to mash.*

Diagnosis: *Under-ripe fruit used.*

Antidote:	Microwave the chopped bananas for about a minute to soften them, leave to cool, and then mash.

Symptom:	Bananas turn black by the time they are served.
Diagnosis:	Bananas will discolour through oxidisation if kept too long.
Remedy:	Add the juice of a lemon to the mashed bananas.

Peach Hedgehogs

Although I have used peaches here, you can hedgehog any stoned fruit. Once the fruit is cooked the dish can be served immediately or allowed to cool. I usually cut off just a sliver of the flesh at the base, so that the fruit halves sit firmly, otherwise they tend to roll around the plate.

Ingredients to serve 2 people
2 whole	peaches

Stuffing
8	amaretto biscuits
25 g (1 oz)	demerara sugar
25 g (1 oz)	whole almonds
1 tablespoon	egg white

Decoration
1 tablespoon	flaked almonds

Method

Cut the peaches in half and remove their stones.

Place the amaretto biscuits, sugar, and almonds in a food processor and whiz. When a rough texture is obtained, add the egg white to just bind the mixture. One very quick whiz should be enough.

Divide the mixture equally between the four peach halves. Stick the flaked almonds into the mixture similar to hedgehog spines.

When required, either grill until the almonds go brown, or place on a baking sheet and bake at Gas Mark 4 / 350°F / 180°C (160°C for fan oven) for about 15 minutes until just soft.

First Aid

Symptom:	Peaches roll around when preparing, baking, and eating.
Diagnosis:	Peaches and most other fruit are round and roll easily.
Antidote:	Cut a sliver off the base to make the fruit more stable.

Symptom:	Peaches have a distasteful furry skin.
Diagnosis:	Acquired taste.
Antidote:	If the peaches are baked correctly, the furry skin should slip off easily before serving.

Baked Nectarines

This is such a simple fruit dish in which you can vary the fruit according to availability. Either keep to a single variety of fruit, or perhaps try a mixture of fruits. I particularly like blackberries and apricots, or raspberries and cherries baked together. Cooking the fruit releases the juices and tempers acidity; making them more acceptable to the sweet toothed.

Ingredients to serve 4 people

4 whole	nectarines
110 g (4 oz)	demerara sugar
225 ml (8 fl oz)	orange juice
3 tablespoons	Grand Marnier® *or* Cointreau®
	Greek yoghurt *or* flavoured cream

Method

Cut the nectarines in half and remove their stones. Lay them cut side up in a shallow ovenproof dish. Sprinkle them with the sugar, orange juice, and liqueur.

Bake at Gas Mark 6 / 400°F / 200°C (180°C for fan oven) for 20 – 25 minutes until tender.

Serve with Greek yoghurt or flavoured cream.

First Aid

Symptom: *Nectarine stones are awkward to remove.*

Diagnosis: *Some stones are more difficult to remove than others.*

Antidote: *Cut the nectarines into quarters and ease the stone from the fruit.*

Plum Fool

You can use any fruit to make into a fool, but in order to get the most flavour out of your chosen fruit it must be puréed or finely chopped. I remove the skin from plums, because I find it chewy in the fool, but you can leave it on if your palate is different to mine. Then it's a matter of blending together the poached fruit with mascarpone or quark § (if you prefer a sharper tang), plus whipped cream, and sugar to taste.

Ingredients to serve 4 people

450 g (1 lb)	plums
50 g (2 oz)	granulated sugar
50 ml (2 fl oz)	water
284 ml (10 fl oz) tub	whipping cream
250 g (9 oz) tub	quark § *or* mascarpone cheese
2 tablespoons	icing sugar

Method

Cut the plums in half and remove their stones. Cut eight thin slices from one of the plum halves, leaving the skin on, cover the slices, and set aside for decoration.

Place the sugar and water into a large saucepan, stir over a low heat until the sugar has dissolved, then add the stoned plums. Simmer gently for 5 minutes, remove the poached plums and let them cool.

Remove the skin from the poached plums and ensure there are no stones. Place the plum flesh in a food processor and whiz until roughly chopped. Put the chopped plums into the refrigerator to chill.

Whip the cream to a stiff peak.

Beat the cheese, add the chilled chopped plums, and mix together. Fold enough icing sugar to your taste into the plum and cheese mixture. Carefully fold the mixture into the whipped cream.

Spoon the fool into individual glasses and decorate with the thin plum slices.

First Aid

Symptom: *Plums are not available fresh, but only in the form of prunes.*

Diagnosis: *Prunes are a suitable substitute for plums.*

Antidote: *Simmer the prunes in the syrup, as for the fresh plums, but for 10 – 15 minutes to allow them to soften, then leave to cool.*

Soft Fruit Jelly

Many people are put off making jelly because of dealing with gelatine, but all you've got to remember is to lightly and evenly sprinkle the powdered gelatine onto the warmed liquid, stir it in, and allow to dissolve. Gently reheat the liquid if the gelatine does not completely dissolve.

This fruit jelly is clear, allowing the colour and shape of the fruit to be admired before eating.

You will need a 1 kg (2 lb) rectangular loaf tin or plastic box.

Ingredients to serve 6 people

570 ml (1 pt)	clear fruit flavoured water
50 g (2 oz)	castor sugar
2 sachets	gelatine granules – from 6 sachet 70 g (3 oz) pack
2 tablespoons	rose water (optional)
450 g (1 lb)	mixed soft fresh (not frozen) small even sized fruit such as strawberries, raspberries, blackcurrants, and redcurrants

Method

In a small saucepan, bring one third of the flavoured water to the simmer. Add the sugar and sprinkle in the gelatine, and while simmering stir until completely dissolved.

Remove from the heat. Add the remaining flavoured water and optionally the rose water. Allow the jelly mixture to cool.

Meanwhile remove any stalks from the mixed fruit and wash them. Arrange a selection of the fruit attractively in the base of the rectangular container. Pour in the cool jelly until it just covers the layer of fruit, and leave it to set.

Mix the remaining fruit together and place gently on top of the set jellied fruit. Pour in the remaining jelly until it covers the fruit, and leave until it is just set.

Pour in any remaining jelly to form a smooth surface, and leave until fully set.

To serve, dip the rectangular container into boiling water for a few seconds (count to 5) and invert onto a serving plate. It is easier to serve slices of the jelly if cut with a warm knife.

First Aid

See the '**Coconut Mousse**' gelatine '**First Aid**' on page 175.

Symptom:	*Gelatine granules are not available, only gelatine sheets.*
Diagnosis:	*Gelatine sheets are more expensive, but give a clearer set.*
Antidote:	*Use 10 sheets of gelatine, and follow the instructions on the packet, or soak them in cold water for 15 – 20 minutes. Remove and drain thoroughly, and squeeze gently to remove excess water. Stir the drained sheets into the hot liquid, in place of the granules, but ensure they are completely dissolved before proceeding.*

Summer Pudding

Here those soft summer berry fruits are encased in a bread igloo, which can vary in size from an individual igloo for one person to a large family sized version.

You will need either six individual 150 ml (5 fl oz) pudding basins, or one large 850 ml (1.5 pint) pudding basin.

Ingredients to serve 6 people

225 g (8 oz)	granulated sugar
275 ml (10 fl oz)	water
110 g (4 oz)	blackcurrants
110 g (4 oz)	redcurrants
110 g (4 oz)	blackberries
110 g (4 oz)	raspberries
225 g (8 oz)	strawberries
12 slices	thick sliced bread
	whipping cream

Method

Place the sugar and water in a saucepan, and stir until the sugar is dissolved. Bring to the boil, and boil for about 5 minutes, until a thin syrup is achieved.

Meanwhile, remove any stalks from the mixed berry fruits, wash them, and cut the strawberries to the size of blackberries. Carefully place all the fruit in a large mixing bowl

Pour the boiling syrup over the fruit, stir **gently**, and leave to cool. When cold, remove all the fruit to a clean bowl with a slotted spoon, and save the fruit syrup.

Trim the crusts from the sliced bread. Cut some slices of bread into fingers to line the side of the basin(s), and cut the remainder into circles to line the top and bottom of the basin(s).

For example, to line six small basins; cut six slices of bread in half and each half into six fingers; then, using pastry cutters, cut a top and bottom circle from each of the other six slices. Use a basin, as a guide, to check the bread will fit.

Lightly grease the pudding basin(s). Dip one side only of each finger and circle of bread in the fruit syrup.

Place a small circle of bread in the bottom of a basin, syrup side facing down. Place fingers of bread around the inside of a basin, syrup side facing out. Make sure there are no gaps between the pieces of bread.

Fill the lined basin with the strained poached fruit. Top the basin with a larger circle of bread, syrup side facing up.

If using more than one basin, repeat this process for each basin.

Cover the basin(s) with cling film and place in a refrigerator overnight. Traditionally, a weighted plate is put on top of the basin to compress the filling, but if you use six small basins, this is not necessary. Keep any surplus fruit syrup in the refrigerator too.

Turn out the summer pudding(s) onto the service plate(s) and spoon over any surplus fruit syrup to obtain a uniform colour. Top with whipped cream and serve.

First Aid

Symptom: *Summer pudding collapses or sticks when turned out.*

Diagnosis: *Bread pressed too firmly and sticks in the basin.*

Remedy: *Line the basin with cling film, before lining with bread, to aid removal of the pudding. When set, unwrap the cling film from the top of the basin, and place the serving plate upside down over the basin. Invert the plate and basin, slip the basin off the cling film clad pudding, and carefully peel away the cling film.*

Cakes and Sponges

See page 76 for guidelines on '**Baking Cakes and Sponges**'.

Chocolate Cake

This is a showstopper of a cake! Well, it worked for me on my debut broadcast on BBC Essex local radio. I took this cake as a talking point, and the team loved it so much that they invited me back the next month. That was in 1995 and I've been back every month since. It has a superbly intense taste, a rich dark chocolate colour, and the texture is very close, so it is easy to slice.

You will need two 20 cm (8") sandwich tins, which have been greased, and the base lined with greaseproof paper.

Ingredients to make an 8" cake
Sponge

175 g (6 oz)	self-raising flour
1 heaped teaspoon	baking powder
110 g (4 oz)	cocoa powder
110 g (4 oz)	caster sugar
1 dessertspoon	black treacle
150 ml (5 fl oz)	vegetable oil

150 ml (5 fl oz)	milk at room temperature
2 medium	eggs at room temperature

Filling

150 ml (5 fl oz)	double cream
1 dessertspoon	castor sugar

Topping

25 g (1 oz)	melted butter
150 g (5 oz)	icing sugar
3 teaspoons	cocoa powder
1 tablespoon	boiling water

Method

This rich chocolate cake is made using the uncomplicated all-in-one method.

Sponge

Sieve the flour, baking powder, cocoa powder, and castor sugar, and mix in a food processor, or alternatively, mix thoroughly with a wooden spoon.

Ensure they are at room temperature, and add the treacle, oil, milk, and eggs to the dry mix.

With a food processor, whiz for 15 seconds on maximum, scrape down, and whiz for a further 10 seconds. Alternatively, with a wooden spoon, beat vigorously for 2 minutes, until thoroughly combined, and the sugar has dissolved.

Divide the mixture evenly between two greased and lined sandwich tins.

Bake at Gas Mark 3 / 325°F / 170°C (150°C for fan oven) on the middle shelf of the oven for about 45 minutes. When cooked the cake should be springy to touch.

Leave to cool slightly before turning out. Peel off the greaseproof paper.

Filling and Topping

Whip together the double cream and castor sugar until the filling is stiff.

Cream together the melted butter, sieved icing sugar, and cocoa powder topping. Gradually add the boiling water and beat well.

Sandwich the sponges together with the whipped filling, and spread the topping evenly over the top of the cake.

First Aid

See the '**First Aid**' section of '**Baking Cakes and Sponges**' on page 76.

Symptom: *Cocoa packet is nearly empty with less than half the required amount.*

Diagnosis: *Always check availability of ingredients before starting a dish.*

Antidote: *Substitute self-raising flour for the missing cocoa powder.*

Baked All-In-One Sponge £ *

This is the quickest of the baked sponge recipes I have provided. The trick is that all the ingredients should be at room temperature. In addition, the extra baking powder gives a quick lift to a quickly prepared cake.

You will need two 18 cm (7") sandwich tins, which have been greased, and the base lined with greaseproof paper.

Ingredients to make a 7" cake

110 g (4 oz)	self-raising flour
1 level teaspoon	baking powder
110 g (4 oz)	castor sugar
110 g (4 oz)	soft butter *or* margarine at room temperature
2 large	eggs at room temperature
	jam *or* marmalade *or* cream

Method

This rich baked sponge recipe uses the quick all-in-one method.

Sieve the flour and baking powder into a large bowl. Add the castor sugar, butter or margarine, and eggs, ensuring they are at room temperature. Beat with a wooden spoon for about 3 minutes until thoroughly blended, and the sugar has dissolved.

Divide the mixture evenly between two greased and lined sandwich tins.

Bake at Gas Mark 4 / 350°F / 180°C (160°C for fan oven) for 25 – 30 minutes until golden brown, well risen, and springy to touch.

Leave to cool slightly before turning out of the tins. Peel off the greaseproof paper, and sandwich the two sponges together with jam, marmalade, or cream. The jam variety is the traditional Victoria sandwich.

First Aid

See the '**First Aid**' section of '**Baking Cakes and Sponges**' on page 76.

Symptom: *Sponge cake is flat, heavy, and thick.*

Diagnosis: *Plain flour used, baking powder omitted, or insufficient beating.*

Remedy: *Use self-raising flour and baking powder. Beat for at least 3 minutes.*

Citrus Yoghurt Cake

I love cakes that are easy-peasy to make, and this creation fully lives up to my expectations. Don't think I've compromised on taste and texture. I haven't. However, I'll let you bite into it and you can decide.

When you mix the orange rind with the sugar and yoghurt, just enjoy the beautiful orange hue that is created. I sometimes substitute another citrus fruit in place of the orange, as they all work equally well.

You will need two 18 cm (7") sandwich tins, which have been greased.

Ingredients to make a 7" cake

Sponge

150 g (5 oz)	plain yoghurt
	rind of an orange
275 g (10 oz)	castor sugar
275 g (10 oz)	self-raising flour – sieved
2 large	beaten eggs at room temperature
110 ml (4 fl oz)	vegetable oil

Filling

2 tablespoons	fine cut orange marmalade

Topping

110 g (4 oz)	icing sugar – sieved
2 tablespoons	juice of an orange

Method

This is a plain yoghurt cake and effectively uses the easy all-in-one method.

Sponge

Beat the yoghurt, orange rind, and castor sugar in a bowl until smooth. Stir in the sieved self-raising flour, beaten eggs, and vegetable oil. Stir the mixture until smooth and lump free. Divide the mixture evenly between two greased sandwich tins and level off the mixture.

Bake at Gas Mark 5 / 375°F / 190°C (170°C for fan oven) on the middle shelf of the oven for 25 – 30 minutes, until golden brown, and springy to the touch.

Allow them to cool slightly before turning the sponges out of the tins.

Filling and Topping

Carefully spread the marmalade over one of the sponges, and sandwich them together.

Place the sieved icing sugar in a mixing bowl, add the orange juice, and stir to form a smooth paste (the consistency of thick double cream). Pour the paste over the top of the cake and spread evenly. Eat and enjoy.

First Aid – see page 76

No Fat Tea Loaf £

My Yorkshire thrift comes to the fore when I make this cake. I'm a tea belly at heart, although sometimes I don't drink the teapot dry, so this is an ideal way of using up the remains of the tea!

You will need a 20 cm x 10 cm (8" x 4") rectangular loaf tin, which is greased, and the base lined with silicone or greaseproof paper.

Ingredients to make an 8" x 4" loaf

225 g (8 oz)	sultanas &/or raisins
175 ml (6 fl oz)	cold tea
225 g (8 oz)	self-raising flour
1 pinch	salt
110 g (4 oz)	demerara sugar
1 large	beaten egg at room temperature

Method

This no fat loaf uses the straightforward all-in-one method.

Soak the sultanas &/or raisins in the cold tea in a large mixing bowl overnight.

Sieve the flour and salt into the bowl of tea-soaked fruit, then add the sugar and beaten egg, and stir until combined.

Place the mixture into the greased and lined loaf tin, and level the top of the mixture.

Place on the middle shelf of the oven to bake at Gas Mark 4 / 350°F / 180°C (160°C for fan oven) for ¾ – 1 hour until well risen, golden brown, shrunken from the sides slightly, and springy to touch.

Leave to cool slightly before turning out onto a cooling tray.

First Aid *– see also page 76*

Symptom: *Tea loaf crust appears rough, tough, and uneven after baking.*

Diagnosis: *Sloppy preparation when levelling the mixture.*

Remedy: *Take extra care to level the mixture, with a moist round-ended knife or clean finger, before baking.*

Sugarless Low Fat Boiled Pineapple Cake

This is a boiled fruitcake without any added sugar and very little fat, but this doesn't detract from the impressive flavour and texture, which is sweet and moist. Tinned pineapple in natural juice plus the natural fruit sugar from the dried fruit make this cake a winner. Well worth making!

You will need a 20 cm (8") cake tin, greased, and lined with greaseproof paper.

Ingredients to serve 6 to 8 portions

425 g (15 oz) can	pineapple in natural juice
450 g (1 lb)	mixed dried fruit
1 teaspoon	mixed spice
2 tablespoons	corn oil
2 medium	eggs at room temperature
225 g (8 oz)	wholemeal self-raising flour

Method

Crush the canned pineapple in its natural juice. Place the pineapple, mixed fruit, mixed spice, and corn oil in a saucepan. Bring slowly to the boil for 3 minutes only and leave until absolutely cold (preferably overnight).

Beat the eggs, then blend the eggs and flour into the fruity mixture in the saucepan. Place the mixture in a greased and lined cake tin.

Bake at Gas Mark 3 / 325°F / 170°C (150°C for fan oven) for about 1½ hours, covering if necessary. Test if done with a skewer.

When cold, store in the refrigerator.

First Aid *– see also page 76*

Symptom: *Boiled cake appears heavy and stodgy after baking.*

Diagnosis: *There are several explanations. Mixture is too wet, flour added to a hot mixture, insufficient baking time, or oven temperature too low.*

Remedy: *Ensure the fruit is boiled for a full 3 minutes. Ensure the boiled fruit mixture is **completely cold** before adding the flour, to prevent destroying its self-raising properties. Check the cooking time with a timer, and the oven temperature with a thermometer, to give the raising agent the correct working conditions.*

Gingerbread £

This is a fine textured cake that is dark, moist, and sticky, with that ginger warmth in every bite. I've tried many recipes, and consider this to be one of the best for flavour, texture, and keeping quality.

You will need a 20 cm (8") square tin, greased, and lined with greaseproof paper.

Ingredients to make an 8" square

110 g (4 oz)	self-raising flour
110 g (4 oz)	plain flour
1 level teaspoon	bicarbonate of soda
1 teaspoon	mixed spice
1 teaspoon	ground cinnamon
3 teaspoon	ground ginger
75 g (3 oz)	butter
75 g (3 oz)	dark muscovado sugar
1 tablespoon	black treacle
1 tablespoon	golden syrup
150 ml (5 fl oz)	milk
1 large	beaten egg

Method

This ginger cake uses the melting method.

Sift the six dry ingredients into a large mixing bowl.

Melt the butter, sugar, treacle, and syrup in a saucepan on a low heat, but **do not boil**. Leave to cool slightly, then add the milk, and stir until combined.

Pour the warm milky syrup into the dry flour mixture and add the beaten egg. Carefully fold together until the mixture is well combined. The mixture should be like a thick batter at this stage. Pour the gingerbread batter into the prepared baking tin.

Bake at Gas Mark 3 / 325°F / 170°C (150°C for fan oven) for about 1 hour, until well risen, firm, and springy to the touch.

Leave the gingerbread to cool completely. Remove it from the tin, still in its greaseproof paper, and wrap in kitchen foil. If you can hold off from sinking your teeth into the gingerbread, it will benefit from a couple of days storage to improve the flavour and texture.

First Aid – *see also page 76*

Symptom: *Gingerbread has sunk in the middle after baking.*

Diagnosis: *In addition to the sunk cake '****First Aid****' referenced above, it may be that too much sugar, or syrup, or treacle was used.*

Remedy: *Ensure the ingredients are measured carefully.*

Oatmeal Parkin

Mention parkin and I immediately think of bonfire night, because traditionally this is when it is eaten. I think parkin is ginger cake with attitude. It's the oatmeal that gives it a coarser texture and therefore satisfies you for longer.

You will need a 23 cm (9") square baking tin, which is greased, and lined with greaseproof paper.

Ingredients to make a 9" square

225 g (8 oz)	plain flour
2 level teaspoons	baking powder
4 level teaspoons	ground ginger
110 g (4 oz)	margarine *or* lard at room temperature
225 g (8 oz)	medium oatmeal
110 g (4 oz)	castor sugar
175 g (6 oz)	golden syrup
175 g (6 oz)	black treacle
4 tablespoons	milk
1 large	beaten egg at room temperature

Method

This ginger cake uses a combination of the rubbing-in and melting methods.

Sift the flour, baking powder, and ground ginger into a large bowl. Rub the fat into the flour mixture until it resembles fine breadcrumbs. Stir in the oatmeal and castor sugar.

Gently heat the syrup and treacle together until well blended. **Do not boil**.

Add the milk, beaten egg, and warmed syrup and treacle to the dry mixture. Stir until thoroughly mixed. Pour the mixture into the greased lined baking tin.

Bake at Gas Mark 4 / 350°F / 180°C (160°C for fan oven) for 45 – 60 minutes until well-risen, and springy to touch.

Allow it to cool slightly before turning out. Keep for a week before eating.

First Aid – *see also page 76*

Symptom: *Parkin is dense and hard after baking.*

Diagnosis: *Syrup and treacle mixture accidentally boiled.*

Remedy: *Watch the syrup and treacle carefully and prevent it boiling.*

Baked Rubbed-In Sponge £ *

If you want to get someone interested in cake making, try this rubbing-in method – it is quick and easy, and gives reliable results. However, the cake will be coarser in texture than one made by the creaming method given later. Also, the top may appear a little domed with a crack along its length, but it should never have a peak.

You will need a 15 cm (6") tin, which has been greased, and the base lined with silicone or greaseproof paper.

Ingredients to make a 6" cake

225 g (8 oz)	self-raising flour
1 pinch	salt
110 g (4 oz)	soft butter *or* margarine at room temperature
110 g (4 oz)	castor sugar
2 large	beaten eggs at room temperature
2 tablespoons	milk at room temperature

Method

Sieve the flour and salt into a large bowl. Rub in the fat until the mixture resembles breadcrumbs. Stir in the sugar, the beaten eggs, and the milk to form a soft consistency. Place the mixture into a greased tin.

Bake at Gas Mark 4 / 350°F / 180°C (160°C for fan oven) for 1 – 1¼ hours until golden brown, well risen, and springy to touch.

Leave to cool slightly before turning out of the tin. Peel off the greaseproof paper, and serve with traditional custard.

Variations

Fruit and Nut

If you want to pep up this sponge cake, try adding the following to vary its taste and look.

110 g (4 oz)	dried fruit such as sultanas, raisins, currants, *or* mixed fruit
50 g (2 oz)	chopped walnuts, hazelnuts, *or* almonds

Add the chosen fruit and nuts to the dry mix, before adding the eggs and milk.

Double Chocolate Chip

If you are a chocoholic this variation should suit you well.

25 g (1 oz)	cocoa powder
75 g (3 oz)	chocolate drops

Replace 25 g (1 oz) of the flour with the cocoa powder, and sieve it in with the remaining flour and the salt. Stir the chocolate drops into the dry mix, just before adding the eggs and milk.

First Aid – *see also page 76*

Symptom: *Sponge cake is flat, heavy, and thick.*

Diagnosis: *Plain flour used or insufficiently rubbed-in.*

Remedy: *Use self-raising flour and rub-in well to incorporate plenty of air.*

Apple, Date, and Walnut Tea Bread

You've probably eaten date and walnut cake, but adding diced apples gives a moist texture to an already winning combination. It is very easy to make, and once baked, it slices beautifully, and is particularly handy for picnics.

You will need a 1 kg (2 lb) loaf tin, greased and lined with greaseproof paper.

Ingredients to make a 2lb loaf

175 g (6 oz)	self-raising flour (optionally wholemeal)
50 g (2 oz)	oatmeal
110 g (4 oz)	margarine *or* butter at room temperature
110 g (4 oz)	castor sugar
1 level teaspoon	cinnamon
225 g (8 oz)	peeled, cored, diced apples §
110 g (4 oz)	walnut pieces – finely chopped
110 g (4 oz)	dates – finely chopped §
2 large	beaten eggs at room temperature

Method

This rich tea bread uses the tactile rubbing-in method.

Sieve the flour. Rub the fat into the flour and oatmeal until well distributed. Mix the sugar and cinnamon into the flour mixture.

Peel, core, and dice the apples. Finely chop the walnuts and dates dates. Beat the eggs. Stir these ingredients into the flour mixture until well blended. Place in the lined loaf tin. Bake at Gas Mark 4 / 350°F / 180°C (160°C for fan oven) for 1 – 1¼ hours until well risen, golden brown, and shrunk slightly from the sides of the tin.

Allow it to cool slightly before turning out onto a cooling tray.

First Aid – *see also page 76*

Symptom: *Oatmeal ingredient is not available or not liked.*

Diagnosis: *Oatmeal simply adds body and fibre to the tea bread.*

Antidote: *Increase the flour (preferably wholemeal) to replace the oatmeal.*

Fatless Whisked Sponge *

This very light and airy textured cake is devoid of fat, except the tiny amount in the egg yolks. It is made quickly, baked quickly, and eaten quickly, since it does not keep long due to its lack of fat. The Catherine wheel shaped Swiss roll is always made using this sponge mix.

You will need two 18 cm (7") sandwich tins, lightly oiled, and their bases lined with lightly greased silicone or greaseproof paper.

Ingredients to make a 7" sponge

3 large	eggs at room temperature
75 g (3 oz)	castor sugar
75 g (3 oz)	plain flour
1 tablespoon	warm water
2 tablespoons	jam *or* puréed fresh fruit *or* cooked apple

Method

Ensure all the utensils and mixing bowls are completely free from grease.

Place the eggs and sugar in a large mixing bowl, and place over a saucepan of hot water, but without the water touching the bowl. Using an electric hand-held mixer, whisk the mixture until it becomes light and creamy, doubles in bulk, and shows the marks of the mixer if trailed across the top of the mixture.

Sieve the flour twice. Fold it into the mixture very gently, while adding the warm water. Spoon equal quantities of the mixture into both lined sandwich tins.

Bake at Gas Mark 4 / 350°F / 180°C (160°C for fan oven) on a middle to upper middle shelf of the oven for 20 – 25 minutes until golden brown, springy in centre, and shrunk from sides slightly.

Leave to cool slightly before turning out of the tins. Peel off the greaseproof paper, and sandwich the two sponges together with either jam or puréed fresh fruit or cooked apple. Serve with traditional custard.

First Aid – *see also page 76*

Symptom: *Baked whisked sponge has a chewy texture.*
Diagnosis: *The mixture was over processed while folding in the flour.*
Remedy: *Use a light gentle folding action to blend in the flour.*

Symptom: *Baked sponge has pieces of raw flour visible.*
Diagnosis: *Insufficient blending of the flour.*
Antidote: *Use as the base of a trifle if the flour cannot be disguised.*
Remedy: *Ensure all the flour is blended without over processing.*

Genoese Whisked Sponge *

Adding cool melted butter to the whisked sponge mixture extends the keeping qualities, as well as improving the taste of this cake. As soon as the butter touches the aerated mixture, you will notice that volume is lost. Therefore, fold in the butter as lightly as possible. I have replaced a small amount of flour with the same quantity of cornflour to aid lightness.

You will need two 20 cm (8") sandwich tins, lightly oiled, and their bases lined with silicone or greaseproof paper.

Ingredients to make an 8" cake

40 g (1½ oz)	unsalted butter
65 g (2½ oz)	plain flour
1 level tablespoon	cornflour
3 large	eggs at room temperature
75 g (3 oz)	castor sugar

Method

Melt the unsalted butter and leave it to cool. Sieve the plain flour and cornflour together.

Break the eggs and sugar in a large bowl, over a saucepan of hot water, but without the water touching the bowl. Use an electric whisk to beat until light and creamy. You should be able to write your name in the mixture without it disappearing.

Sieve half of the flour mixture into the beaten eggs and sugar. Using a metal spoon, gently fold the ingredients to combine them.

Fold in the cooled melted butter and the rest of the flour as carefully as you can to avoid losing volume. Do not over-mix. Divide the mixture equally between the two sandwich tins.

Bake at Gas Mark 5 / 375°F / 190°C (170°C for fan oven) for 20 – 25 minutes until golden brown.

Leave to cool slightly before turning out of the tins. Peel off the greaseproof paper, and sandwich the sponges together with either jam or marmalade.

First Aid

See '**First Aid**' for '**Baking Cakes and Sponges**' on page 76 and for '**Fatless Whisked Sponge**' on page 197.

Symptom: *Baked whisked sponge has heavy close texture.*

Diagnosis: *Butter was added while hot, or the mixture was over mixed.*

Remedy: *Allow the butter to cool before adding, and combine the ingredients as lightly as possible.*

Steamed Jam or Marmalade Sponge £ *

This is pure comfort food, and at times everyone needs a little comforting. Once you have the basic recipe, you can tailor it to your vision of comfort. Do this by adding such nuggets as a handful of dried fruit, a dollop of syrup, a sprinkling of candied ginger, pieces of chocolate, or slivers of nuts. The store cupboard version of this comfortable steamed sponge has jam or marmalade topping.

You will need a ½ litre (1 pt) pudding basin, which has been greased.

Ingredients to serve 4 people

50 g (2 oz)	margarine *or* butter at room temperature
50 g (2 oz)	castor sugar
1 large	egg at room temperature
1 tablespoon	milk at room temperature
110 g (4 oz)	self-raising flour
2 tablespoons	jam *or* marmalade

Method

This is a plain steamed sponge that uses the creaming method.

In one bowl, cream the fat and sugar together until soft and light in colour. In another bowl, beat the egg, add the milk, and stir together.

Add half the milky egg, and half the flour to the creamed mixture, and blend well. Add the remaining milky egg and flour, and mix until thoroughly combined. The mixture should be a soft dropping consistency. Add a little more milk if necessary.

Place the jam or marmalade in the bottom of the greased basin, top with the sponge mixture, and level off until smooth.

Cover the basin with kitchen foil or greaseproof paper, and ensure it is secured with string. Steam in a large saucepan half full of water for 1¼ – 1½ hours.

Leave to cool slightly before turning out of the basin. Serve with custard.

First Aid – *see also page 76*

Symptom: *Steamed sponge cake is wet and soggy.*

Diagnosis: *Steam or droplets of water have got into the pudding.*

Remedy: *Ensure the basin is watertight with a secure foil or greaseproof cover, and only half fill the saucepan with water. Put a small pebble in the saucepan, so it will rattle as an alarm, if the water boils dry, and prevent burning.*

Symptom: *Steamed sponge cake is dry and heavy.*

Diagnosis: *Unbalanced recipe, insufficiently creamed fat and sugar, or poorly incorporated milky egg and flour ingredients.*

Remedy: *Ensure self-raising flour is used. Cream the fat and sugar until light and fluffy. Lightly fold in the remaining ingredients.*

Baked Creamed Sponge £ *

This is the most traditional method of creating a baked sponge, and forms the basis of the well-known Victoria sandwich.

You will need two 18 cm (7") sandwich tins, which have been greased, and the base lined with greaseproof paper.

Ingredients to make a 7" cake

110 g (4 oz)	soft butter *or* margarine at room temperature
110 g (4 oz)	castor sugar
2 large	beaten eggs at room temperature
110 g (4 oz)	self-raising flour
1 level teaspoon	baking powder
	jam *or* marmalade *or* cream

Method

This rich baked sponge recipe uses the traditional creaming method.

In a large bowl, cream the fat with the sugar until light in colour, and creamy in texture. Beat the room temperature eggs, and blend a tablespoonful at a time with the creamed mixture, until well combined. Sieve the flour, and gently fold into the sponge mixture.

Divide the mixture evenly between two greased and lined sandwich tins.

Bake at Gas Mark 4 / 350°F / 180°C (160°C for fan oven) for 25 – 30 minutes until golden brown, well risen, and springy to touch.

Leave to cool slightly before turning out of the tins. Peel off the greaseproof paper, and sandwich the two sponges together with jam, marmalade, or cream. The jam variety is the traditional Victoria sandwich. Serve with custard.

First Aid – see also page 76

Symptom: *Baked sponge is flat, heavy, and thick.*

Diagnosis: *Plain flour used, insufficiently creamed fat and sugar, or poorly incorporated egg and flour ingredients.*

Remedy: *Ensure self-raising flour is used. Cream the fat and sugar until light and fluffy. Lightly fold in the remaining ingredients. Check the eggs are at room temperature.*

Rich Fruitcake

In order to get the best from this cake, buy the luxury quality dried fruit with added cherries, glacé pineapples, and apricots. It is worth paying that little bit extra, for a richer fruitier taste. This is particularly worthwhile when the cake accompanies a birthday, anniversary, or Christmas celebration.

You will need a 20 cm (8") round cake tin, greased and lined with greaseproof paper.

Ingredients to make an 8" cake

225 g (8 oz)	butter at room temperature
225 g (8 oz)	dark brown sugar
1 tablespoon	black treacle
450 g (1 lb)	good quality dried mixed fruit
275 g (10 oz)	plain flour
1 pinch	salt
4 large	eggs at room temperature

Method

In a large mixing bowl cream the butter, brown sugar, and black treacle until well combined. Add the mixed fruit and stir well.

Sieve the flour and salt together in a separate bowl.

Add one egg and a quarter of the flour and salt mixture to the fruitcake mix, and stir until well combined. Repeat with each egg and quarter of the flour and salt, until all the ingredients are combined. The fruitcake mix should have no pockets of white flour and should be of uniform colour.

Place the mixture in a greased and lined 20 cm (8") round cake tin.

Bake at Gas Mark 2 / 300°F / 150°C (130°C for fan oven) on the lower middle shelf of the oven for 1 hour, and then reduce to Gas Mark 1 / 275°F / 140°C (120°C for fan oven) for 2½ to 3 hours, until:

- The cake is firm to the touch.
- The cake has shrunk slightly from the sides.
- A skewer comes out clean when inserted into the middle of the cake.

Leave the cake to cool in the tin before turning out onto a cooling tray. When cold, wrap the cake in cling film, or store in an airtight plastic box until required.

First Aid – *see also page 76*

Symptom: *Fruitcake has a hard, humped, crusty top.*

Diagnosis: *Probably too hot an oven, or too long a cooking time.*

Remedy: *Check the oven temperature and cooking time. Cover the cake tin with a square of thick brown paper with the edges folded down, and increase the cooking time slightly, to obtain a softer crust.*

Biscuits and Scones

See the earlier chapters '**Are You Picking the Best Ingredients?**' and '**How Do You Cook With Confidence?**' for general advice and guidance.

Scones £ *

Scones take their name from the town of Scone in Scotland. Originally, they were baked on a girdle † over a peat fire. Nowadays, apart from girdle † scones, they are baked in an oven. Very good scones can be made using sour milk or buttermilk with equal quantities of bicarbonate of soda and cream of tartar instead of baking powder. † Girdle is the Scottish word for griddle.

Ingredients to make 6 to 8 scones

Alternative with self-raising flour

225 g (8 oz)	self-raising flour
1 level teaspoon	baking powder
½ level teaspoon	salt
25 – 50 g (1 – 2 oz)	fat
150 ml (5 fl oz)	fresh milk

Alternative with plain flour

225 g (8 oz)	plain flour
2½ – 3 level teaspoons	baking powder
½ level teaspoon	salt
25 – 50 g (1 – 2 oz)	fat
150 ml (5 fl oz)	fresh milk

Alternative with sour milk

225 g (8 oz)	plain flour
1 level teaspoon	bicarbonate of soda
1 level teaspoon	cream of tartar
½ level teaspoon	salt
25 – 50 g (1 – 2 oz)	fat
150 ml (5 fl oz)	sour milk *or* buttermilk

Method

Preheat the oven to Gas Mark 8 / 450°F / 230°C (210°C for fan oven). Lightly grease a baking tray.

Sieve the flour with the other dry powdered ingredients into a mixing bowl. Rub in the fat, aerating the flour at the same time. Make a deep well in the flour mixture, pour in almost all the milk, and mix to a soft spongy dough with a palette knife or round-ended knife, adding extra milk as necessary. On a floured surface, knead the dough very lightly until it is just smooth.

For traditional scones, lightly knead the dough into a ball, and then flatten the ball to 2.5 cm (1") thick, and cut it diametrically into six or eight triangles.

Otherwise, roll the dough to 2.5 cm (1") thick, and use 5 cm (2") or 7.5 cm (3") cutters to obtain round scones. Repeat with the off-cuts until all the dough is used.

Brush the scones with beaten egg for a glossy crust, or brush with flour for a soft crust. Bake the scones on the greased baking tray at the top of the preheated oven for 7 to 10 minutes until well risen and brown.

Sweet or Savoury

You can make the plain scones to use as you would bread or, with minor additions, you can create sweet or savoury variants.

With the addition of 40 g (1½ oz) castor sugar to the dough, they become the bases for a Devon cream tea.

The addition of 50 g (2 oz) finely grated strong cheese turns them into a savoury quick snack. Alternatively, you could add your favourite chopped herbs.

First Aid

Symptom: *Scones fall over to one side during baking.*

Diagnosis: *Dough was uneven or twisted by the cutter.*

Remedy: *Try to roll the dough as evenly as possible, and push the cutter straight down and lift straight up without any twisting motion.*

Symptom: *Scones lose their shape whilst baking.*

Diagnosis: *Recipe imbalance due to excess liquid or sugar in the dough.*

Remedy: *Check your recipe against my ingredients above.*

Symptom: *Scones are biscuit-like and crumbly in texture after baking.*

Diagnosis: *Recipe imbalance due to insufficient liquid in the dough.*

Antidote: *Use the scones as a crumble topping for poached fruit.*

Remedy: *Check your recipe against my ingredients above.*

Apple, Sultana, and Cinnamon Cakes

The fat usually used to make such cakes is here replaced by quark, which is a skimmed milk cheese, so it is low in fat. It can be purchased from supermarkets, and may be used extensively in cooked dishes, or as a low fat substitute for cream or curd cheese in many recipes.

Ingredients to make 8 cakes

225 g (8 oz)	self-raising flour
1 teaspoon	baking powder
1 teaspoon	cinnamon powder
50 g (2 oz)	castor sugar
50 g (2 oz)	quark §
1	eating apple
50 g (2 oz)	sultanas
50 ml (2 fl oz)	skimmed milk

Method

Sieve the flour, baking powder, and cinnamon into a large mixing bowl. Add the sugar and rub in the quark.

Core and peel the apple and cut into fine dice §. Stir the diced apple and sultanas into the mixture. Add the milk and stir thoroughly.

Form into eight even sized balls and flatten slightly to form a fishcake shape. Place on a greased baking tray.

Bake at Gas Mark 6 / 400°F / 200°C (180°C for fan oven) on the middle shelf of the oven for 20 – 25 minutes until well risen, golden brown, and just firm.

These cakes will not keep more than a day, so eat them quickly!

First Aid

Symptom: *Cinnamon cakes soon become dry and stale.*

Diagnosis: *There is no fat in the recipe, so prone to going stale quickly.*

Remedy: *Eat the cakes on the day of baking, or store in an airtight container, or freeze any surplus cakes and defrost and eat when required.*

Fruity Coconut Bars

These are soft textured, almost cake-like biscuits, ideal for the tuck box, or served with a refreshing cup of tea.

You will need a shallow 20 cm (8") square tin that is greased and lined with greaseproof paper.

Ingredients to make about 12 bars

110 g (4 oz)	wholemeal flour
1½ teaspoons	baking powder
110 g (4 oz)	brown sugar
225 g (8 oz)	dried fruit
75 g (3 oz)	desiccated coconut
½ teaspoon	cinnamon
¼ teaspoon	ground ginger
¼ teaspoon	ground nutmeg
2 large	eggs
75 g (3 oz)	margarine
1 tablespoon	milk

Method

Mix the flour, baking powder, sugar, dried fruit, coconut, cinnamon, ginger, and nutmeg together in a large mixing bowl.

Beat the eggs, melt the margarine, and add them with the milk to the dry mix. Combine until well mixed, and place in a greased and lined shallow square tin.

Bake at Gas Mark 4 / 350°F / 180°C (160°C for fan oven) for 50 minutes until well risen, golden brown, and shrunken slightly from the sides of the tin.

Leave to cool and cut into fingers for serving.

First Aid

Symptom: *Sugar was not added to the biscuit mixture before baking.*

Diagnosis: *Sugar adds sweetness and a moist texture.*

Antidote: Make some icing from 110 g (4 oz) sieved icing sugar and a little hot water to form a creamy paste, and after baking and cooling the biscuits, drizzle the icing over them.

Millionaires Shortbread

What a decadent name for a biscuit! It's the nearest I'll get to be wealthy, so I make and eat them all the time. What you get is a variety of textures and flavours in one biscuit, with a crisp base, chewy toffee filling, and dark bitter chocolate topping. This sounds like the start of a commercial!

You will need a greased 10 cm x 20 cm (4" x 8") oblong tin.

Ingredients to make about 12 biscuits

Base

100 g (4 oz)	margarine *or* butter
50 g (2 oz)	castor sugar
150 g (6 oz)	plain flour

Filling

110 g (4 oz)	butter
110 g (4 oz)	castor sugar
225 g (8 oz)	tinned condensed milk
2 tablespoons	syrup

Topping

110 g (4 oz)	dark chocolate §

Method

Base

Cream the fat and sugar together until soft and light in colour. Add the flour and mix until completely combined. Roll out and place in a greased oblong tin.

Bake at Gas Mark 4 / 350°F / 180°C (160°C for fan oven) for 15 – 20 minutes until firm and slightly coloured. Leave to cool completely.

Filling

Melt the fat with the other ingredients and simmer for about 10 minutes stirring constantly. Pour the filling onto the cool base and leave to cool completely.

Topping

Melt the chocolate § and pour onto the cool filling. Leave to cool before cutting into squares.

First Aid

Symptom: Millionaires shortbread toffee filling is burnt.

Diagnosis: Filling can easily acquire a burnt flavour while making.

Remedy: Ensure the toffee filling mixture is simmered and stirred constantly until it thickens and changes colour.

Orange Crisps

These thin lace-like biscuits are just the thing to serve with strong coffee at the end of an enjoyable meal. I love the simplicity of making these little gems; whiz in a food processor, roll into a log, chill or freeze until required, then slice thinly and bake quickly. Magic!

Ingredients to make 2 dozen biscuits

50 g (2 oz)	almonds – finely chopped
50 g (2 oz)	candied peel – chopped
	finely grated zest of orange
40 g (1½ oz)	plain flour
50 g (2 oz)	softened butter
50 g (2 oz)	castor sugar

Method

Place everything in a food processor and whiz to form a smooth dough. Wrap in cling film or greaseproof paper and roll into logs 2.5 cm (1") diameter. Chill for at least 30 minutes. They can be frozen at this stage if desired.

Remove the cling film or greaseproof paper and slice the logs very thinly. Lay out on a lightly greased baking sheet.

Bake at Gas Mark 3 / 325°F / 170°C (150°C for fan oven) for 10 – 15 minutes until lightly brown. Cool on a wire rack.

First Aid

Symptom: *Orange crisps appear dark brown when baked.*

Diagnosis: *Biscuits over-cooked either at too high a temperature or for too long.*

Remedy: *Make a note against the recipe of the oven shelf used, temperature setting, and cooking time. Next time adjust one of these variables and keep an eye on the biscuits. Repeat this process until light brown biscuits are achieved.*

Flapjack

Adding crushed Cornflakes® to the oat mixture makes these flapjacks less solid than the more traditional plain oat variety. I sometimes vary the flavour by adding dried fruit or candied ginger, or replacing some of the flour with cocoa powder, and then dipping them in chocolate.

You will need a Swiss roll, or similar, rectangular tin 35 cm x 15 cm (14" x 6").

Ingredients to make 2 dozen slices

225 g (8 oz)	butter *or* margarine
2 tablespoons	golden syrup
225 g (8 oz)	granulated sugar
110 g (4 oz)	porridge oats
110 g (4 oz)	self-raising flour
175 g (6 oz)	crushed Cornflakes®

Method

Gently melt the butter or margarine with the syrup in a saucepan. **Do not boil**.

Mix all the other ingredients together thoroughly in a bowl. Add the melted syrup mixture to the bowl and combine thoroughly. Spread the mixture into a lightly greased Swiss roll tin.

Bake at Gas Mark 5 / 375°F / 190°C (170°C for fan oven) on the middle to top shelf for 15 minutes until just firm.

Cut into fingers whilst still warm and leave to cool in the tin. Store the cool flapjack in an airtight container.

Variations

If you want to vary the basic recipe, you could add **one** of the following ingredients to the above dry mixture.

50 g (2 oz)	dried fruit e.g. sultanas, currants, raisins
or 50 g (2 oz)	glacé cherries – chopped
or 50 g (2 oz)	nuts of any variety – chopped
or 50 g (2 oz)	chocolate drops
or 50 g (2 oz)	stem ginger – finely chopped

First Aid

Symptom: *Flapjack has a hard and crunchy texture after baking.*

Diagnosis: *Either the syrup mixture was allowed to boil or the flapjack was over-baked.*

Remedy: *Ensure the fat and syrup mixture does not boil as this makes the flapjack hard. Bake until just firm to touch because it will firm up as it cools.*

Easter Nests

These are fun things to make at any time of the year, especially with young at heart people in mind.

Ingredients to make 8 nests

75 g (3 oz)	butter *or* margarine
3 tablespoons	syrup
3 level tablespoons	cocoa powder
110 g (4 oz)	Cornflakes® *or* Shredded Wheat®
1 packet	chocolate speckled eggs

Method

Put the fat, syrup, and cocoa powder in a large saucepan. On a gentle heat, stir the mixture until the fat has melted, and the cocoa powder has dissolved.

Take off the heat and add the Cornflakes® or shreds of Shredded Wheat®. Coat the cereals in the chocolate mixture until completely covered.

Place tablespoons full of the cereal mixture onto silicone or greaseproof paper to form eight nests. Add the chocolate speckled eggs whilst the mixture is still soft. Chill until firm to touch.

First Aid

Symptom: *Cocoa powder is not available.*

Diagnosis: *Must ensure all ingredients are available before starting recipe.*

Antidote: *Substitute the fat, syrup, and cocoa with chocolate that has a high proportion of cocoa solids. Melt the chocolate § and coat the cereals.*

Ice Creams and Water-Ices

See the chapter '**What Kitchen Equipment Do You Need?**' for advice on freezers and ice cream makers, and '**How Do You Cook With Confidence?**' for guidelines on frozen food safety.

The best-before date for home-made ice cream is about one week, because it soon loses its flavour due to the lack of additives, emulsifiers, and colourings used in commercial products.

Vanilla Ice Cream and Variations

This is the time-honoured original ice cream flavour that we all know and love, but with a little imagination there are many flavoured variations that you can evolve from the basic recipe.

Ingredients to serve 6 people

570 ml (1 pt)	milk
1 pod	vanilla
4 large	egg yolks
150 g (5 oz)	granulated sugar
1 teaspoon	cornflour
275 ml (10 fl oz)	whipping cream

Method

Place the milk into a heavy-based saucepan. Halve the vanilla pod and scrape the seeds out into the milk. Then chop the pod finely and add to the milk. Bring the milk to the boil, take off the heat, and leave to infuse for 15 minutes.

Cream the yolks, sugar, and cornflour until smooth, thick, and light in colour. Bring the milk back to the boil and pour in the egg mixture, stirring constantly. Whilst on the heat, stir the mixture until it begins to thicken, but do not boil.

Remove from the heat and strain the mixture through a sieve into a bowl, while pressing down on the vanilla pieces to extract as much flavour as possible. Leave the vanilla custard to cool completely.

Whisk the cream until floppy, and gently combine with the vanilla custard. At this point, you can use an ice cream maker to churn and chill the custard. Alternatively, place the custard in the freezer for 2 hours. Remove, and whisk for 30 seconds with an electric hand mixer.

Keep the ice cream in the freezer until required to be served.

Other Flavours

Instead of using vanilla pods, you can substitute a variety of other flavours. Here are my suggestions.

Rum and Raisin Ice Cream

Soak 75 g (3 oz) raisins in 3 tablespoons of dark rum, preferably overnight, and add to the custard with the whipped cream. Substitute dark brown sugar for the granulated sugar.

Chocolate Ice Cream

Break 75 g (3 oz) good quality chocolate § into the milk during simmering.

Orange or Lemon Ice Cream

Grate the zest of two oranges or lemons, and add to the milk while simmering.

First Aid

Also see the '**First Aid**' section for '**Lavender Ice Cream**' below.

Symptom: *ice cream is too hard to scoop easily.*

Diagnosis: *Probably kept too long in the freezer. You should eat ice cream more often.*

Antidote: *Put the tub in the microwave oven for 10 seconds just before serving, and use a really hot scoop dipped into boiling water between use.*

Lavender Ice Cream

If you enjoy the perfume of this cottage garden plant, you will appreciate the aromatic taste of this ice cream, which mimics exactly how it smells. I serve it with blackcurrants, either simply poached or in a tart. The acidity of the fruit seems to complement the floweriness of the lavender.

Unfortunately, you cannot buy fresh lavender flower heads. You either have to grow your own lavender, or be friendly with someone who does. Do not use dried lavender, sold for flower arrangements, which may contain inedible preservatives.

Ingredients to serve 6 people

15 g (¾ oz)	lavender flower heads
570 ml (1 pt)	milk
4	egg yolks
110 g (4 oz)	castor sugar
275 ml (10 fl oz)	double cream

Method

Wash the flower heads twice in salty water, and rinse clean in fresh water. Place the flower heads in the milk, and bring to the boil. Remove the heat and leave to infuse for 10 minutes until the flowers turn grey.

Whisk the egg yolks and castor sugar together until white and creamy. Strain the infused milk into the whisked egg and sugar mixture, and discard the flower heads.

Return to the heat, and stir constantly, until the mixture coats the back of a wooden spoon. Leave to get completely cold.

Whip up the double cream until floppy. Gently fold the cream into the lavender flavoured mixture.

At this point, you can use an ice cream maker to churn and chill the mixture. Alternatively, place the mixture in the freezer for 2 hours. Remove, and whisk for 30 seconds with an electric hand mixer.

Keep the ice cream in the freezer until required to be served.

First Aid

Also, see the '**First Aid**' section of '**Vanilla Ice Cream**' above.

Symptom: *Ice cream left in freezer more than 2 hours without whisking.*

Diagnosis: *Forgetfulness.*

Antidote: *If still fluid, whisk as usual, but if solid leave in freezer, as only the texture is slightly affected.*

Remedy: *Use a timer, your oven timer, clock radio, telephone, etc.*

Instant Marmalade Ice Cream

If you haven't made ice cream before, try this simple version. The only condition is that the marmalade or jam you use must have at least 45 per cent fruit content. After it has been made the ice cream is ready for consumption as soon as it is firm enough to shape.

Ingredients to serve 4 people

350 g (12 oz) jar	marmalade *or* jam preserve of any flavour
275 ml (10 fl oz)	double cream

Use home-made or bought preserve with a high proportion of fruit to sugar. I recommend at least 45 per cent fruit content.

Method

Tip the preserve into a large bowl, and cut up any large peel with scissors into 0.5 cm (¼") lengths. Beat with a wooden spoon to remove lumps. Whip the cream until stiff and fold into the preserve until thoroughly blended.

Place in a plastic container and then into the freezer for a couple of hours. This is one of those ice creams that does not need to be beaten while it freezes, and it can be served straight from the freezer.

Consume within one week.

First Aid

Symptom: *Ice cream needed to serve more people than planned.*

Diagnosis: *Extra guests arrive unexpectedly.*

Antidote: *Dip the plastic container in hot water for 20 seconds, run a knife around the sides to loosen the ice cream, turn it out onto a suitable plate, and return to the freezer until required. To serve, use a hot sharp knife, dipped in boiling water, to slice the ice cream into the desired number of portions.*

Instant Liqueur Ice Cream

This is a cheat's ice cream, that you can truthfully say you've flung together in an instant. You will find nothing like it in the shops, but it will taste as if it should be there, with the big boys.

Ingredients to serve 6 people

570 ml (1 pt)	double cream
400 g (15 oz) carton	ready-made custard
~3 tablespoons	your favourite liqueur such as brandy, dark rum, *or* Amaretto®

Method

Whip the double cream until floppy, and fold it into the ready-made custard. Add the liqueur of your choice to taste, but do not add too much, otherwise the mixture will not set.

Place in a plastic container and then into the freezer for 2 – 3 hours until set. This is one of those ice creams that does not need to be beaten while it freezes, and it can be served straight from the freezer.

Consume within one week.

First Aid

Symptom: *Ice cream will not set.*

Diagnosis: *Too much liqueur added.*

Antidote: *Use within a few days as a liqueur custard sauce.*

Remedy: *Stick to recommended quantities of ingredients.*

Frozen Yoghurt £

This is a different way of serving yoghurt with a pudding, instead of the traditional dollop on the side. Try it!

Ingredients to serve 6 people

570 ml (1 pt) tub	yoghurt, either low fat *or* full fat
200 g (7 oz)	castor sugar *or* honey
150 ml (5 fl oz)	double cream

Method

Beat the yoghurt and castor sugar or honey until smooth. Lightly whip the double cream and stir into the mixture. Pour into a plastic container and freeze for at least 4 hours until required.

Other Flavours

Optionally you can add your favourite fruit flavouring to the yoghurt just before freezing. Here are my favourite suggestions.

Strawberries, Raspberries, or Blackcurrants
225 g (8 oz)	crushed berry fruits

Raisins
110 g (4 oz)	raisins

Stem Ginger
50 g (2 oz)	stem ginger

First Aid

Symptom: *Frozen yoghurt in a low fat variant is required.*

Diagnosis: *Healthy diet needs reduced fat intake.*

Antidote: *Use low fat yoghurt and leave out the double cream, but consume within a week to enjoy it at its best.*

Ruby Red Grapefruit Granita £

A granita is a refreshing way to end a meal, a real palate cleanser, and it looks so colourful. It is a flaked water ice, similar to a sorbet, but fluffed up like snow-flakes using a fork. I usually serve it in tall glasses with pieces of fresh ruby red grapefruit.

Ingredients to serve 6 people

Syrup
110 g (4 oz)	granulated sugar
275 ml (10 fl oz)	water
1 teaspoon	whole juniper berries – crushed

Flavouring
570 ml (1 pt)	ruby red grapefruit juice
50 ml (2 fl oz)	gin

Method

Syrup

Stir the sugar, water, and crushed juniper berries to the boil in a saucepan, and simmer for about 5 minutes. Leave to infuse off the heat for 1 hour. When completely cold, strain off the juniper berries and discard the berries.

Flavouring

Add the grapefruit juice and gin to the cold juniper syrup and stir well. Place the liquid in a shallow container in the freezer.

Remove every hour and break up with a fork until flaky ice crystals form. This process takes about half a day to complete.

Once the ice crystals have formed, and appear loose and free flowing like snow-flakes, store in a plastic container in the freezer until required. This granita will not stick together like a sorbet but remains loose and flaky.

First Aid

Symptom: *Grapefruit is not a favourite flavour.*

Diagnosis: *People have different tastes.*

Antidote: *Substitute any other pure juice, but ensure it has a good flavour.*

Index